Motor Boat
and Yachting
Manual

Motor Boat and Yachting Manual

Eighteenth Edition

Edited by
Tom Cox

Consultant Editor
Commander R. L. Hewitt M.V.O. R.N. (Rtd)
Editor – Motor Boat and Yachting

EDWARD STANFORD LONDON

Edward Stanford Limited
(Member of the George Philip Group of Companies)
12–14 Long Acre London WC2E 9LP

First Published 1907
Eighteenth Edition 1973
© Edward Stanford 1973

Printed in Great Britain by
BAS Printers Limited

PUBLISHED AND DISTRIBUTED IN SOUTHERN AFRICA BY

DAVID PHILIP, PUBLISHER

3 SCOTT ROAD, CLAREMONT, CAPE PROVINCE

ISBN 0 540 00966 0

Contents

Appendices

Foreword

Over the years, since it was first published in 1907, the style and content of the *Motor Boat and Yachting Manual* has steadily moved with the times. The various editions sit in my office bookcase and are interesting to browse through on those all too rare occasions when the level of correspondence in my 'In' tray has reached the low water mark; they also provide a useful source of reference to the sport during the twentieth century.

This new edition has been completely re-written, with the aim of giving the modern motor boat enthusiast as much information as possible about the design, construction and practical operation of his craft. It has, perforce, been written in general terms, without detailed descriptions of specific makes of engines and the like, but such matters should be adequately covered by makers' handbooks—although it has to be admitted that these are not always as informative as one would wish.

Since the last edition appeared in 1963 there has been something of an explosion in the numbers of pleasure craft afloat, with many newcomers to the sport. Tom Cox—a regular contributor to *Motor Boat and Yachting*—has compiled the information with the motor boat owner principally in mind, but most of the contents are equally applicable to the auxiliary-powered sailing yacht, and there are few boats nowadays which do not have an engine of some kind or other. Much of the book should be of value to sailing folk and there is indeed a separate chapter on sailing cruisers and the growing breed of motor sailers.

Foreword

Perhaps the greatest difference between motor and sailing boats is the comparative ease with which the beginner can climb aboard a power driven yacht and go places—or try to. At first sight, steering a motor boat doesn't seem so very different from steering a car; because of this apparent simplicity it's not too difficult to get into trouble, particularly in tidal waters, and hence the importance of some of the later chapters which deal with matters of safety and sea-sense.

Above all, a motor boat's safety is often dependent on the reliability of her engine and its ancillary equipment. It is therefore vital for any owner to ensure that these items are kept in first class order. To do this he must have some knowledge of how they function and of the attention they need, while these matters have become increasingly important in an age when many owners now undertake a substantial proportion of the maintenance work on their boats and engines.

Dick Hewitt

Preface

The rather longer than average interval since the last edition of the Manual means that this is almost an entirely new publication in content. Some things are not very amenable to change and chapters dealing with the construction of a wooden boat, and the handling of power craft appear much as before, but there is a lot of new material, and many new contributors whom it is my pleasure to thank.

In fact, I am very happy to present the reader with a considerable gathering of talent. John Teale has provided a design chapter in which the groundwork of the subject is treated surely but lightly; John injects information painlessly, and with a smile. Dermot Wright reviews electronic navigation aids, and his run down on how and what provides an informed guide to the latest equipment.

Ian McLeod-Baikie's piece on yacht medicine comes from a source of some eminence and I am grateful that when I consulted him he did not insist on his usual fee! He offers some sound advice besides valuable instruction in first aid.

When I first read Brian Roger's article on the origins of our weather I thought it opened a new window for those trying to grasp the fundamentals. I am still of that opinion because he treats the nub of the matter without the assumption that we know something about it already. Another thing is that apart from illustrating three basic cloud types we are free from all those confusing cloud pictures. Andrew Phelan seems to have made a corner with his very readable articles on the law as it affects the owners of small craft; in this book

Preface

he has also had an exercise in compression, and he has covered a lot of ground in the space available.

I owe a great deal to John Liley, and my grateful thanks go to him and to Dick Hewitt, past and present editors of *Motor Boat and Yachting*, for permission to use material which had previously appeared under my name in the Journal. Dick Hewitt also read the manuscript and I thank him for giving his time to this and for his cogent suggestions.

There are many others who also contributed to the sum of material in this book, both directly and otherwise: The manufacturers and suppliers who gave both information and illustrative material, and all those others unnamed from whom I garnered pieces of wisdom. And at the end, I give my especial thanks to Janet Cole who typed the MS; her understanding of the requirement was a real help to my efforts.

Tom Cox
Whitstable

chapter 1

All Kinds of Small Craft

The vessels briefly defined here are those which will probably be of most interest to the amateur boat owner. Only basic types have been described since the finer technical differences may be more usefully discussed in the design chapter. Of the twelve types of boat discussed, eleven are yachts, and as such their first distinguishing mark is the burgee which will be flown from the masthead or the highest hoist. The ensign worn aft may be either Red or Blue according to the status of your club and whether you have an Admiralty warrant, and it should be noted that only the Royal Yacht Squadron is entitled to wear the White Ensign which is otherwise exclusive to the Royal Navy. The ensign which all British yachts are entitled to wear is the Red Ensign which is the Merchant Navy's 'Red Duster'.

THE DINGHY (Figs. 1.1. and 1.1a.) is the smallest vessel in serious use afloat, it is an open boat propelled by oars, sail or power. In its smallest sizes, 7 to 10ft in length, it is used mostly as a tender to a larger vessel. Bigger dinghies may be used for angling, and of course they also comprise a vast number of sailing boats in the dinghy racing classes, normally in the range 10 to 20ft. Dinghies can be round bilge or hard chine and they may be of the stem or pram variety. Pram dinghies have a bow as well as a stern transom.

MOTOR LAUNCHES (Fig. 1.2.) may have family connections with large and staunchly built dinghies or they may be more sophisticated craft with half decking and perhaps also a cuddy or shelter forward. The power may be outboard or inboard but in general the term 'launch' is more indicative of a large, open or half-decked boat with an inboard power unit.

All Kinds of Small Craft

Fig. 1.1

Fig. 1.1a

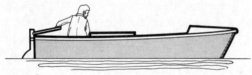

Fig. 1.2

Fig. 1.3

Fig. 1.4

RUNABOUTS (Fig. 1.3.) are small, fast motor boats, they may have inboard or outboard engines and they are generally semi-displacement or planing craft, mostly open but sometimes with a wheel shelter. A high power/weight ratio is necessary for performance and from boats of this kind one may see the development of ski craft which are very similar and also the high performance small racing craft. They are normally hard chine but the hull may have a conventional, a cathedral or a catamaran section (see Figs 2.1 and 2.6).

POWER WEEKENDERS (Fig. 1.4) have much in common with the larger runabouts in-so-far as they may have the same sort of hull but with a small cabin added, in fact many of them are based on a hull moulding which may be finished as either a runabout or a midget cruiser and which for want of a better term we call a weekender. A typical example would have two berths, a small facility for cooking and perhaps a WC. The power would probably be outboard and it could range from about 10 to 50hp or more.

FISHERMAN (Fig. 1.5.) types can be either day boats with a small cabin for cooking and shelter or they may have accommodation suited to a small cruiser with two or more berths, a galley and a separate toilet. The feature which distinguishes both types is a large cockpit with plenty of elbow room for the anglers. They will usually be powered with in-board engines or inboards with outdrives.

MOTOR CRUISERS (Fig. 1.6.) of the displacement type probably still comprise the majority of this class but the Express Cruiser is becoming increasingly popular. The traditional displacement boat will be round bilge and may boast a variety of sterns but the transom is most often met. It may be either an aft cockpit or a centre cockpit boat with the accommodation divided into fore and aft cabins; the cockpit may have either a wheel shelter or, on the larger vessels, there will probably be a wheelhouse, often of sufficient size to make a useful contribution to the general accommodation. The power is supplied by single or twin inboard engines and currently the twin diesel engine installation is most popular.

EXPRESS CRUISERS (Fig. 1.7.) as the name implies are medium to fast boats, mostly of either semi-displacement or planing type; the hulls are mainly hard chine but they may have softened chines. The sections are mostly conventional and within this description may be found shallow, medium and deep Vee bottoms of either warped plane or monohedron form. The accommodation may be much as in a displacement cruiser but the power/weight ratio will necessarily be much higher and the usual installation nowadays is two diesel engines which are frequently turbo charged to obtain the required power within a compact overall size. But some of the smaller craft might have inboards with outdrives.

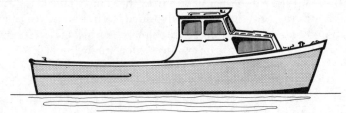

Fig. 1.5

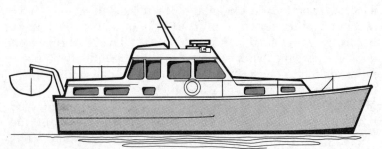

Fig. 1.6

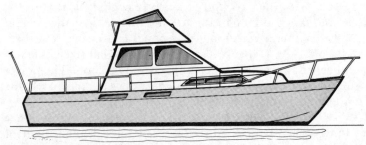

Fig. 1.7

Fig. 1.8

MOTOR SAILERS (Fig. 1.8.) are the sort of compromise cruisers indicated by the name, they are sometimes called 50/50s but this rarely means that they are equally capable under power or sail, it is more often the engine that gets the employment and the sail may only be useful when off the wind. However, a new breed of motor sailers may soon be with us—there are already some examples; in brief these are true sailing boats with full capability under sail, plus a very big auxiliary engine. The apt description is 100/100s.

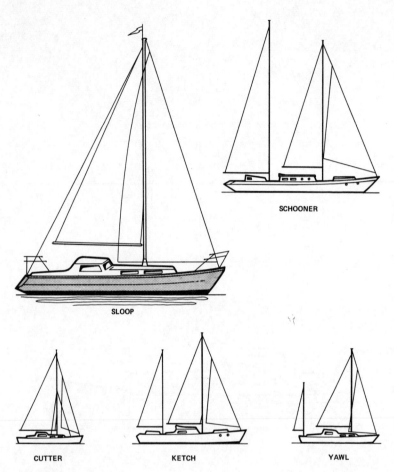

SCHOONER

SLOOP

CUTTER

KETCH

YAWL

Fig. 1.9

SAILING CRUISERS (Fig. 1.9.) come in a multitude of guises, their universal distinction being that they are all primarily dependent upon their sails and the engine is an auxiliary or secondary means of propulsion. They may be anything between 18 and 50ft or more in length and they may be rigged as sloops, cutters, yawls, ketches and, less frequently, schooners. They may have fin keels, twin keels or centreboards and their capability varies from estuary sailing to world cruising.

6

MULTIHULLS (Fig. 1.10.) were at one time the preserve of the more adventurous sailing man but there are now power catamarans and also sailing trimarans and catamarans with sufficient power installed to make them motor sailers. Since multihulls do not roll and catamarans particularly have big deck and cockpit areas they are popular with many as family cruisers. A sloop rig with the mast set well aft is characteristic.

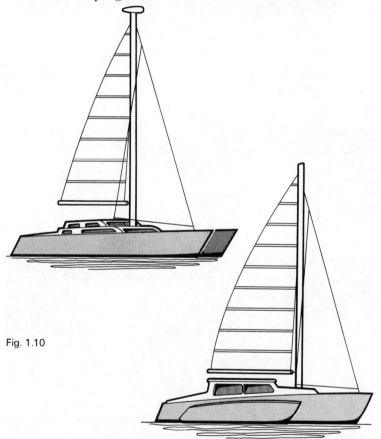

Fig. 1.10

MOTOR YACHTS (Fig. 1.11.) will generally be recognised by their lines and their size—the term is not often used for boats of under 45ft—and in common with all yachts they do not have their name on the bows as is usual with a commercial vessel. Well glazed superstructures and lack of cargo hatches

7

Fig. 1.11

Fig. 1.12

is another identification, and a fair amount of rake and sometimes streamlining of the superstructure is another feature of recently built vessels.

LIFEBOATS (Fig. 1.12.) operated by the RNLI now fall into three main categories: the small, inshore, inflatable boats powered by outboard engine; the traditional double ended boat which may be about 40 to 50ft LOA and perhaps self-righting, and the larger vessels up to 70ft long which are coming into service for long range offshore work. There are other intermediate designs employed in some areas such as high powered dories and other fast motor craft but they are not in general use.

chapter 2

Design

Yacht design, whether sail or power, is both an art and a science. The science bit comes in selecting the best hull shape for the duties the boat is expected to perform. The art, in presenting the details of this shape in attractive a manner as possible and generally in turning out a good-looking craft. Though beauty is in the eye of the beholder, or so they say, the professional yacht designer will usually produce a vessel that most people will agree looks right, combining elegance with practicality. The amateur, or the man who thinks that money spent on a design is money wasted, is more likely to draw out something in which no flight of the imagination has been spared and which may look superb on the drawing board, but which appears strangely incongruous on the water where it is seen from all sorts of unflattering angles. Similarly he may design a boat in which nothing has been allowed to stand in the way of stern utility, and looks it. So the art comes in combining these two extremes.

However, the first task of any designer is to select that suitable hull form and so in this chapter we can consider the factors that influence his choice.

First of all let us ponder the basic principles. A conventional sailing vessel, for instance, with an outside ballast keel can never attain any vast speeds, for however hard the wind may blow the boat will heel correspondingly to spill some of the breeze from its sails. In a super hurricane with the wind providing immense theoretical horsepower, the craft will probably be lying over on its side unable to use any of the force available. Thus the sailing boat has to be designed to slip through the water as easily as possible to take advantage of every bit of breeze it manages to convert into useful power. Since it will never be going terribly fast, shapes needed for high speed need not be considered. Cut off the ballast keel and install a motor in this vessel and you would have a highly efficient low-speed power boat.

Sticking to this sailing business for a moment longer, the racing dinghy can be considered. Here the fact that the crew can use their weight more effectively than a ballast keel to keep the craft upright means that the dinghy is capable of higher speeds than the normal yacht. Hence we are moving into a different speed category and the hull shape is influenced accordingly. The shape of the bottom of a sailing dinghy with slight modifications would do well for a medium speed power boat, and indeed this form is often used for it is still pretty efficient even at very low velocities.

We have now, however, reached a turning point, for if we want to go even faster than the best racing dinghies a hull form is required in which a great deal is sacrificed in the search for speed and which will eat up the horse-power when trundling along at a modest rate of knots. Even so, there are plenty of possibilities open and factors such as whether the vessel is meant to zip about only in sheltered waters or whether fast averages offshore are required will again influence the final choice.

So much for the generalities, let us now get down to a bit of detail. First of all, one definition is called for. This is speed/length ratio and is given by the expression $V/\sqrt{L}$, where V is speed in knots and L the waterline length of the boat in feet. If one had a craft 25ft on the waterline and doing 5 knots, its speed/length ratio would be $5/\sqrt{25}$, which is 5 divided by 5, or 1. If this vessel were doing 10 knots its speed/length ratio would be $10/\sqrt{25}$, or 10 divided by 5, which is 2, and so on. That $\sqrt{}$ sign means square root, incidentally, for those whose school days are lost in the mists of time.

There are two main things that reduce the speed of a boat as it moves through the water. The first is frictional resistance and the second, wave-making resistance. These are two rather fearsome-sounding terms for easily understandable actions. Taking frictional resistance first, water is a viscous fluid and thus it will take some energy to push a boat through it, however slowly, due to the friction on the vessel's bottom. The greater the area of the bottom the greater the resistance, naturally enough, and if the water were to run up the sides of the boat as well it would meet friction there too and even more energy would be absorbed.

A rough, barnacle-encrusted bottom will offer more friction as will any objects that protrude beneath the vessel such as rudders, centreboards, propellers, fins or anything you like. Travelling at low speeds and slipping quietly through the water, the sea will tend to behave itself and not rise above the line where the craft floats, apart from occasional waves, of course. But should throttles be opened and speed increased, water will try and climb the boat's sides as it is forced apart by the craft cleaving its way along. Should it be able to wet the sides, frictional resistance will be increased and so fast boats are normally Vee bottomed and many fit rails along the corner between bottom and sides. This corner is called the chine. Both the angle and the rails are meant to induce the water to fly off into space at that point rather than ascend still higher, and Fig. 2.1 shows this action. On craft with very steeply Vee'd bottoms additional rails may also run along the bottom. Their action is just the same as a chine and the same Fig. 2.1 shows this.

The second main form of resistance is wave-making. Here we have to ponder on one important boat characteristic. As it moves through the water it makes waves and the length between crest and crest of these waves is governed entirely by the speed of the boat and by no other factors at all. Thus a 250,000 ton super-tanker, 1,200ft long, makes exactly the

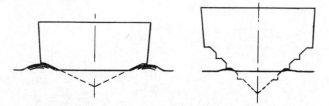

Fig. 2.1 Chines and spray rails are both designed to deflect water away from an area of the sides or bottom.

same length of wave at, say, 8 knots as does the smallest outboard dinghy. If you don't believe in this wave business, have a look at a tug, for instance, travelling fairly fast. There will be the crest of a wave at its bow, then a deepish trough, and then another crest somewhere near the stern. If you could measure the distance between crest and crest you could tell how fast the tug was going. Though a dinghy may make a shallower wave, it is still there and there is no escaping it.

Well, here are some boat speeds and corresponding wave lengths.

Boat speed (knots)	Wave length ft	M	Boat speed (knots)	Wave length ft	M
3	5·0	1·64	8	35·6	11·68
4	8·9	2·92	9	45·0	14·76
5	13·9	4·56	10	55·6	18·24
6	20·0	6·56	11	67·3	22·08
7	27·2	8·92	12	80·1	26·28

The list could be extended ad infinitum, but let us think of its significance. Firstly, there will always be a crest at the bow and then another crest so many feet further astern; between the two there is a hollow. Now, if we had a vessel 20ft long on the waterline for example, at 6 knots the aft crest would be at the transom, but at higher speeds the crest would be moving away astern and the back of the boat settling into a hollow.

Fig. 2.2 shows a vessel about 48ft on the waterline at two speeds. On the left it is doing about 7 knots and is nicely balanced on two wave crests along its length and so is riding level. The right hand sketch shows it at about 11 knots. The distance between the crests is now a bit over 67ft and thus a good deal more than her waterline length. The stern is beginning to settle in the trough between the crests, and

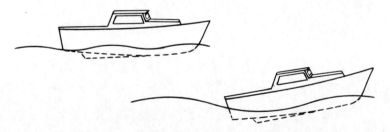

Fig. 2.2   A 48-footer running at, left 7 knots and, right 11 knots.

increasing speed more would bring the centre of that trough nearer the transom and put the boat at a still greater bows-up angle. All vessels regardless of their shape or size behave in this way.

Obviously the way out of this difficulty is to drive the boat hard and up onto that forward crest. This can be done with sufficient power plus a suitably-shaped bottom. Neither is normally any good without the other but just before going on to these considerations, one more feature of these waves ought to be mentioned.

Length between crests is governed solely by speed, as has been said, but the height of the waves, or the depth of the trough, whichever way you like to consider it, is controlled mainly by the weight or displacement of the vessel. A light boat will make shallower waves than a heavy one and so will have a less deep trough to settle into and thus will never attain such a steep bows-up angle.

So, on what has been said so far it would appear that there are two ways of achieving speed without bothering too much about bottom shape. The first is to make the craft as long as possible, for this will delay the point when the aft crest passes the transom—a 55-footer for instance would still be on two wave crests at 10 knots—and the second is to make the boat as light as possible. Not only will less power be required, for making shallow waves clearly requires less energy than making deep ones, but the bows-up angle will be less and it might be possible to increase speed without having to provide vast amounts of power to push the boat up what amounts to a steepish hill. The hill will be there, but it will be more of a gentle incline.

In the sailing world, an International 10 square metre Canoe goes fast because it is long, thin and light. In the power boat field, the pre-War Camper and Nicholson 50-footers of very light construction could do 20 knots with only 100hp installed. Neither of these featured what we might call planing hull forms.

As has been indicated that forward wave crest can be climbed provided sufficient power and a suitably-shaped bottom are available. Power requirements are obvious, but what about that bottom? Perhaps the wings of an aeroplane would serve as an example. In Fig. 2.3 the left-hand sketch shows the sort of thing one might expect on a normal single-engine private 'plane, not some military jet with thousands of horsepower waiting to be unleashed. The wing span, or

Fig. 2.3 You might expect to see the wings of a 'plane as in the left-hand sketch but would have doubts as to performance if they were angled up as on the right.

spread, is fairly wide and with that you would reasonably expect adequate lift with the power available. If, on the other hand, the wings were only half as long you would be justified in anticipating much less lift. Whether the thing would get in the air at all would be open to doubt but should that be managed and the engine failed in flight the gliding performance would probably be lamentable.

Just the same thing applies to the bottom of a boat designed for planing and high speed. It must be fairly wide for it to develop enough lift to allow the craft to climb that hill in front of it and then proceed happily with limited power. A narrow-sterned boat, or even worse one that was double ended (pointed at both ends), would be a miserable failure in a high speed role, however easily it might slip through the water at low velocities.

Looking now at the right-hand picture in Fig. 2.3 we have a 'plane with sharply upwards-raking wings. Studying this on the ground one might feel that it would go reasonably well as long as there was plenty of power available, but that again its gliding performance would be perilously near that of a sack of bricks. Correct once more, and a boat with that shaped bottom, called a deep Vee, will plane well provided it is endowed with a sufficiently powerful engine.

So then, the designer has a selection of possible hull shapes to choose from. For a craft intended for tootling up and down the Thames or other inland waterways where speed is never required, a nicely rounded streamlined hull, perhaps even with a pointed stern, will do fine since it will be highly efficient and sparing of fuel. For another boat intended for rather greater speeds, up to say speed/length ratios of 3, this first shape will be modified to give it a more buoyant stern so that it does not sink too deeply into its own trough, and provides enough lift for some attempt to be made to climb that forward crest. And remember that the propeller churning around beneath the stern is tending to scoop water away and to aggravate the situation. For higher speeds still, a wide transom is dictated.

However, the next client asks for real racing speeds and here demands change again. Previously we needed good beam, particularly at the transom, and the weight of the boat concentrated somewhere around the middle of the craft so as not to aggravate the tendency to sink down by the stern. Now we require a narrow vessel, and the narrower the better, coupled with a concentration of weight at the back. The reason for this latter feature is to prevent the trim becoming too flat, for if it is there is more boat than required in the water with a consequent rise in frictional resistance. It will be appreciated that the main lifting part of the bottom is towards the stern and the faster one goes the greater the lift and the greater the force raising the transom and depressing the bows. Now the boat has to climb that forward crest through the application of brute force at the propeller, largely unaided by suitable stern sections.

One consequence of all this and particularly the gathering of weight near the transom is that the boat tends to 'porpoise', or undulate through the water. In Fig. 2.4 the left-hand sketch shows a really fast boat running in calm water. The centre of gravity of the vessel, which is the centre of all the weights combined, is acting downwards aft of the point where the hull meets the waterline. The boat is happy enough to run like this though the trim is too flat for efficiency. The right-hand drawing shows what often happens as the craft is driving forward. Here the bows-up trim and the shove of the propeller has caused the situation where the centre of gravity is ahead of that meeting between the hull and water. Obviously the boat cannot sustain this attitude and the bows will drop until the forward edge of the waterline is again in front of the centre of gravity. A few moments later and the right-hand situation may be repeated, only for the bows to drop once more. This can continue indefinitely until speed is reduced or increased markedly and is called, as has been stated, porpoising.

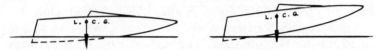

Fig. 2.4   If the centre of gravity falls ahead of the forward edge of the waterline the bows of a boat must drop. This is called porpoising.

Anyway, we now have a boat of roughly the shape we want for the speed required but it can still be refined or even completely changed in hull lines, though still adhering to the general principles of the basic form to make it suitable for offshore work.

At sea what we want is a craft that maintains a reasonably dry deck i.e. plenty of transverse stability, which does not tip or roll too much under the action of waves or even when all the crew suddenly concentrate on one side of the cockpit, that will travel over waves without too much pounding, and which will run in a reasonably straight line even in rough water without undue struggling at the wheel or tiller. All these features are really equally important though some may have to be sacrificed to make way for outstanding qualities in others, and all may be achieved in a number of different ways. Let us take them in order.

A dry deck is promoted by deflecting water away from the sides of the boat by the use of the previously discussed chine and/or rails, plus the use of flare in the sections. If you look ahead to Fig. 2.8 and the lines plan of a motor sailer, it will be seen that the sides of the boat lean outwards and this will obviously discourage water from running up them and then flopping on deck to everyone's discomfort. So flare is a good thing, though it is best in moderation. Some boats are seen with this feature greatly exaggerated and first impressions are that these wildly canted sides must be the ultimate in making for a dry deck. Unhappily this is not so and they have two main disadvantages. The first is that at high speeds wind catches under these sides and tends to lift the bows making steering very difficult and even dangerous as the bows swing from side to side meeting waves at varying angles and inducing many to hit the craft squarer than they normally would and so to break on board. Even at normal speeds wind funnels along under this flare and the sea which has been deflected outwards is carried along with the breeze until it comes to the point on the boat, usually about one-third of the way back from the bow, where the flare is not so pronounced, whereupon it leaps gaily on board.

Transverse stability may be provided in many ways. Clearly a craft with a bottom shaped like the left-hand sketch in Fig. 2.1 will be steadier than one with the deeply Vee'd section of the right-hand drawing, though at high speed the latter will be stable enough, rather in the way that a bicycle becomes manageable once under way however wobbly it may be at rest or very low speeds.

Anything sticking below the bottom of the vessel will help matters and Fig. 2.5 shows the midship section of a craft with both bilge keels and a skeg. The former are useful on round bottom boats and need not be long for them to be effective. For example, 5ft in length would be ample for a 35-footer and they would then be about 9in deep. The skeg, or false keel, plays a valuable part too in damping down rolling and thus promoting stability but it will be dealt with again in a few moments. Recall, though, that all such objects add to the wetted surface and frictional resistance of a boat and so may not be suitable for high speed craft.

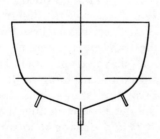

Fig. 2.5   A round-bilged boat with bilge keels and skeg, both as aids to reduced rolling.

Nevertheless, the obvious way to increase transverse stability is to employ a multihull form such as a catamaran, sea sled or gull wing. The two distinct hulls of the first are too well known to require description but the sea sled could be worth mentioning. The left-hand sketch of Fig. 2.6 shows a diagrammatic view of one. It will be seen that two hulls are joined at a centreline tunnel that sweeps down from the bow to give a flat transom. This latter feature allows high speed to be attained as in conventional craft. Since the two hulls are continuously joined the constructional problems on a sea sled are fewer than on a catamaran. A development of the sea sled is the gull wing shown in the right-hand sketch of the same Fig. 2.6. This has a main central hull with balancing sponsons at the sides and such a shape obviously provides a very stable platform at sea.

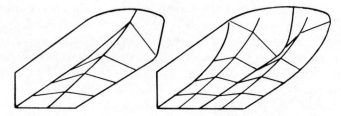

Fig. 2.6 Diagrammatic, fish views of, left, a sea sled and right, a gull wing hull.

In addition both sea sleds and gull wings, together with catamarans, having widely spaced hulls tend to run in a straight line at sea, and not to require too much work at the wheel. For a conventional craft to do this requires a certain amount of thought on the part of the designer. Have a look at the left-hand part of Fig. 2.7. Here a vessel with its skeg cut off a long way from the transom is travelling fast in a following sea. It has overtaken one wave and stuck its bows in the back of the next wave ahead and in doing so has naturally slowed down. The bottom picture shows what happens next. The weight or inertia of the boat is acting through the vessel's centre of gravity (cg) and driving it forward. However, the boat is pivoting about its centre of lateral resistance (clr) and the result is that the craft is bound to sheer off to one side or

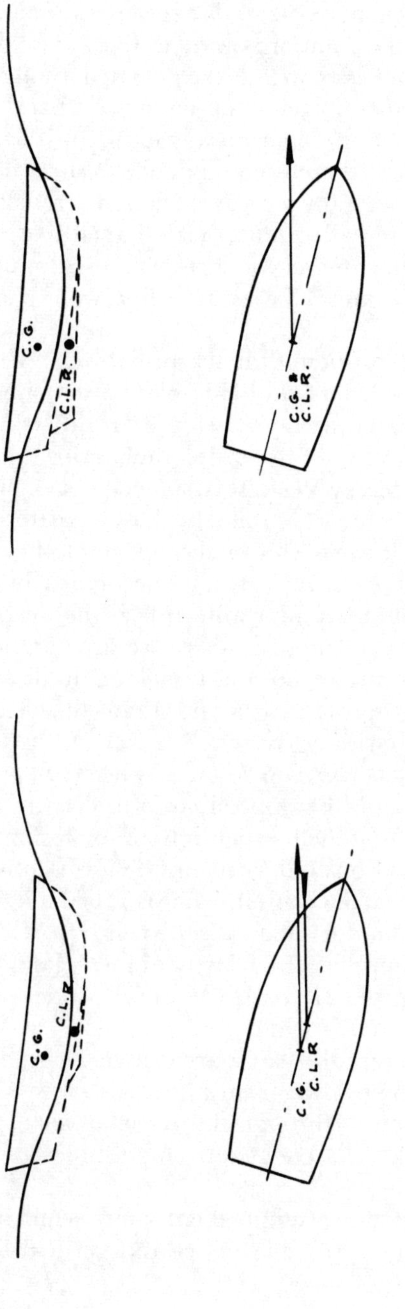

Fig. 2.7 A vessel with its centre of lateral resistance too far forward may be a pig to handle in a following sea.

broach. This can be very dangerous especially if the sheer takes it into a position broadside to the waves. The right-hand sketch shows a vessel with a skeg carried a long way aft in the same predicament. Here, the clr is well back and the forces tending to drive the boat on and to pivot it are acting in the same line so that there is no tendency to sheer off course.

A long skeg again increases frictional resistance and when high speeds are called for a boat shaped like that in Fig. 2.4 may well be the answer for this straight-running requirement. Its centre of lateral resistance lies well back, as can be imagined.

As for the non-pounding feature, a well Vee'd section such as that on the right-hand side of Fig. 2.1 should give a soft ride as should both the sea sled and gull wing. For normal speeds, and even up to quite high cruising velocities, the length of the steeply Vee'd section need not extend further back than 'midships for it is unlikely that a greater length of boat will ever be thrown completely clear of the water. But for racing when the entire craft may become airborne it certainly makes for a more comfortable ride if the deep vee is carried right back to the transom. Here we are compromising again as this greatly angled bottom is lacking in lift and will require more power to push it along than the flatter, yet more uncomfortably-riding, vessel.

All that has been said so far has been expressed in general terms for it would be impossible to deal with the subtleties of design or its detailed execution in this chapter. However, having decided on hull form the designer must put his ideas on paper and he does this in what is called a lines plan. Such a drawing of a motor sailer is shown in Fig. 2.8 though it has been a bit simplified for clarity. Lines plans are frightening looking things yet are basically simple, so let us glance at this one and see what is what.

Three views of the yacht are drawn. A profile; a plan view (that is, looking down from above); and a body plan which consists of sections through the vessel at various points. In the plan shown, the sections are superimposed on top of the profile.

Apart from the sections mentioned, which are assumed to be cut straight across the vessel and vertical to its waterline,

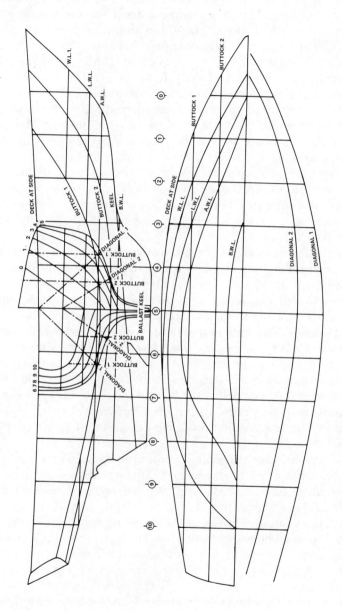

Fig. 2.8   Simplified line plan of a 40ft motor sailer.

three other types of section are shown. The first of these are the waterlines. This is a confusing term for the boat is not meant to float at any of them and the old expression, level lines, might be better. What happens is that the designer draws in the waterline at which he expects the craft to float, and this is normally marked as LWL (Load Water Line) and then draws sections parallel to this line above and below it. Such sections are, therefore, horizontal slices through the boat at different heights and are marked on this plan as W.L.1., A.W.L. and so on. Where the slices are cut is shown on the profile and the shape of the slices on the plan view.

Next, vertical slices are assumed to be made parallel to the fore and aft centreline of the boat and at varying distances from this centreline. These are called buttock lines. Where the slices occur is shown on the plan view and their shape on the profile.

Finally, more slices are taken diagonally across the boat. Their position is given on the sectional view and their shape plotted on the plan view. Though these diagonals would obviously cut the deck if continued to their full length, only the shape relating to the bottom or sides is drawn.

It should be mentioned here that only one side of the boat is drawn on any sectional or slice view and that, by convention, the bow of the craft is drawn to the right with the forward half-sections shown to the right of the centreline and the sections of the back half of the boat to the left of the centreline. In this plan, ten sections have been drawn on the body plan and section five on the profile view doubles up as the centreline for the body plan.

There are four waterlines, two buttocks and two diagonals drawn on the plan reproduced. In fact there were twelve waterlines, four buttocks and five diagonals plotted on the original lines plan. Anyway, having slaved away at this drawing and eventually achieved the shape he wants the designer gives measurements to various spots so that the builder can reproduce his ideas exactly on the full size boat. In this case a grand total of 277 different measurements were given. Most of them were incorporated in what is called an offset table—which is simply a list of dimensions so that sections, waterlines, buttocks and diagonals can be accurately drawn.

This lines plan is that of a motor sailer and it might be as well to conclude this chapter with a brief dissertation on these craft which raise endless problems in design. The problem is to combine the varying demands of good sailing performance with good performance under power.

As has been said, for simple sailing no real heed need be taken of high speed requirements, yet the man who buys a motor sailer wants to be able to travel a bit faster with his motor switched on than he would ever do under sail alone. As discussed the boat is likely to meet that awkward condition when its stern starts to sink into the trough of its pressure wave. On a power boat we could counter this by widening the transom and giving it plenty of buoyancy, but such a shape, with its inherent poor low-speed qualities, would wreck the performance under sail. Thus a compromise must be reached. Here an overhanging, or counter, stern has been chosen. This allows a good shape of boat in the water before it starts to squat by the stern with increase of speed under power, but when this squat does occur a new length of boat is presented to the water and adds buoyancy and lift to the stern. Though the counter stern is not as efficient for speed as the pure, wide, immersed transom it is a reasonable compromise.

With its outside ballast keel necessary for sailing performance, wetted surface and frictional resistance on a motor sailer are far greater than is desirable for power boating and this, in turn, means that the propeller should be as large as possible for maximum 'urge'. Of course this is not desirable from the pure sailing viewpoint as the drag of a large propeller is considerable. Yet it must be accepted. It is compromise, compromise all the way with a motor sailer which is probably the reason why so few good ones have been designed. Most are either sailing vessels equipped with over-large auxiliaries but with unchanged hull forms, or power boats with masts and sails stuck on top. The former won't motor and the latter won't sail.

On that note we will cease. Yacht designing is a fascinating profession and though it has only been possible here to give the barest outline of what is involved you may now be able to understand the problems, or at least some of them, and the various methods of overcoming them.

B

chapter 3

Construction

In the last edition of this book timber was in vogue to the extent that a whole chapter on this subject was devoted to building in wood, but most boat owners will be aware of the impact which glass reinforced plastic has had on the building of yachts and small craft of all kinds in the intervening years. At the last International Boat Show in London about 90% of the vessels displayed were moulded GRP and of the remaining 10% only some of these were timber, competing with steel and ferro-cement.

Speaking generally, GRP has become the favourite material for most small vessels because it has advantages in both construction and in ownership. The increasing demand for small boats would scarcely have been met by building in the traditional material since mass production would be difficult and the necessary skilled labour is no longer available. From the owner's point of view, whilst some may see the passing of timber with genuine regret, there is a nearly universal appreciation of the benefits which GRP has brought in reduced hull maintenance.

Part 1

WOOD BUILD

Planked Boats
These may be built with either flush fitting planks—carvel build (Fig. 3.1.) or the planks may overlap—clinker build (Fig. 3.2.). Both require frames and timbers which are permanent to the structure although some small clinker built

boats, such as racing dinghies, are without timbers (ribs) and depend for their strength and rigidity upon all of the planks being glued where they overlap.

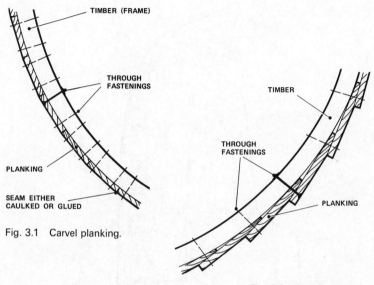

Fig. 3.1 Carvel planking.

Fig. 3.2 Clinker planking.

On all boats the main constructional member, which provides the backbone, is the keel (Fig. 3.3.). This extends for most of the length of the boat and, in a wooden vessel which is to be planked, it will be of sufficient depth and width to make a rigid base for the remainder of the structure (Fig. 3.4.). The keel always provides the bottom member of the canoe body or hull proper and deepening below this, so as to form a skeg or a fairing for a ballast keel, is known as the deadwood. To provide a landing for the bottom-most planks, which are known as the garboards, a piece of wood wider than the keel is bolted on top known as the hog. The stem, which with its apron makes the landing for the ends of the planks at the bow, is joined to the keel with a long sloping joint called a scarph.

Assuming that the boat is not to be double ended (in which case it would have a stern post with a similar function to the stem) the panel of wood called the transom will be joined to

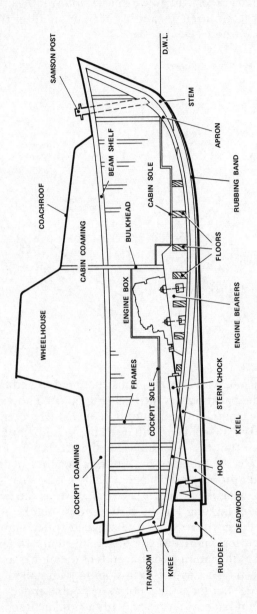

Fig. 3.3 The main structure of a wooden boat.

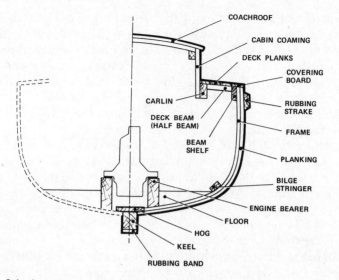

Fig. 3.4 A section through the hull in way of the engine.

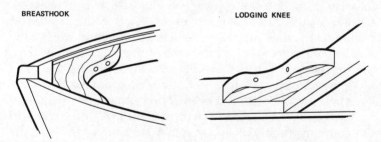

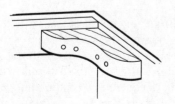

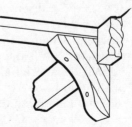

Fig. 3.5 Breasthook and knees.

the keel at its after end with the aid of a knee. The transom may be flat or eliptic in plan and it may be raked fore or aft, the knee being shaped to suit. The transom is often framed, which means that it has an extra thickness of wood round its edges so as to give a wider landing for the ends of the planks or, if the frame is set inside the edges of the transom, by the amount of the plank thickness the ends of the planks can be covered or hooded.

Before the hull can be planked up moulds must be set up on the keel, these are temporary frames cut to the shape of the sections of the hull as drawn by the designer for the different stations. With the keel, stem, transom and moulds set up, the first longitudinal members can be put on. These are the beam shelves which are recessed into the moulds running from stem to stern, one on each side. They are bent both to the curve of the hull in plan (around the moulds) and also to the sheer line which is the curve shown at the deck in profile. A stringer will be put in at about the turn of the bilge on each side and these will also be recessed into the moulds so as to allow for the thickness of the ribs which will pass outside them. Next some strips of wood called ribbands, running fore and aft, may be screwed temporarily to the moulds, particularly about the turn of the bilge, so that when the timbers are put in they will take the correct curve. The hull might have some sawn frames as well as timbers and if the latter are thick in section they may be steamed before fitment.

Where the longitudinal beam shelves meet the stem and the transom, they will be secured with a breasthook at the forward end where the included angle between the two shelves is less than a right angle, and quarter knees at their separate junctions with the transom which will make more than a right angle (Fig. 3.5.).

Planking up, whether for clinker or carvel starts with the garboard strake, that is the one nearest the keel on each side, and is carried on alternately port and starboard so that the spring in the planks does not cause the hull to distort as the work proceeds. The ribbands will of course need to be removed as planking progresses. Cross members are put in, taking up the slope of the planking on either side and bolted down to the top of the keel. These are the floors which in dinghies are often dispensed with by running the timbers across the top of the keel so that a timber may be continuous from one gunwale to the other. A flat board going the length of the keel over the top of the floors, or timbers if they are taken across as described, is known as the keelson. It is not always fitted and is more likely to be seen in open boats. If bilge keels are to be fitted, the stringers will have been located so that they can be through-bolted to these.

It is convenient to put in the engine bearers prior to decking—if it is to be a cabin boat—and these should be as heavy in section as is consistent with the general scantlings of the hull and the power to be used. They should also be as long as is practical, the aim being to spread the load through the hull. The bearers should take up on the floors and the skin of the boat if it is a motor vessel, but for a sailing vessel with a light auxiliary motor it serves to take the load on the floors only provided they are substantial and sufficient in number.

Fitting the deck beams across the boat with their ends lodged in the beam shelves is the next operation. These will have some camber so that the deck sheds water quickly and, if the boat is to have a coachroof and side decks, the beams fore and aft of the opening will be joined by two longitudinal pieces called carlins. Half beams at the same frequency as the full deck beams join the carlins to the beam shelves and provide the support for the side deck. The cabin coaming, which is the side of the coachroof, is screwed to the inside of the carlin and stands up to take a light beam shelf at the top so that the coachroof beams may be located. The carlins and the coamings may follow a straight line or they may be curved as the shape of the hull. A number of the half beams will probably be reinforced by hanging knees where they join the beam shelf, and the full beams at the ends of the cabin will also have lodging knees where they meet the beam shelves.

Plywood makes a stronger deck than laid planks although the latter looks very nice. Marine ply is also cheaper and less likely to leak. If the deck is planked, the plank at the edge of the deck is called the covering board because it goes over the top of the beam shelf, the ends of the timbers, and the top strake of the hull planking. Sometimes a thin plank deck is laid on top of plywood but in any case it needs to be caulked.

in the seams with one of the proprietary compounds. If the boat is carvel built the hull planks will also be caulked unless they are edge glued. A marine plywood deck can be finished off by canvassing over, covering with glassfibre (using epoxy resin) or deck paint. The deck edge is often given a narrow strip of wood on top, which is called the toe rail. This is very useful both to keep feet inboard on slippery decks and to prevent gear from sliding straight overboard, but it should have some breaks in it to allow water to drain off the deck.

The coachroof is finished similar to the deck, using marine ply. Sometimes two thin sheets of ply are laminated together strengthening the roof and holding its curvature with less assistance from the beams, which can be lighter in consequence.

There are other means of planking boats such as double diagonal, where the first layer of planks is put on at an angle of about 45° to the horizontal line of the keel and the second layer at 90° to the first. Frames are still required but they may be fewer than in a carvel or clinker boat, and the individual planks are much thinner so that the finished thickness of the skin may be less than with conventional planking. Watertightness is ensured by putting a layer of calico, with thick paint on both sides between the two layers of planking, which are fastened with copper nails and roves as with a carvel boat. The effect is to obtain a semi-monocoque structure which has considerable strength in the skin but may still be lighter than carvel or clinker build.

Seam and batten, where wide planks are used with a batten behind the joint which is recessed into the frame, is sometimes used but this is obviously better suited to hard chine boats.

Another method is strip planking, which is suited to round bilge boats. It is a form of carvel build using very narrow strips of plank of approximately equal width and depth which are edge nailed together. The narrowness of the strips enables them to be pushed down on top of each other to accommodate the curve of the hull and so dispenses with the spiling or marking out of planks which is necessary in conventional carvel building. The result naturally has too many joints for caulking and the strips are normally edge glued. It does not compare with ordinary carvel construction but is probably a convenient way to make a mould for a cold moulded ply hull.

Marine Plywood

This is of course the home builder's favourite material because it comes in large panels, in various thicknesses, is easy to work, and modern resin glues have made it thoroughly reliable. It has lent itself to the construction of hard chine and double chine sailing and power boats for a number of years, and whilst professional boatbuilders have mostly abandoned it for GRP, most kit boats are marine ply. Because of its cleanliness and convenience one cannot see it being overtaken for this purpose by any other material for some time to come.

A marine ply boat requires a frame but there is less of it. For an open boat the keel, stem, chines, half a dozen frames and the transom suffices because of the integrity of the skin which is to be put on. Similarly with a cabin boat, the number of frames required will be small compared with the timbers in a boat of traditional build, and internal bulkheads will also serve as frames wherever they occur in the design. The accepted means of fastening both the frames and the hull panels on a plywood boat is with one of the resin glues assisted by bronze screws at strategic points of stress.

There are two important points to be made in the use of marine plywood first, that it should be to the proper British Standards specification BSS 1088 and second, that all edges are protected to prevent the ingress of water, this may be done with paint or a thin solution of resin glue. It is best not to put any covering on external plywood or to make any joint to it without first applying either glue or paint, e.g. the quadrant strip which may fill the angle between the deck and the coachroof coaming should, if it is not glued, be applied after painting or varnishing in the angle. The same could be said of the latter in the use of solid wood but it is rather more important with plywood, which has thin veneers which might lift in continuously damp conditions if not sealed as suggested.

Hot and Cold Moulded Ply

A moulded ply boat is one in which the ply veneers are applied separately, one on the other, using a complete form or mould to obtain the desired shape. The veneers are put on diagonally so as to cross each other at more or less right angles and glue is spread between each layer, the veneer being held down temporarily by small staples from a hand stapling tool. Sometimes the final skin is laid fore and aft, otherwise if there are three veneers, which is quite usual, the last one will be laid in the same direction as the first.

Part 2

GLASS REINFORCED PLASTICS

Conventional Lamination in a Mould

What is now known familiarly as a GRP boat is likely to have a hull which has been laid up (laminated) with alternate applications of glass cloth or loose fibre mat, and polyester resin in a mould—which is probably constructed of similar material. The mould will have been taken originally from a form or 'plug' which is exactly the shape of your finished hull, the plug will be male and the mould female. Since GRP allows designers great scope there is no point in their being held to earlier shapes which sometimes arose from the limitations of previously popular materials. Most plugs are therefore custom built for their purpose (Fig. 3.6.) although some may

Fig. 3.6 Hull mould for 32ft trimaran. Cox Marine.

be properly built as wooden hulls and subsequently finished as complete boats—thus getting two for almost the price of one—but not quite! Early exponents of GRP construction sometimes took advantage of this facility by taking moulds off all sorts of unlikely craft in order to save the cost of a proper plug, and indeed so hurried was their work that planking scarph joints, fastenings etc. were all faithfully reproduced in the mould.

It will be apparent that unless a great amount of work is done on the mould, the finished hull moulding can be no better than the plug from which the mould was made, and it is in the degree of finishing required for a good plug that much of the expense arises. Beyond this the mould will get several layers of hard wax before use and the occasional re-surfacing during use. These wax coatings have to be polished right out and a lot of elbow grease is needed. A release agent may be applied to the mould surface before the moulding is laid up and this is the last operation before laminating starts with the application of the gel coat.

A gel coat is an initial application of resin, brushed or sprayed onto the mould surface. It may be pigmented to the desired hull colour using the lay up resin or it can be obtained as gel coat already pigmented. Its purpose, apart from providing a hull of the desired colour, is to cloak the strands of glass in the mat or cloth being used, and to give a hard, impervious surface. Sometimes a thin tissue of glass cloth is put on after the gel coat to protect it from pressure from the first layer of glass mat, but it is not always used, and it depends upon the part-curing time allowed for the gel coat before lamination begins (Fig. 3.7.).

There is no optimum schedule for the use of glass mat and/or glass cloth in laying up a hull moulding and every moulder has different ideas in the matter. In fact there is one method of moulding where resin and glass fibres are sprayed into the mould together so that a random matrix is formed, but this calls for considerable operator skill and knowledge of his equipment, otherwise the thickness of the hull may vary.

It is quite a usual practice to use cloth or layers of mat and cloth when it is expected that the stresses will be high, as for instance in the bottom of a fast power boat, but many power

Fig. 3.7 GRP construction at Hurley Marine. The upturned hull mould, right, has been sprayed with gel coat and one lamination of glassfibre mat has been layed up in the lower half.

boats and lots of sailing cruisers are laminated with chopped strand mat only. Chopped strand mat (csm) is, as its name implies, short filaments of glass lying in random directions and bound together in the form of a mat of varying thickness according to the requirement. The weight quoted for a mat is in ounces and it states the number of ounces per square feet. The total weight of the finished lamination, that is, layers of glass in the moulding, indicates the scantlings of the hull and a typical example for a sailing boat of about 20 to 23ft using csm could be 8 to 10oz on the topsides and 12 to 15oz in the bottom.

Whether mat or cloth is used, it is laid into the mould on wet resin, being stippled against the mould surface with brushes and having air bubbles removed by small hand rollers of various designs, the popular one being rather like a row of washers. It is important that the resin is forced up through the glass mat so that the binding agent is dissolved and the mat permitted to 'drape' or conform with the mould shape. The ideal is the minimum resin required to effect complete wetting

34

Fig. 3.8 Deck and superstructure moulding for the Fairways Fisher.

out of the mat, extra resin adds nothing but weight, but it is no handicap to have a slight surplus until the final layer of mat is put on, thereafter any pools of resin seen on the final surface are weight and waste.

GRP mouldings shrink slightly on curing and this facilitates removal from the mould, the curing time will depend upon the resin mix and the temperature, but it is important that it is long enough to reach the 'setting' stage as distinct from the hard, rubbery condition which precedes it before removal from the mould. The process incidentally is irreversible, polyester is a thermosetting resin and although you may soften the surface a little with acetone, it is insoluble.

In laying up, the glass and resin is taken beyond the hull sheerline which will be scribed into the mould and the moulding is trimmed back to the line after removal. The LWL may also be scribed into the mould and any other positions which need to be marked for drilling or positioning hull fittings.

For a cabin boat the deck, cockpit and superstructure are usually moulded in one piece and the procedure is the same as for the hull in that a female mould is used. But in this case the moulding is rather more complex (Fig. 3.8.), as will be the interior mouldings which, if they are put in instead of joinery, will generally constitute the major part of the interior arrangement in just one or two pieces. Bulkheads, bunk bases, lockers and cabin sole can all be accommodated in one or more integrated mouldings which will be put into the hull (perhaps with most of their fittings) before the deck is bonded on.

The attachment of the deck can either be mechanical via a flange or overlapping joint, using rivets or nuts and bolts, or it can be with a resin bond employing strips of glass mat or cloth to overlap the joint. However, if the resin is to make a good bond with the two mouldings to be joined, it is necessary that they should not be allowed to cure for too long and that the surfaces to which the resin and mat is to be applied are well roughened up so that whiskery ends of glass are exposed.

Sandwich GRP Construction
This form of construction can be undertaken using a conventional, female hull mould, with the advantage that the

Fig. 3.9 Expanded plastic core material layed up on male mould for GRP sandwich construction; GRP outer and inner skins will follow.

outside skin has a gel coat which is impervious and has a high finish. But to do this denies some of the cost saving which can be made by using an elementary male form, a saving which it is claimed enables one-off hulls to be produced economically by this method. Although the male form may be rudimentary by comparison with the framing of a conventional boat, since it is only of a temporary nature, it does nevertheless have to be accurate and the lines still have to be lofted and the moulds set up properly if a good hull is to be taken from it. For hulls of suitable shape e.g. without tumblehome or integrated decks, it is possible to use the form for more than one vessel. It also, however, becomes dependent upon the method of attachment used for laying up the sheets of expanded foam on the male mould, which is the first part of the building operation. With any amount of in-curve above the maximum moulded beam, destruction of the form becomes inevitable, or at any rate it must be mostly dismantled to be withdrawn (Fig. 3.9.).

The sandwich consists of GRP/semi-rigid foam plastic/

GRP, and the core material is laid first. It needs some skill to tailor the material to the required fairness but the application of the GRP outer skin which follows is more a practised than a skilled operation. Much emphasis is placed upon longitudinal strength and uni-directional weave glass cloths are frequently used to obtain this. For the necessary combination of minimum thickness and weight with maximum strength, glass cloth may be used almost wholly for the outer laminate of the sandwich, mat being employed only for securing internal bulkheads, fillets etc.

The next stage of the work on the outer skin takes up rather a lot of time. It does not call for skilled labour but the finished appearance and the local fairness of the hull depend upon care, and much tedious work in flushing up the weave of the cloth with resin filler, fairing minor bumps and hollows, followed by sanding. The process is repeated until the desired surface is achieved. The subsequent lay up of the inside skin of the hull after removal of the form does not offer any particular difficulties, compression pieces can be inserted in way of chain plates etc. and attachments made in the same way as in a conventional GRP moulded hull.

In the absence of a gel coat, the outside of the hull is finally finished with polyurethane which will act as a sealant as well as providing a good appearance. This is an important part of the process because any strands of glass fibre which might be exposed in the final sanding operation can be hygroscopic and leaching out would occur in the course of time, as it does where damage is neglected on any GRP boat. Consequently, although the core material may be resistant to water absorption, the maintenance of an unimpaired surface finish is as important in sandwich construction as it is on any ordinary glassfibre hull.

It is claimed for the process that cost saving becomes worthwile on vessels of over 30ft and that the bigger the boat the more significant the economy. Apart from this aspect, the method does seem to offer structural advantages in larger GRP craft, where a great weight of material may be necessary purely to obtain the required rigidity, plus local stiffening which is to be avoided if possible. The sandwich built hull can, by comparison, be both light and rigid, it has a high tensile skin and stresses are spread more evenly through the structure because there need be no sudden changes of section through the addition of stiffening members.

Vacuum Press Moulded GRP

This is a process using a mould and lay up materials as for a conventional moulded GRP hull, with two differences. Firstly, a layer of sisal mat is incorporated in the lay up (generally half way through the laying up schedule so that the number of layers of glass mat or cloth used is symmetrical on either side of the sisal). Secondly, the complete lay up is covered with a polythene sheet and the air evacuated so that the laminations of glass and sisal plus resin are subjected to pressure against the mould.

The effect of the sisal is to provide a passage for the resin laterally to all parts of the moulding so that there are no dry areas and a complete wet out is obtained. The vacuum ensures that all air is driven out before the flow of resin and the moulding, when cured, is free from inclusions and has a wall strength somewhat higher for its thickness than a conventional moulding. A gel coat is used in the ordinary manner and the pressure provides a very high surface finish.

There are certain advantages in the process beyond the mechanical improvement of the moulding and these should appeal to professional moulders. The process is clean, resin is only poured once into the mould, no brushes, rollers or handwork with resin are required and the whole of the lay up process is dry. The labour requirement is less, and those needed for conventional lamination using one mould can be employed in laying up two to three moulds in the same number of hours. Finally, the vacuum pump is not expensive and there is only a small amount of additional equipment.

Part 3

Metal Hulls

Steel is frequently the first choice for building motor yachts and inland waterways boats, but it is not greatly employed in this country for motor cruisers and sailing vessels below 45ft although the Dutch yards produce many craft in steel that are smaller than this. Similarly, aluminium may be the first choice for the superstructure of a motor yacht but it finds little employment as a material for building hulls although it is eminently suitable for that purpose. The first cost will be higher but it has a negligible maintenance requirement (Fig. 3.10.).

For a small boat, metal is much more difficult to form to sweet lines than wood or glassfibre, also the equipment needed to build in metal is much more expensive. Further, aluminium in particular, poses its own problems in making welded joints which leave the material free from distortion, although the welds themselves may be thoroughly sound using an inert gas-shielded process.

Perhaps one of the so far unused techniques such as explosive forming may be taken up in the future for the flow production of small metal hulls but in the case of steel there are two kinds of exponents to date. Those who build hard chine craft calling for a minimum of metal working and those who are principally employed in building fully framed

Fig. 3.10 Completing the steel hull and aluminium superstructure plating on a 109ft luxury yacht. Camper and Nicholson.

vessels. Clearly, the work required for the latter category does not encourage the building of small hulls.

The principal members for a fully framed hull of steel or aluminium are similar to those of a conventionally built wooden boat and they have the same names. The obvious, major difference is that they do not have any timbers but the frames which replace these have exactly the same purpose, as do the keel, stem, stringers, deck beams and so on. But with some hard chine boats the hull is built on somewhat different principles, with fewer frames and a much greater reliance on the shell plating for the strength of the structure.

The welding of a modern steel boat is speeded up by using the CO_2 electric arc process with a continuous wire feed. Similarly, improvement has been made in overcoming corrosion by using pre-coated metal, which comes from the steel works already epoxy-zinc painted and needs to be cleaned off only in the area of the weld. This can be easily and promptly repainted so that corrosion does not have a chance to get an initial hold. The use of such pre-painted steel is not universal, but it seems to be a great step forward, and the results when seen at the end of construction are certainly impressive.

Part 4

Ferro-Cement and Cement-Fibre
There are not many yards building with ferro-cement but those who are involved have developed the process to a point where it can certainly take its place with the other constructional materials. Further, it has some specific advantages for use in waters known to be unkind from the aspect of borers and fouling. There are, however, a growing number of builders in the amateur field who see it as a method whereby one may acquire a fairly large boat at a low cost and a task which is within their range of skills.

The basis of a ferro-cement boat is a set of accurately made frames, shaped and welded up so that they can be set up with longitudinals to make the foundation of the metal armature. The completed armature will have on it perhaps six or more layers of half inch chicken wire laid up close together so that there are very few apertures remaining of any size. The job of plastering up with a mixture of cement, sand and pozolan (the latter ingredient improving the workability and strength of the mix) is best left to professionals as it all has to be done in one continuing operation. Major bulkheads and tanks inside the hull can also be of similar material, otherwise the interior is completed by joinery in the usual way. The deck and superstructure can similarly be either ferro-cement or timber.

Cement-fibre is quite different from the above in that there is no steel armature and the hull is a monocoque, depending upon a sandwich construction which uses an expanded foam plastic as the core and the outer layers of glassfibre mixed with aluminous cement which is sprayed on as a random mix. The initial procedure is much as for GRP sandwich construction in that the core is first layed up on a wooden form or male mould. The outer skin of the sandwich is then sprayed on and when it has cured, the mould is removed and the inner skin sprayed into the hull. The deck and superstructure can be similarly formed by making a suitable mould. Ordinary abrasives can be used to rub down the outer surfaces, and the boat can be finish painted with conventional materials.

Part 5

Vacuum Forming and Foaming
To date only comparatively small hulls have been produced on vacuum forming presses but it is a suitable and very rapid method for the production of plastic dinghies. By using inner and outer mouldings, with the space between filled by a foam plastic, a rigid and lightweight boat can be made (Fig. 3.11.). Various plastics may be used and it is somewhat dependent upon the availability of sufficiently large sheets, but a popular material employed for dinghies of about 12ft LOA is ABS, which forms easily and gives mouldings of consistent wall thickness. The hull shells so made are reasonably resistant to abrasion but there is the possibility of some deterioration over a long period through the ultra violet in sunlight. One of the principal attractions of a small boat made in this manner is that it can suffer a lot of damage without losing its buoyancy.

Fig. 3.11 Durafloat dinghy being taken from the jig in which the inner and outer halves are sealed together and filled with foamed plastic.

chapter 4

Practical Details

Part 1

BUILDING IN WOOD

The Moulds

Assuming that we have decided to build a round-bilge open launch and that we have drawn out the body plan on the floor or on sheets of hardboard, the next step is to make the moulds, which can be of any common wood of $\frac{1}{2}$ to $\frac{3}{4}$in in thickness. Since the planking will be laid round the moulds, the latter must be smaller than the sections by the thickness of the planking.

Great care must be taken in transferring the lines from the floor to the timber for shaping, and an excellent method is that used by many boatbuilders. Short iron nails with large heads, of the type used for fastening roofing felt, are filed flat on one side and a number of these are placed, flat side downwards at six inch intervals, exactly on the lines drawn on the floor.

The mould timber is then laid carefully over the nails and pressed down, thus causing the nail heads to sink into the grain of the wood and remain there. On lifting from the floor a thin batten can be held to the nail heads and a pencil line drawn for cutting purposes.

The mould of one side of a section is first cut to shape, and a duplicate is then made, the two being braced together with cross-ledges at the waterline and sheerline, care being taken to keep the ledges square. Two or more pieces of timber jointed together by means of ledges can be used for each half-section to avoid wastage. All moulds (and the transom) being prepared, the next step is to set them up in position.

To commence, a centreline is drawn on the floor with thwartship lines to mark the positions of the sections. At the mid-section a vertical strut (A) (Fig. 4.1.) is set up, one edge against the centreline and one face against the section line. The mould of the mid-section is then nailed to this strut at a convenient height from the ground. Diagonal struts (B,B) are set up to keep (A) vertical and rigid, and to hold the mould perfectly square to the centreline, similar struts (C,C) are set up on each side. Small boats are usually commenced bottom upward, so the mould is set up inverted.

The procedure is exactly the same with the other moulds, and care must be taken not only to get them square and level,

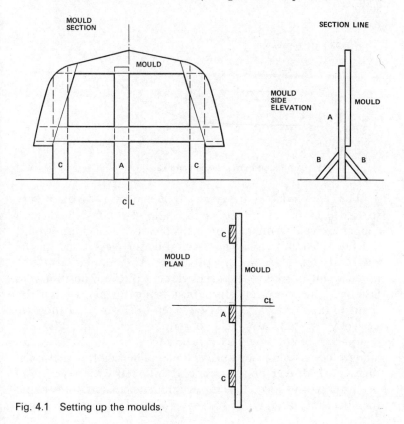

Fig. 4.1 Setting up the moulds.

but at the correct height from the floor, in order that they may follow the sheerline given in the design. It is usual to place the midship and all forward moulds with their forward faces over the correct section line. After moulds have their after faces over the section line. The object is to allow the planking subsequently put on, to touch one edge of each mould at the designed point, although the error would never amount to much, as the moulds are very thin relative to the length of the boat.

Keel, Stem and Stern Post
Assuming all moulds to be in place and their positions carefully checked, the keel (or hog) must be planed up to the designed shape, as also must the stern post or knee and the stem.

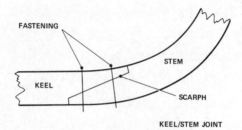

Fig. 4.1a   The scarph joint between stem and keel.

The stem and keel are generally joined by a scarph, a very strong form of joint (Fig. 4.1a.) and through-bolted with copper or yellow-metal bolts as indicated, steel bolts would quickly be eaten by sea-water. A rabbet or recess is cut in the keel and stem to take the planking. The moulds are then notched out to receive the keel, which is put into position and fastened, the stem and stern post being further secured by struts to the floor. Care must be taken to ensure that they are perfectly upright, any bias to right or left would give the completed boat a twisted appearance and would have an adverse effect upon her performance. The whole structure is then checked over once again and stiffened with braces and ties wherever needed. Battens are nailed to the moulds along the sheerline, and other battens are bent at various points over the moulds to make sure that they are all nicely 'faired up'. These also to provide support for the timbers, which, in carvel construction, must next be put in place.

Timbering

Timber stations must now be marked off on the keel, taking care in arranging the spacing not to come against any of the moulds. At each station a wedge-shaped notch is cut out to fit the timbers. These latter, perhaps of American elm, are planed to the correct dimensions, or, as a boatbuilder would say, to the correct scantlings, and steamed in a steam-charged box until they are quite pliable. They are then taken out, the ends cut to fit the notches in the keel, and then bent to fit firmly under the battens, being tacked to the sheer battens. No time must be lost in fitting the timbers after steaming, as they soon cool and lose their pliability. In the case just quoted we have described timbers butted into the keel, but the process is somewhat different for timbers which are continuous from gunwale to gunwale and carried over the keel—or, rather, under it, as we are building bottom up.

Planking

Now we come to the most difficult part of boatbuilding—planking up. This is the method for carvel construction. The 'midship mould is first marked out in equal sections corresponding to the finished width of the planking, which must always be narrow enough to make a fair curve round the bilge. Then a 'spiling' batten has to be used to plot in turn the shape of each strake. The plank nearest the keel (known as the garboard strake) is the first to be dealt with. The spiling batten must be as long as the strakes and 4in wide, with a straight line down its centre. Tack a ribband to the moulds where the first seam will come. Tack the spiling batten to the moulds between this ribband and the keel rabbet, and mark in the distances on the batten from its centreline to the rabbet and the ribband. Dot in these distances on the plank that will form the garboard strake, join up the dots and saw out. The plank may only touch the rabbet at a few points, but the greatest clearance must be measured and set off at a number of stations from the bottom of the rabbet on to the plank. If the plank is then cut away to the series of dots so obtained, it will have

47

nearly the correct curve to fit the rabbet. The plank is then fitted in place, the edge being previously chalked, and planed away with a fine plane where the chalk marks show the points of contact, until a perfect fit is obtained. The procedure with the rest of the planking is similar, the ribbands being removed one by one and replaced by strakes. If close seams are used, the edge of each plank is given a coat of thick varnish as it is put in place. A common method is to make the seams wedge-shaped when, to make them water-tight, they must be caulked with boat cotton. The seam is then filled with putty or some other stopping. The planking is through-fastened to the timbers with copper nails.

Turning Over, Fitting Gunwales
After planking, the boat is turned over, with the moulds still in her, and the gunwales are steamed and bent to shape, being through-fastened in position. Next, the nails of the planking are clenched off either on roves or by cutting them off within a quarter of an inch of the wood and hooking them over. One or two breasthooks may then be fitted, also quarter knees at the stern, and then the moulds can be taken out, the sides of the boat being prevented from flattening in by struts between the gunwales.

Floor Frames and Stringers
Templates, or thin wood patterns, of the floor frames are then made and the floors cut and fitted with chalk in much the same way as the planking. They are joggled over the keel and through-fastened to it, also to the planking. Water courses, or limber holes, must be cut in each floor, otherwise pumping water out of the bilge will afterwards prove a very tedious business, involving the separate draining of a number of compartments. Next the bilge stringers must be steamed and bent to shape and through-fastened, being either joggled over or butted against the tapered ends of the floors. The stringers are not joggled over the timbers, but laid over and through-fastened to them.

Framing and Planking a Hard Chine Boat
In the case of the hard chine, Vee bottom type hull, the permanent frames of the vessel are made up on the floor, and

temporary moulds are not necessary. The timber should be planed ready for use and the lines taken off the floor by the method recommended when making the moulds for a round-bilge boat.

Each frame must be assembled on the floor, care being taken to see that the edges of the timber are faired with the lines. Wooden brackets are fastened across the joints with a good-quality marine glue, and through-clenched with copper nails of a stout gauge on roves or washers. Temporary stretchers to secure the tops of the frames while building progresses should be fixed in position with screws, as the assembly of each unit is completed. The datum line should be clearly marked, and the frames numbered. The frames are set up, as in the case of moulds for the round-bilge craft, and notched to receive the hog so that the garboard strake lies fair. Chines are the next step, they must be sawn and planed to shape, bevels being taken at each station.

Frames are notched to receive them, and metal brackets, usually of galvanized mild steel, are used to secure the two members together with screw bolts. Care must be taken to see that the curve of the chine is sweet, and that all the frames fair perfectly. Any discrepancies must be corrected at this stage or a badly shaped hull, with the imperfections magnified in the eyes of the builder, will result.

When stringers and deck shelves are fitted the builder may proceed immediately to the planking stage.

For many years marine plywood has been deservingly popular for planking hard chine cruisers, runabouts and dinghies, as it is light and strong. Modern adhesives and factory techniques have removed the fear of parting laminations.

Plywood can be bent to conform to simple arrangements, the limiting radius being governed by the thickness and nature of the material. It is, however, possible to increase the radius by steaming. Compound curves to any marked degree are not possible, and for this reason the design of a boat should be carefully studied before deciding to substitute plywood for other methods of planking. It is not, however, wise to depart from the specification without consultation with the designer. The edges of exposed plywood should be sealed before fastening in position, also on meeting faces, with paint or resin glue.

Engine Bearers
In fitting the bearers, templates are used in the same way as with the floors, but the work of fitting is altogether more elaborate. Great care must be taken to get them correctly spaced and parallel. Through fastenings must be employed to hold them rigidly in position. Stiffening is effected either by struts to the stringers or by knees. The false keel, if specified, must now be through-bolted in position, the faces of the joint being well varnished or treated with a bedding preparation, as indeed all joints should be.

Sterntube Chock or Shaft Log
The tapered chock for the sterntube is then ready to be fitted. It will be cut nearly to shape from the design, being afterwards accurately fitted to the keel or hog and bolted in position. Naturally, there must be room between the two lines of bolts for the shaft and sterntube, the chock is bedded on a mixture of red and white lead.

Shaft Line—Boring
We are now in a position to mark out the shaft line and bore the sterntube chock to take it. The line on the design must be produced forward and aft, giving a point at which it touches the stem, also its position vertically under the transom. The corresponding points on the actual boat can then be marked (Fig. 4.2.). Next, we want two intermediate points, one just forward of the sterntube chock inside the boat, the other a foot or so aft of the point where the line comes outside the keel. These points must be carefully marked on pieces of wood nailed in place.

With the help of the points thus obtained, a small auger

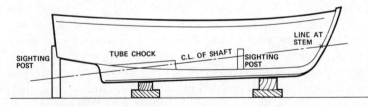

Fig. 4.2 Marking off the shaft line.

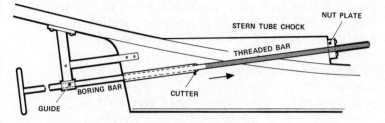

Fig. 4.2a   Boring the sterntube chock and deadwood.

can be put through the chock on the correct line, after which the hole is finished to the right diameter by means of a boring bar and cutter, usually fitted with a screw thread working in a nut plate (Fig. 4.2a.). The same drawing shows the guide used to preserve alignment.

Painting and Varnishing
All bare wood should receive at least one coat of priming paint before two undercoats and two topcoats of enamel. Generally, one of the thin primers, normally based on aluminium, is most suitable.

Between the priming and first undercoat a good rub down with a fine sandpaper should be given, but between subsequent coats, wet and dry paper should be used. This wet and dry paper is dipped in water occasionally to clear it of its dust.

On varnish work, the first coat on bare wood should be diluted with white spirit, and subsequent coats rubbed down with wet and dry paper. At least four coats should be aimed at.

Paint schedules for wooden, GRP, steel and ferro-cement boats are given at the end of this chapter.

WOODS USED IN BOAT CONSTRUCTION

The following lists show various kinds of wood commonly employed for different parts of a craft. Other timbers which have been introduced to the market in recent years have proved suitable for certain requirements.
Keel—English elm, African mahogany, iroko or English oak.

Stem and stern post floor frames and wood knees—English oak (natural crooks), oak, iroko or mahogany laminations. Note—Steel floor frames, if galvanized, may be used with advantage in large craft.

Engine bearers—Pitch pine, Oregon pine.

Timbers (bent)—American elm, English oak, or (for dinghies) ash. Laminated timbers can also be employed.

Timbers (sawn)—English oak (natural crooks).

Deadwoods and false keels—English oak and elm and also iroko are suitable for both purposes. Pitch pine, Oregon pine and African mahogany may be used for false keels.

Gunwale, beam shelves, and stringers—Oregon pine, pitch pine, mahogany and English oak or larch.

Deck beams and carlines—Oak, Pitch pine, Oregon pine.

Planking—Teak, mahogany, cedar, Pitch pine, Oregon pine, silver spruce, English oak, iroko, wych elm or larch. Marine grade plywood is also suitable for chine hulls and moulded construction.

Deck—Teak, mahogany, Oregon pine, Pitch pine, iroko, cedar, silver spruce, red and white deal (if covered with painted cotton or plastics material), marine grade plywood.

Coamings—Mahogany, pitch pine, teak and marine grade plywood.

Covering board—Where the deck is laid in narrow planks, a teak or mahogany covering board should be fitted; and, in some cases, a centre plank as well.

Thwarts and other seats—Teak, pitch pine, mahogany, Oregon pine, English oak, larch, red or white deal.

Bulkheads—The same as for seats, except that cedar may be used in very light craft. Marine plywood is frequently employed. Panelling of some proprietary composite material, such as Masonite, is also used.

Flooring and floor bearers—White or red deal, or marine ply. Sometimes teak gratings are employed. Risings and mouldings should be of mahogany, teak or pine.

Rudder and tiller—The rudder and steering gear on most yachts would be of gun-metal or galvanized mild steel, but in small motor dinghies and square-sterned yachts' launches it is usual to fit an oak, mahogany, teak or marine ply rudder with an ash or oak tiller.

NOTES ON TIMBER

Abura—A pale reddish-brown to light-brown wood of fairly fine even texture and of medium hardness. It works fairly easily, but requires care in nailing and screwing. Suitable for interior use as an alternative softwood. Weight 36lb per cu ft.

Afara—This is another softwood suitable for interior work. It is of pale straw colour to light yellow and is of medium hardness. Weight 35lb per cu ft.

Afrormosia—Widely employed for planking and decking. A yellowish-brown timber, moderately hard, strong, rot resistant and stable. Fairly easy to work but stains when in contact with ferrous metals under damp conditions. Weight 44lb per cu ft.

Afzelia—An African wood, very resistant to rot, hard, strong and stable. It is suitable for keels, stems and other structural members. Of reddish colour, it is moderately hard to work. Weight 48lb per cu ft.

Agba—A durable wood suitable for planking, decking, super-structure and other purposes. It is yellowish pink and yellow-ish brown in colour. The grain is similar to mahogany and is of medium hardness. Timber should be selected free of gum. Weight 30lb per cu ft.

American Elm—The rock elm is the best variety, and should be light in colour and extremely close-grained. It can be obtained in long lengths, but it is rarely free from shakes, and therefore much has usually to be cut to waste. It is very tough, but it is not suitable for any planking where it will be alternatively wet and dry, as, under those conditions, it is very liable to rot and to warp. Under sea water it is extremely durable, but it does not last so long in fresh water. Weight 50lb per cu ft.

Ash—Although a hard and excellent timber in many ways, ash is not generally recommended for boatbuilding owing to its low resistance to decay under damp conditions. However, it can be used fairly confidently for dinghy construction as these boats normally spend much of their time high and dry. Young pliable wood should be selected and well treated with Cuprinol or the wood preservative. The weight is in the region of 44lb per cu ft.

Elm—English elm is only suitable for keels, deadwoods, and planking below the waterline. It is not suitable in positions where it is alternatively wet and dry. Great care must be exercised in choosing elm, as it is frequently full of bad knots and shakes. Sap is not so harmful in elm as in any other wood. Its weight is about 35 to 43lb per cu ft when seasoned.

Freijo—A medium hard, stable and rot-resistant wood suitable for planking and decking. The colour is yellowish-brown. Although of coarse texture, it is easy to work, but is not always readily available. Weight 37lb per cu ft.

Guarea—Another wood sometimes employed for planking and decking. It is moderately resistant to decay and is light-pinkish or orange-brown in colour. This wood is of medium hardness, but is not particularly stable. Weight 37lb per cu ft.

Idigbo—With careful selection idigbo can be used as an alternative to oak. It is resistant to decay but is not as strong as oak. Idigbo is pale yellow to light brown in colour and is of coarse texture and medium hardness. Weight 36lb per cu ft.

Iroko—With careful selection this wood can be employed as an alternative to teak. It is very resistant to decay, is strong, hard and generally stable, although irregular grain may result in some distortion. It is light yellow when fresh, but ages to medium brown or dark reddish brown. Weight 41lb per cu ft.

Larch—Larch is tough, durable and fairly light, with either a straight or crooked grain, but it is very scarce and of poor quality in the South of England. It can be obtained in Scotland, Wales and Northern Ireland, and is suitable for planking. It must not, however, be supposed that it is as hard and durable as oak, or as tough as American elm, but it is lighter than either. It frequently entails much waste in working. Seasoned, it weighs about 35lb per cu ft.

Mahogany—Honduras and Philippine mahoganies are the finest timbers of their kind, but unfortunately they are not very plentiful and the boatbuilder must probably content himself with African mahogany. It is a tough wood and hard to finish, but it is widely employed for planking large and small craft. It can be obtained in long lengths and good widths. It weighs 35lb per cu ft.

Makore—A durable and stable timber suitable for underwater planking. It is generally of straight grain, fine even texture, hard and fairly strong. Weight 39lb per cu ft.

Oak—British-grown is far superior to any of the foreign oaks for all ship and boatbuilding purposes where crooked timber is required, but Japanese and American oak may be used for straight work, where toughness is not quite so essential. The straw-coloured oak with a fine grain is usually the toughest, and, if possible, it should be felled in the winter. Be careful to see that there are no sappy places or bad shakes in the wood and that it is not of a dark-reddish colour with an open grain. Next to teak, oak is the most durable wood used in boat-building. The weight of seasoned English oak is 46 to 48lb per cu ft.

Obechi—An alternative soft timber for interior work, but is not resistant to decay and consequently needs preservation. It is a creamy-white wood and, considering its light weight, possesses good strength properties. Weight 24lb per cu ft.

Oregon Pine—Similar to pitch pine, but much lighter and not so strong or durable; easy to work and tough, it is very suitable for all work where pitch pine is too heavy and great durability is not quite so important. Weight 33lb per cu ft.

Pitch Pine—A very tough and durable wood suitable for the planking of sea-going cruisers intended for rough work; also for the keels of light racing boats and for gunwales and stringers in any class of craft. It is heavy and difficult to work, owing to the resin clogging the tools. It is obtainable in long lengths. Weight about 41lb per cu ft.

Sapele—This wood, moderately resistant to rot, hard and strong, is suitable for planking and decking. Although it is not particularly stable, it can also be employed for joinery work, as it finishes and polishes well. It is somewhat similar to mahogany in appearance. Weight 40lb per cu ft.

Seraya, White—A pale straw-coloured wood of medium to coarse grain and moderately resistant to decay. Can be employed for planking and decking. It is of medium hardness. Weight 35lb per cu ft.

Silver Spruce—A good timber mainly used for spars and occasionally for planking on dinghies. It can be obtained in good sizes and entails but little waste in conversion. Weight about 28lb per cu ft.

Teak—Teak is the most durable wood known for boatbuilding, including planking, decks, hatchways and all sorts of deck

c

fittings and joinery work, and provides a very handsome finish when varnished, or for interior work, polished. Its weight, however, is against its use for planking small craft, although it is used for rubbing bands, seats, etc. It is not quite as heavy as oak and weighs between 40 and 45lb per cu ft. The so-called oiliness of teak is not due to any oil content, but to a natural resin which acts as a preservative. This resin when dry is slightly crystalline, and it is the effect of that on cutting tools which has probably given rise to the myth of hardness. Teak is a very poor bending wood, and so its use for steamed timbers is ruled out. Its natural straight growth, coupled with the fact that only the highest grades are imported into this country, precludes the possibility of finding anything in the nature of a naturally grown crook for stem or knees, as in the case of oak.

It is an expensive timber and users, or would-be users, of teak must know how to assess their requirements and how to order to keep the cost as low as possible. Do not, for instance, order a board 12in wide where two boards of 6in will do, or a length of 14ft where two 7ft lengths would be all right.

However, because there need be very little waste, teak can be considered an economical timber in use when taking into account long life and low maintenance costs.

Utile—A reddish brown wood with irregular striped grain. Is durable and often used in lieu of mahogany for planking, thwarts and coamings, but is generally rather heavier at 34 to 47lb per cu ft.

Western Red Cedar—A popular wood for building dinghies and decking. It takes a good finish and is fairly durable, but lacks resilience and is readily bruised. Weight 24lb per cu ft.

White or Red Deal—Names commonly applied to Scots pine. *Northern pine*, Norway fir or spruce, Swedish and Finnish fir, etc.; also known as European red or white wood. This timber is suitable for covered decks and interior work. Selected stock is sometimes used for planking. Weight 27 to 32lb per cu ft seasoned.

Wych Elm—Wych elm is usually paler than English elm and is considered to be a better-quality timber, being of straighter grain and finer texture. It is widely used for clinker construction. Seasoned weight, about 43lb per cu ft.

PLYWOOD IN BOATBUILDING

Plywood, as previously mentioned, is now widely used in boatbuilding, but it must be borne in mind that not all grades are suitable for boatbuilding purposes. Only material conforming to the British Standards Institute's BS 1088 should be employed as planking, decks, cabin tops and for other exterior purposes. Woods used in the manufacture of marine plywood include African mahogany, sapele and makore.

Laminated stems, knees and other boat members come within the scope of the amateur builder, there being various synthetic resin glues on the market which are waterproof and do not require heat for setting. All that is required to make a laminated member is a jig of the shape required, made up of stout timber, sufficient strips of wood $\frac{1}{4}$ to $\frac{3}{8}$in thick and wide enough to make up the member, also a number of large G cramps or joiners' sash cramps, and, of course, a quantity of glue which must be used according to the makers' instructions. The strips are coated with glue, pulled into the shape of the jig by the aid of the cramps and left until set. The resulting member will be as strong as, if not stronger than, one fashioned from solid timber.

For panelling, the opportunities offered by decorative plastics-faced hardboard and plywood should not be overlooked. They have the advantage of requiring no painting or other maintenance apart from washing down, and retain their freshness under reasonable wear and tear conditions from season to season.

Part 2

COMPLETING A GRP HULL

Working with glass mat and resin is more a matter of practice than great skill. The very ease with which it can be manipulated, and the manifold possibilities which open up once a small amount of experience has been gained with the material, can sometimes lead to usage which will not pass critical examination. When joining GRP to GRP, or wood to GRP, or taping on fittings, etc. it must be borne in mind that the curing of the GRP basic moulding will make a great difference to the strength of the bond achieved with subsequent joints and attachments.

On breaking apart a GRP joint for test purposes, it will often be found that the attachment has depended almost wholly upon intimate contact without fusion. The joint will frequently part with only the minimum disturbance or the tearing of the fibres in either component. It is possible that the joint face will have few signs of anything ever having been attached to it, although considerable force is required to tear it apart.

In the fitting out of a GRP hull it would therefore be wise to assume that the state of cure of the mouldings is such that you can expect no fusion between the old and the new resin, but by adequate roughening up of both components you may achieve an intimate mechanical bond. It is desirable too that besides aiming at a mechanical bond at the joint faces, the joint itself is designed as far as possible to be mechanically strong through the disposition of the components. A simple illustration of this is given in Fig. 4.3. and if the general idea is assimilated you will have a much stronger boat.

A GRP hull obtained for fitting out at home can often be obtained in several different stages of completion. It may be a bare hull shell, a hull and deck either separate or bonded together, or a hull with deck and superstructure separate or bonded. Also of course interior mouldings will often be available, separately or incorporated. Unless you are only interested in a GRP hull shell to be subsequently finished with wood superstructure and furniture, it is clearly advantageous to obtain the hull and deck bonded together. One good reason being that big GRP mouldings, although they may have adequate strength, can be quite floppy until the interior mouldings and the deck/superstructure is bonded on. At the factory the hull will probably be in a jig or cradle during the bonding operation so that everything is lined up, and you will not have that advantage. Another thing is that due to the changing curvature, particularly in a round-bilge hull, and the fact that you are unlikely to have any markings for stations, thwartship or longitudinal levels inside the hull, you could

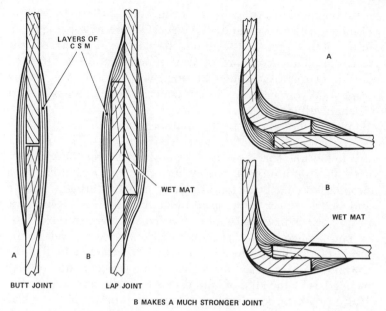

LAYERS OF
C S M

WET MAT

A

B

WET MAT

A   B

BUTT JOINT   LAP JOINT

B MAKES A MUCH STRONGER JOINT

Fig. 4.3   Joining glassfibre panels and mouldings.

have considerable difficulty in positioning the interior furniture and bulkhead mouldings in exactly the right places. It
depends upon how much confidence you have in your ability
to cope, and you will also need assistance if only for lifting,
if you are starting from scratch.

The builder supplying the mouldings will generally
provide the resin and glass materials you need for your task,
and, if it is convenient to you, he will often also let you see
similar craft being assembled so that you may learn at first
hand. The extent of the drawings and specification provided
will depend very much upon the extent of the builder's trade
in kits. Some have very complete arrangements to meet the
requirements of the home builder.

To return to basic considerations, and assuming that you
have acquired a bare hull to finish with a wood superstructure
and interior joinery. You may have your hull completely bare,
but if it can be obtained with fore and side deck moulding you
will find it easier to attach your superstructure and, as

mentioned before, you will be working on a stiffer base. A hull supplied with a fore and side deck will preferably have an upstanding flange at the inner edge of the deck. It will be seen that if the coaming of your superstructure is attached outside of this by through bolting, with the use of a sealing compound you will have a joint which is both water-tight and mechanically sound.

Where there is no deck moulding you will need to fit a beam shelf as in a wooden boat (see Chapter 3). This member will follow the sheerline, and being high up on the topsides, with the possibility of having any fastenings covered by a rubbing strake, it can be attached both by through bolting and matting over with resin and csm (Fig. 4.4.). Once the beam shelf is in construction proceeds as for a wooden boat excepting of course where attachments have to be made to the inside of the hull. The only method of attachment feasible without drilling holes in the hull skin, which is not recommended, is by the kind of joint discussed earlier in this chapter. That is, by a thorough roughening of the surface of the inside hull where the floor, stringer or bulkhead is to be situated, and then securing with a fillet consisting of layers of strips of

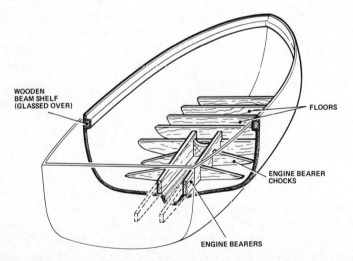

Fig. 4.4 Disposition of wooden floors, engine bearers and engine bearer chocks in a GRP hull. All of these members would be glassed over as indicated by the wooden beam shelf.

glass mat, stippled on with resin and a brush, and then compacted with a small roller. If the member to be attached has a reasonable surface area on the joint face, as for instance an engine bearer, floor or stern chock, it can be bedded on wet mat or resin and filler before being glassed in.

The wood must be new and absolutely clean and a medium sanded surface will hold quite well. In the case of a bulkhead it will only be possible to secure with fillets, but a floor or an engine bed can be attached much more securely and protected from oil and water by glassing right over (Fig. 4.4.).

In order to save wastage of material, and in the interest of closer joints, it is best to make templates for all members which have to mate with any curved part of the hull. These can be made of cheap wood or even stiff cardboard, which can be tacked onto a batten if necessary to make it more rigid. But before making any templates it is essential to set the hull up and mark some interior reference points for longitudinal and thwartship levels, and verticals which will make a proper right angle with these.

If the LWL has been scribed into the mould you will have a line on the moulding to guide you when you set up the hull. Otherwise you will have to make some marks from figures obtained from the hull drawing and connect these so as to obtain a line on the outside of the hull which you can level it up to. Having got the hull in the attitude, lengthwise and laterally, which you believe to be correct, and having secured it against movement, you are now able to provide yourself with a datum inside the hull.

You will no doubt have made some rough drawings of your arrangement inside the hull, and one of the things you will have decided is the height of the cabin sole (which on many small boats will also decide its length and width). Cut templates of the foremost and the aftermost floors or bearers under the sole and adjust them for your required height. A further adjustment will be necessary with a light batten laid fore and aft across to get them horizontal, longitudinally and athwartships, with the aid of a spirit level. On cutting and fitting the floors from the templates, you will achieve a horizontal datum from which most other things can proceed. The longitudinal placement of the floors will have been indicated earlier by drawing a string or wire taut between the bow and the centre of the transom, and dropping a plumb bob from this as required to get section station and other measurements between bow and stern. It should be noted that floors are not essential in a GRP boat, and a factory built vessel may not have any, but when fitting out a bare hull from scratch they can be useful in providing a datum and base from which to work, besides acting as cabin sole bearers and reinforcement for bilge keels.

If the main members are truly vertical it will assist when attending to later joinery, and all floors and bulkheads should be checked for accurate placement with either the plumb line or a spirit level with a cross bubble.

The remainder of the joinery will follow according to your inclinations. Such things as bunk and locker fronts can either be secured by strips of mat with resin making a fillet inside, or a light stringer can be matted to the hull and the bottom of the bunk front screwed to this (Fig. 4.5.). If you can think ahead so as to have drawn or visualised all of the attachments required to the hull before boxing in too much with furniture, you will save time later, e.g. glassing in small wood bearers for the WC, pads for attaching bilge pumps, etc. and pads and glass reinforcement for chainplates and staunchion mounting.

If your hull has a GRP deck, through fixings in direct

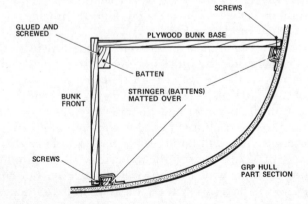

Fig. 4.5 Glassing in stringers and battens to provide location for bunk bases and fronts in a GRP hull shell.

tension with a suitable pad and large washers and glass reinforcement is in order. But if you have a wooden deck, unless the chainplates have been bonded into the topsides during moulding they will need to be put on pads which have been glassed onto the inside of the hull and through-bolted so that they are in sheer. In this case the fitting may either be on the outside of the hull or on the inside with the eye emerging through the deck.

If you are going to put bilge keels on your hull, whether for protection or for sailing, and there is no drawing to consult, it should be arranged that the bolts for these go through the floors. If these are absent or of insufficient span, wide bilge stringers should be glassed into the bottom on each side of the boat so that the bilge keel bolts can come up through them.

Engine bearers need close consideration in hulls of all kinds and with a GRP boat the same basic requirement is there, that is for the load to be spread as far through the hull as possible. Since these will be higher than the floors (if floors are fitted) in a small boat their length is immediately restricted by the cabin sole requirement. Where the floors, if present, are not to be the cabin sole bearers the engine bearers can be half jointed so as to sit on these and the bottom of the hull, and taken fore and aft for as far as is convenient. There should be no through fixing to the hull skin as in a wooden boat, but they should be completely glassed in onto the bottom and to the floors too after glueing and screwing at the half joint (Fig. 4.4.). Remember to keep limber holes in the floors clear when applying the csm and resin. It is a good idea to get some short lengths of dowelling and, after waxing, insert them through the limber holes before completing the glassing in of the floors, but you should remember to remove them whilst the resin glass is still at a 'doughy' stage.

For most of these glassing in operations either one and a half or 2 oz chopped strand mat will be found convenient and two or three laminations should be put on as a minimum according to weight for light bulkheads, etc. Three or four for main bulkheads and floors, and four to six for engine bearers. The suggestion is approximate but should give an adequate margin of strength for displacement power boats and sailing vessels with auxiliaries up to about 25ft LOA. Significant increase of either LOA, or power to achieve express cruiser speeds will call for a judicious scaling up of these suggestions. The dimensions of the wood bearers prior to glassing in will be much the same as for a wooden boat. Similarly, if there are no convenient floors to give lateral support you will need to incorporate some cross chocks to keep the bearers vertical, and these also should be glassed in with the bearers. In the event that no floors are called for in the design, the cross chocks obviously have great importance, and an adequate number must be incorporated to support the engine bearers, particularly in way of the engine.

Engine bearer data is scarce, but an example may serve as an indication. In a range of GRP cruisers fitted with diesel or petrol engines of up to 50bhp, fully glassed in wood bearers of approximately $3\frac{1}{2}$in width with an average depth of about nine inches have proved adequate over a long period. As previously mentioned, bearers should extend fore and aft as far as possible, and be tied in with the boat structure—hull and floors.

Whether for power or sailing auxiliary, the requirement for the sterntube chock is much the same as for a wooden boat excepting of course that its attachment to the hull will be by glassing in as for the floors and engine bearers. It may be that you will also be making provision for the rudder tube in this area if it is not an outboard hung rudder. A convenient way to tackle these two requirements is by fitting a short piece of hardwood into the bottom of the hull, rather like a false hog, so that it is on the centreline and runs from the transom forward, at least as far as where the face of the sterntube chock will be. This should be bedded onto the bottom of the hull on wet mat and resin, or one of the glass fillers and resin. When set, the sterntube chock can be glued and screwed to the top of it in the required position, and the whole lot matted over to the hull, i.e. glassed in. The after end of the hog piece will provide either a seat for a bottom flange on the rudder tube, which can be screwed to it, or additional bearing area, if the tube is to pass through and be glassed in.

APPLICATION OF RESIN/GLASS

There are basic considerations for the resin and glass which you will use in bonding your attachments to the GRP hull.

It is likely that your materials will be provided by the moulder on request, if not he will tell you where you may obtain supplies. The standard polyester resin which you will probably use (since epoxy resin is very much more expensive) is very much like syrup in appearance and viscosity. Although it has a shelf life, which means that it must be used within a certain time before a natural setting process sets in (polymerisation), it will not normally 'cure' (harden or polymerise) unless a catalyst is added, and the process can also be speeded up by the addition of an 'accelerator'. This accelerator may be added by the user to combat cold conditions, temperature being one of the factors affecting the time for curing. But some may have been added to the resin at the factory in conformity with the moulder's requirements. Most resin supplied for amateur use has an accelerator incorporated, but more may be needed for abnormal conditions.

A resin which has had an accelerator incorporated prior to delivery will still not cure in the ordinary course of usage without a catalyst being added. It is important for you to know what you are using and you should obtain the supplier's recommendation. The other way out is to conduct some small experiments before starting on the proper job.

In every case you will of course need to add a catalyst in the recommended quantity to the resin you are about to use immediately, since even the slowest mix is liable to 'go off' or start to polymerise within an hour. Your brushes will also start to harden in this period and since they are expensive, and it is an irreversible process, you should plunge them into acetone immediately after use. This acetone, incidentally, will be useful also in cleaning and slightly softening areas on cured mouldings which you have roughened up in order to bond on another member. You should also acquire a suitable barrier cream and a recommended hand cleaner before you start operations.

You will probably not need to use any other than chopped strand mat (csm) for all of the work involved in fitting out a bare GRP hull shell, although cloth of various weaves and rovings, which are unidirectional filaments, are available for specialized uses. You should obtain the grade known as 'E' glass which is more resistant to moisture, and in order that you get the easiest application when stippling the material into corners, fillets, etc., it is recommended that you use $1\frac{1}{2}$ and 2oz material. You will find it much easier to put on an extra laminate rather than cope with a thicker mat. The csm, which is composed of random, short filaments, is held together in its mat form by a binder, and this must be soluble by the resin so that complete wetting out is achieved and the relaxed mat is enabled to 'drape' in conformity with the mould, corner or fillet to which it is being applied. In nearly all cases you will find that the best tool for pushing the material into the required places is a good quality paint brush with sufficient bristles to be stiff enough for stippling without being hard. Brushes from 2 to 3in are the most generally used for this work.

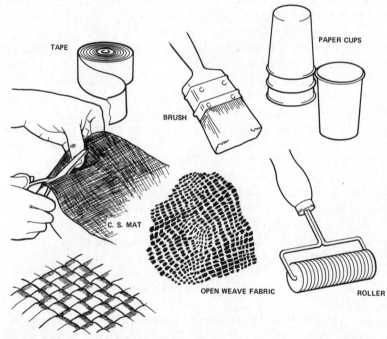

Fig. 4.6 The tools and materials for GRP work. The use of throwaway paper cups for the resin enables small quantities to be conveniently made up and, except for brushes and rollers, cleaning problems are avoided.

A liberal brushing of resin should be put on the work area before applying the first layer of mat. This should then be stippled until the resin comes up through it and it can be seen that a complete 'wet out' has been achieved. The next layers of resin and mat are applied in the same manner and so on until the required laminate thickness is obtained. As far as possible force the resin up through the mat rather than brushing it over the top. When all of the layers of glass have been applied the whole must be consolidated by a thorough rolling, so that all entrapped air is removed and one solid matrix is obtained. You will need rollers in one or two sizes to effect this last job satisfactorily, and for the type of work under discussion from 1 to 2in width would be most useful (Fig. 4.6.).

It should be remembered that the curing time will depend greatly upon the ambient temperature. If you are operating on a really warm day you will have to move fast to use resin which has been compounded for use in about 65°F. Similarly, the temperature of the workpiece itself may vary a lot especially if it is exposed to the sun. Working in a hull first thing in the morning will give quite different conditions from those to be experienced at midday and you must either make allowance for your usual resin mix or alter it to suit.

PAINTING SPECIFICATIONS

These example painting schedules are taken from the Yacht Painter's Manual published by International Yacht Paints and we are glad to acknowledge the information provided.

Painting Wooden Yachts

Topsides, Superstructure, Spars, Cabins, Boottops (if not subjected to fouling) and bottoms of craft kept ashore. Also Decks with grit added.
Priming (if required):   Metallic Pink Wood Primer
Undercoat: Undercoat for Interlux Yacht Enamel
Topcoat: Interlux Yacht Enamel
(Undercoat can be mixed with a small amount of enamel to give a flat finish for interior work.)
Alternative spec.: Prime if necessary as before then,
Undercoat: As above or 101 Polyurethane

Topcoat:	101 Polyurethane

Boottops and Bottoms either permanently afloat or drying out.

Priming (if required):	Metallic Pink Wood Primer
Undercoat:	Lake Racing or Hard Racing or Extra Strong Hard Racing or Anti-fouling Boottop.
Topcoat:	As for undercoat.

Boottops and Bottoms which are permanently afloat.

Priming:	As before, if necessary
Undercoat:	Underwater undercoat
Topcoat:	Kobe Anti-fouling or Interplastic or Cruiser Anti-fouling.

For stoppers use Trowel Cement or Interpad above water; Metallic Primocon below water.

Iron Keels and underwater Ironwork.

Condition:	Rusty, shot blast or wire brush. Galvanized or Zinc Sprayed, wash with fresh water.
Primer:	Five coats of Metallic Primocon
Finish:	As for wooden hull
Condition:	Anti-fouling in good condition. Apply Undercoat and finish with Anti-fouling as for wooden hull.

Lead Keels and Bronze Propellers

Condition:	Damaged, clean with emery cloth. Apply one coat of Underwater Undercoat followed by five coats of Metallic Primocon. Anti-foul as for rest of hull.
Condition:	Anti-fouling good. Apply one coat Undercoat and Anti-fouling as for rest of hull.

Varnishing Wooden Yachts

Exterior varnishing

Scheme 1: One coat Blue Peter Marine Varnish thinned with 20% White Spirit if on bare wood, then three to four coats of Marine Varnish. On old varnish, rub down and apply two coats Marine Varnish.

Scheme 2 :   One coat 101 Polyurethane Varnish thinned with 20% White Spirit if on bare wood, then three to four coats of 101 Polyurethane Varnish. On old varnish, rub down and apply two coats 101 Polyurethane Varnish.

Scheme 3 :   One coat of Moisture Cured Polyurethane Varnish thinned with 10% MCPV thinners, if on bare wood, then three to four coats of MCP Varnish. On old varnish, rub down and apply two coats MCP Varnish.

Scheme 4 :   One coat 707 Penetrating Wood Primer for bare wood, then three to four coats of 707 Polyurethane Varnish. On old varnish rub down and apply two coats of 707 Polyurethane Varnish.

Interior varnishing

As above with alternative use of Matt Cabin Varnish to finish on Scheme 1 and Eggshell Polyurethane Varnish finish on Scheme 4.

Glassfibre Yachts. First painting and repainting

All surfaces

For first painting remove all traces of wax or silicone polish with Oil Removing Fluid, then prime with Glassfibre Primer.

The Glassfibre Primer is required only for new GRP and it must be overcoated within twenty four hours. Thereafter the paint schedule for new and repainting GRP is:

Topsides, superstructure, etc.

| Undercoat: | Undercoat for Yacht Enamel |
| Topcoat: | Yacht Enamel |

Alternative spec.

| Undercoat: | Undercoat for Yacht Enamel or 101 Polyurethane |
| Topcoat: | 101 Polyurethane |

Boottops and Bottoms which are either permanently afloat or drying

If not previously painted, prime as above, then for first painting and repaint:

| Undercoat: | As for wooden hulls |
| Topcoat: | As for wooden hulls |

Boottops and Bottoms which are permanently afloat

If not previously painted prime as above, then for first painting and repaint:

Undercoat: As for wooden hulls
Topcoat: As for wooden hulls

Iron Keels and Bronze Propellers

As for wooden hulls.

Steel Yachts

Topsides, Superstructure, etc.

For bare plate, new or repaint: shot blast or wire brush then Bare Plate Primer then:

Undercoat: Undercoat for Yacht Enamel (two coats).

Topcoat: Yacht Enamel.

Alternative spec.

Undercoat: Undercoat for Yacht Enamel and one coat 101 Polyurethane.

Topcoat: 101 Polyurethane.

For stainless steel: Prime with one coat Self Etch Primer and one coat Bare Plate Primer if above water, and one coat Metal Primocon if below water. The undercoat and the finish coat is as for steel.

Boottops and Bottoms which are either permanently afloat or which dry out

New or bare metal prime with two coats Metal Primocon then Primocon Filler if necessary followed by two more coats Metal Primocon. Allow more than five days for drying.

Undercoat: As for wooden hulls
Topcoat: As for wooden hulls

Boottops and Bottoms which are permanently afloat

For new metal use Metallic Primocon for undercoat allowing twenty four hours drying, otherwise:

Undercoat: As for wooden hulls
Topcoat: As for wooden hulls

Aluminium and Zinc Sprayed Boats and Galvanizing

Topsides, Superstructure, etc.

Before priming degrease aluminium with carbon tetrachloride. Wash zinc spray and galvanized iron with fresh water.

Priming:	Self Etch Primer then Light Alloy Primer if bare metal
Undercoat:	As for steel hulls
Topcoat:	As for steel hulls

Boottops and Bottoms permanently afloat or drying

New metal, Self Etch Primer then four coats of Metallic Primocon. Allow at least five days drying.

Undercoat:	Undercoat for Boottop and Bottoms (new metal; no undercoat required if previously painted.)
Topcoat:	Extra Strong Hard Racing Anti-fouling White two coats.

Boottops and Bottoms permanently afloat

Prime as before for drying bottoms and bottoms then undercoat with another coat of Metallic Primocon if new metal, otherwise use Underwater Undercoat.

Topcoat:	Light Alloy Anti-fouling two coats.

Painting Copper Bottoms

Clean surface with emery cloth.

Undercoat:	Underwater Undercoat
Topcoat:	Kobe Anti-fouling or Interplastic

Ferro-Cement Boats

Topsides, Superstructure, etc.

Allow ferro-cement one month to cure before priming and on new surfaces use two coats Primer for Ferro-Cement with Interpad Filler between if required.

Undercoat:	Undercoat for Yacht Enamel, two coats for new surfaces
Topcoat:	Yacht Enamel

Alternative spec.

Undercoat:	Undercoat for Yacht Enamel plus one coat 101 Polyurethane if new, otherwise: one coat 101 Polyurethane
Topcoat:	101 Polyurethane.

Boottops and Bottoms permanently afloat and drying

New surfaces prime with three coats of Epoxide Resin

71

Practical Details

Composition facing up with Interpad between if required, otherwise, for repaint:

Undercoat: As for wooden hulls
Topcoat: As for wooden hulls

Boottops and Bottoms permanently afloat

New surfaces prime with two coats Primer for Ferro-Cement and Interpad if required, then for new and repaints:

Undercoat: Underwater Undercoat
Topcoat: As for wooden hulls.

Anti-fouling for Ferro-Cement may also be applied direct to the bottom when cured. If a change of anti-fouling is desired later the Anti-fouling for Ferro-Cement must be insulated by one coat of Metallic Primocon.

Decks

After priming, if necessary, according to the foregoing specifications for the various materials, all painting is similar with one coat of Deck Paint followed by another coat of ordinary or Non-Slip Deck Paint.

Aluminium Alloy Outdrives

For first painting degrease with White Spirit.

Priming: Self Etch Primer then two coats
                                    P.U. Primer for Steel and Light
                                    Alloy
Undercoat: 708 Polyurethane White
Topcoat: Extra Strong Hard Racing White
                                    Anti-fouling two coats.

For repainting, wire brush any damaged areas before re-priming.

Rubber Dinghies

May be resurfaced with one or more coats of Coating for P.V.C.

Chain Lockers, Bilges, Tank Exteriors

After priming, if necessary, according to the foregoing specifications for the various materials, all painting is similar

with Danboline Red or Grey two coats. The priming of ferro-
cement may be varied though by using two coats of Cement
and Plaster Primer.

Recommended Grades of Rubbing Down Paper

Grades of paper commonly used range from 100 to 400
with 500 or 600 occasionally for removing blemishes from a
surface which is to be burnished to a high gloss.

The use of wet and dry paper used wet is not recommended
on bare wood.

100 or 120	Use along the direction of the grain to remove remnants of loose paint after burning off or stripping. Sand down again with a finer paper.
180 or 200	Use on new wood or wood burnt off as above after 100. These grades are too coarse for rubbing down wood which is to be varnished.
230	For rubbing down old enamel prior to under-coating.
280–320	For rubbing down wood to be varnished and rubbing down new undercoating which is to be enamelled.
320	For rubbing down varnish or enamel and undercoating.
400	For rubbing down freshly applied enamel.
400, 500 or 600	For removing blemishes from finished paint-work.

chapter 5

Interior Design

Few aspects of boat building have shown more progress in recent years than the design of accommodation, especially in the smaller yachts. To some extent this has depended upon modification of profiles and external shape generally, which would not have been tolerated in earlier times when hull lines were unalterable boundaries for any kind of requirement down below. If, for a few years, and in answer to popular demand the pendulum tended to swing the other way so as to run near to a caravan approach to the problem, there are few examples of such building left today, and great strides have been made to make boats that are liveable without appreciable sacrifice of either appearance or performance.

In order to achieve the desired end, considerable ingenuity is often shown in the treatment of small craft layouts. Some features have been successfully borrowed from other spheres (the dinette) and others have been developed and practised to an extent which makes clear the value of their contribution (quarter berths). These are solid gains, as is the development of marine domestic equipment such as inexpensive WC's of small overall dimensions, and galley furniture which is not so far removed from the facilities one might expect to find ashore. But caution is needed in assessing the worth of much that is offered in the way of features and gadgetry proposed to extend the range of accomplishments afloat. It is hardly possible to be specific, but in general it should be borne in mind that things which operate with delightful ease at the Boat Show will not always be amenable to different angles of attack, such as may be enforced at times when at sea, or even when you are being rocked gently at a mooring.

It has been a habit for some designers and builders of small boats to proclaim the number of berths they have managed to accommodate as a principal attraction or description of the vessel. It is certainly something a prospective owner needs to know but perhaps too much emphasis is laid upon it, to the exclusion of other considerations which become more important as the number of berths increases. Sleeping and sailing are not the sole preoccupations of a crew, they also need room to move about, to hang their clothes and to stow their gear. If there are more than two or three in the boat's complement they will also need some washing facility besides the galley pump, and so it goes on. Those who ignore these requirements in the beginning may well find their lack of foresight the beginning of a general disenchantment for both them and their families.

In very small boats whether power or sail there is very little room for subsequent additions in the layout. The provision made for lockers and general stowage in relation to the number of berths needs careful consideration, unless you are prepared, as many owners are, to account one of the berths as necessary stowage space. This is a good approach anyway to the question of crew numbers, and much more conducive to a happy ship. There is, after all, enough crowding when you step ashore and it may be assumed that one of the reasons you took to the water was to find a bit more elbow room.

It has been remarked that the supposed accommodation requirement for the smallest cruisers appears to vary greatly according to whether they are sail or power. A sailing boat of less than 20ft LOA will frequently boast four berths whereas a power vessel of about that size will more likely have two. It is true that claims may be made that there are berths in the cockpit, etc. but in this connection we are entitled to consider only berths under permanent cover as being eligible in the count. Nevertheless even here there can be some bending of the truth, as for instance one boat which was marketed as having five berths of which it would be reasonable to consider only three as being worthy of the name, the other two were located, one on the cabin sole and the other on the galley top. Actually this was a very pleasant little three berth cruiser, but in view of the 'berth hunger' exhibited by so many prospective owners, few would have dared to call it such.

The accommodation arrangements shown here offer several approaches for sail and power vessels of various sizes, but whether plans, sections or photographs, there are some things which cannot be made clear and which need to be remembered when looking at catalogue illustrations generally, unless they are very comprehensive. The height over a quarter berth is as important to the occupant as its length and breadth and the same thing may be said for berths under a foredeck. Cooks last longer when the galley is near the hatch opening, and also if they can either stand up straight or be seated on a stool. Headroom is not as important in the WC compartment as it is in the galley—unless a washbasin is in there too. Stowage space below berths is nearly useless unless it has a bottom which can be reached and is closed off from the bilges. Avoid too many detachable pieces of furniture and also those items which are claimed to 'hinge down', 'fold up', 'slide out' and permutations of these manoeuvres. In a small vessel some of this will no doubt be necessary, but a simple solidity is a great virtue in any fitment or equipment aboard a boat.

It may be of some help if you try to visualize your accommodation requirement not only in terms of the numbers to be catered for, but also your probable use of the boat in regard to season and range. The Scandinavians, who certainly have summers no better than ours, and they are a good deal shorter, make much more of their vessels by putting many of the facilities into a bigger cockpit which, although it can be protected by a canopy gives every opportunity to make the most of a sunny day. Many of their boats are arranged so that they can cook, eat and lounge without going below. If, as you may well think, you are going to use your vessel as much as possible when the sun shines and you do not intend to do any long open water crossings, then an honest acknowledgement of the limitations of your use could provide you with a better vessel for your purpose.

All but two of the vessels mentioned in this chapter are GRP (the Otter is a planked boat and the Maas is all-welded steel). Most GRP boats nowadays have some form of lining to combat condensation and this may take the form of a separate internal moulding for the superstructure, or some kind of fabric lining such as vinyl cloth, which may be mounted on light panels or stretched between battens so as to make a neat interior finish. Whichever method is used a lining is well worth having on a GRP or a metal boat. On larger power boats which might have a considerable amount of wiring for electrical services it is probably better to have the lining on demountable panels so as to improve accessibility.

The Pacific 550 (Fig. 5.1.) makes a good accommodation example in the midget cruiser or power weekender class; she is 18ft LOA and has a beam of 6ft 6ins. The two berth layout, with a galley and toilet facility on either side of the cabin entry, is typical of the arrangements in many power craft of about this size. The berths can be bridged with a centre piece so as to make room for two adults and a child, and there is the possibility of two more temporary berths in the cockpit under a canopy. Headroom is restricted in a boat of this size but the after ends of the berths give sitting accommodation.

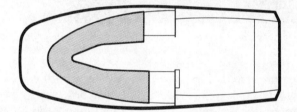

Fig. 5.1 The Pacific 550, a weekend boat designed for outboard power. It has a big cockpit and two berths with a toilet and galley space on either side of the hatch entry.

The marginally bigger Shetland 570 and the Dolphin 20 are other examples in this class with somewhat similar layout plans but more headroom.

Loosely termed 'family cruisers', this sector of the pleasure boat field offers a wider variety in size and accommodation arrangements than any other. An attempt at definition still leaves a multitude of boats anything between 20ft and perhaps more than 40ft LOA, with aft and centre cockpit vessels and an indefinite number of layout permutations within these two major classifications. There are, however, other broad differences besides these and they may be noted

Fig. 5.2 Showing the two tier berth arrangement in the bows of the Natant 23.

as 'all-cabin boats', 'big cockpit' or fisherman type boats, and craft which tend to provide a balance between these rival accommodation claims. Clearly, the bigger the boat, the smaller the problem in this connection but a small vessel which offers a nice solution is the Natant 23. (Fig. 5.2.). An attractive and space saving feature in this boat is the use of two levels in the cabin in order to telescope the sleeping accommodation. By raising the wide berth which spans the bows above the level of the settee berths on either side of the cabin, the feet of the latter can be run partly under those above, thus shortening the length to much less than the 13ft or so which would otherwise be needed. However, it is not claimed that the forward berth would accommodate other than two children in comfort although the two settee berths are of adequate size. The space so saved provides for a galley to starboard and an enclosed toilet compartment on the other side. It also enables a larger amount of boat to be given to the cockpit, and the

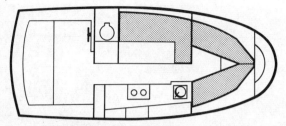

Fig. 5.3 The ample beam of the Seamaster 23 gives room for a two berth dinette with galley opposite as well as two berths in the bows.

general usage of space on this boat serves as an example of what can be provided without unusual cramping or gadgetry on an overall length of under 24ft.

Another example and perhaps more typical of space distribution in a vessel of this approximate length is the Seamaster 23 (Fig. 5.3.), where considerably more of the boat is devoted to the cabin and room is found for full length berths in the bows with a dinette converting into a double berth placed aft of this to port. There is still room for a toilet compartment on that side and the galley takes up the full length of the cabin to starboard. This arrangement gives somewhat less room to the cockpit but it is a popular layout which, with minor variations, may be seen on many small cruisers. Incidentally, both the Natant and the Seamaster have standing headroom.

Moving up in size, the Apollo 32, which is a Scandinavian design, shows what can be done with 32ft LOA (Fig. 5.4.). It is a more or less standard layout for a centre cockpit boat

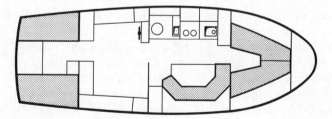

Fig. 5.4 Apollo 32. A comfortable displacement cruiser with six berths, two in an after cabin. See also Fig. 5.5.

Fig. 5.5   Saloon in the Apollo 32 with dinette and galley.

and allowing for some variation in the main cabin, as regards the disposition of the dinette, galley and toilet compartment, the arrangement is, of necessity, much the same for many centre cockpit vessels. To say this however is not to diminish the fact that the cabin in the Apollo 32 is particularly attractive with an unusual shape for the dinette which is most practical and comfortable in use. (Fig. 5.5.).

The Senior 31 in its aft cockpit form provides five berths ex the cockpit, two of these being the convertible dinette (Fig. 5.6.). Quite a lot of length is left for the cockpit in this boat and the space is further extended by having an open, shelter wheelhouse. The engines being fitted with 'Z' drives, take up little space right at the after end of the vessel. It will be seen from the plan that it is possible to close off the forecabin and aft of this a generous area is given to a toilet compartment and a good galley.

It seems that fewer displacement power cruisers in the

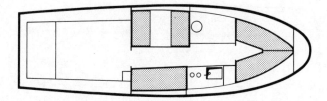

Fig. 5.6   The aft cockpit version of the Senior 31. Five berths, two in a dinette.

35 to 40ft range are available nowadays due to the growing demand for more speed. A good example of the accommodation possibilities available on a boat of this kind is the Otter 40 (Fig. 5.7.), which, although first launched in 1969, is still instructive from the point of view of family accommodation, catered for in a manner which gives privacy when desired yet affords large general areas when the crew is gathered together. The big wheelhouse is of course the social centre of the ship, but the facilities adjacent to the great cabin aft make this

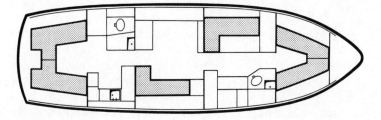

Fig. 5.7   Otter 40, a sea-going displacement boat with excellent family accommodation.

compartment available for use either as a saloon or a stateroom which can be closed off from the rest of the vessel. The centre cabin and the forecabin also offer privacy if needed, with a separate toilet compartment which is available to either, or they can be opened up into one open plan area. It will be seen that the galley is placed so that it can serve either the great cabin or the wheelhouse/saloon with equal facility.

Express cruisers offer a wide selection of layouts and tend frequently towards open plan arrangements particularly in regard to saloon and galley facilities. In the Laguna (Fig.

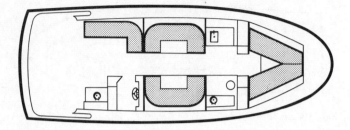

Fig. 5.8   The Laguna 10 metre Express Cruiser. Note the symmetrical arrangement of the settee berths in the main cabin each one of which makes up into a double.

5.8.), which is fitted with a high output generator, all of the cooking is by means of plug-in equipment, electric kettle, broiler, etc., so although the galley itself is not portable it is possible to cook or brew up at more than one position in the boat. This is very well suited to the layout of the vessel which has a 'sedan' or aft saloon which, by means of glazed sliding doors, can be opened right up to the cockpit in clement weather. The symmetrical arrangement of settee berths in the main cabin is another interesting feature of this vessel.

Another express boat with the sedan feature is the Souter 50 but this craft is big enough to permit a very different treatment down below where, as in big ship practice, the cabins are on either side of a companionway (Fig. 5.9.).

The Ocean 40 offers an attractive variation on layout for a 39ft boat, the features including three separate two berth cabins, apart from additional berths in the saloon, and a sundeck at bridge level.

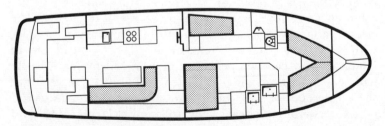

Fig. 5.9   Souter 50, an express cruiser with a big deck saloon/wheelhouse and sleeping accommodation in three cabins.

Vessels in the motor yacht category, which would be over 45ft LOA obviously give many more possibilities for variation in accommodation arrangements and when the size approaches 100ft, then luxury can be extended to the provision of cabin suites complete with their own bathrooms. A noteworthy example of a modern yacht in this category is the 'Lucy', a 109ft TSDY built by Camper and Nicholson. She provides for only six people in the passenger accommodation but each cabin is equipped with everything to make it a self-contained suite. Of the crew accommodation for four, two of these are in separate cabins. The general accommodation provides a large saloon/dining room and a verandah lounge. Both the main and the crew galleys are all-electric.

Since sailing cruisers require rather finer ends to make their way along, the accommodation, size for size, tends to offer rather less space than in power vessels, particularly in the smaller boats, although as mentioned earlier it is often the case that a large number of berths are offered in relation to size. There are of course the usual champions and examples of both open plan and closed cabin arrangements but although the claims of privacy may still be valid on any vessel it is perhaps a mistake to pursue this idea too far on the smallest cruisers, since the result can be a very 'boxed-in' atmosphere down below. Perhaps open plan with curtains is a better arrangement for boats of about 20ft LOA. However open plan the layout may be in regard to berths it should be noted that there is rarely any advantage, and perhaps some danger, in trying to conserve space by having portable galley equipment. This should not only be firmly fixed but located with a view to use both under way and when in harbour.

In small sailing cruisers it is generally the demand for the fourth berth which causes layout problems unless there is enough beam to permit the incorporation of a dinette. The open plan Snapdragon 600 is a good illustration of the spacious effect which can be achieved in the cabin of a small sailing vessel. But provision for cooking and eating is far from ideal and it will be seen that this arises again from the provision of four berths in a vessel of just under 20ft LOA. The effect of this tends to turn a capable little cruiser into a day sailer.

83

There is another trend which must militate against the best use of space in the smallest vessels and that is the tendency to provide only full length berths irrespective of the family requirement. In many boats two full length berths plus two smaller berths for children would be quite adequate.

A slightly larger boat designed in the USA and known here as the Alacrity 22 shows what can be done when the beam is increased, in this case to 7ft 8in. But again the temptation to put in an extra berth has not been resisted and although the dinette and the fore berths give bunks for four people, the galley unit has been put on a slide so that a fifth berth can be suggested.

The Westerly Pageant is only 19in longer than the Alacrity but is considerably deeper in both hull and superstructure. With this additional space and a reconciliation to having one short berth, the designer has been able to incorporate a completely enclosed WC compartment, a fixed galley with a sink and gimballed stove, four to five berths, and headroom through the main part of the boat.

One good reason for an adequate galley facility on a small sailing cruiser is that they are capable of venturing much further abroad than a power boat of similar size, but because they are inevitably slow by comparison, substantial meals are required en route.

There are few very small motor sailers and the standard boats which are available are big enough to be able to offer reasonable accommodation plans. The Nauticat 33 is a good representative of her kind with well arranged accommodation for family sailing. The Maas 34, which is built with three layout options is similarly capable of catering for a family of up to six in some comfort below and, additionally has, in the Countess version, a big cockpit for fishing or lounging.

chapter 6

Kits for Amateur Construction

It is apparent that boats intended to be built at home or by home builder's hands must have some limitation as to choice of material and complexity of construction, although in saying this, one remembers fabulous examples of home built craft which have defied this generality. However, a sort out of what is available today in kit craft shows that there is an enormous choice within the limits of easily handled material such as marine ply and also less practised methods (in the UK) such as ferro-cement, and to this we may add GRP shells for amateur completion.

Design, whether for power or sail seems to originate from two sources. Those who specialize in the design of craft for the amateur builder, by far the most prolific architects in the field, and designers of nominally professionally built boats. The builders of the latter may make a kit alternative available, although even this appears more often to be inspired by the builder extending into kits or shells rather than an initiative by the naval architect. In fact, there seems to be little duality in the designer's role—he is either a kit man or not!

To some extent this division of interest is also apparent in the suppliers who may come under the kit boat heading in that there are those who specialize to the exclusion of any craft which is not obtainable as a kit. They have considerable expertise in not just the provision of the basic kit, but kits in carefully defined stages with meticulous provision of all requirements with regard to instructions and the inclusion of the last small screw. This kind of supplier may be seen as the foundation of the true kit boat business.

Kits for Amateur Construction

The advent of GRP has naturally raised an interest in this material for the home builder, and since the nature of the stuff does not lend itself readily to home building from scratch, the GRP kit boat is never less than a hull shell. This will most likely be from the same mould as those boats which the builder is accustomed to complete in his own yard. Hence, the supplier of a GRP boat as a kit is rather more likely to have a large interest in supplying completed boats.

Some producers of GRP boats do depend greatly upon the supply of shells and complete kits as a valuable part of their business which supplements sales, particularly during the latter half of the year. Their arrangements are such as to provide a sound service to the customer which remains efficient through continuing use in the same manner as the marine ply kit boat experts, but with others it is a more casual affair which may only achieve some importance when trade for completed boats is not so good. The distinction may be subtle but it appears to us to be present and it behoves the potential customer, who may very well be a novice as regards construction, to consider carefully how much assistance and instruction he may need, or may be available, from any particular supplier.

A given design may or may not be exclusive to a particular supplier of kits and this applies particularly to kits having marine ply as the principal material of construction. With GRP shells, the opposite is generally true, so basically one only has a choice of supplier for a given craft if it is a ply boat.

The number of stages at which one may buy a kit varies also according to material. As an example, with marine ply you may have four or more stages from some suppliers: 1. A basic kit of cut and shaped wooden parts. 2. A frame kit with all frames made up ready to set up on the keel. 3. A frame kit with all other wood parts including planking or skin material supplied. 4. A completed shell, with or without superstructure if available, but less paint and fittings.

There can be variations on the kit stages as described above according to supplier, but excepting for the very popular dinghy kits such as are produced in hundreds, a reasonable amount of flexibility may be found in the supplier's attitude towards individual requirements.

A kit for a ferro-cement hull may seem a bit nebulous anyway and one might tend to shudder at the thought of what could comprise a truly basic ferro-cement kit, a couple of yards of sand and cement, some lengths of steel rod and a drawing? Actually the essence of a ferro-cement kit is completely shaped and welded frames which, if tied together correctly give a satisfactory hull framework. It really does not matter who supplies the chicken wire and the aggregate for plastering but the frames and detailed drawings are essential for most aspiring builders.

The final success of the operation, supposing one is to undertake the major part of the building, depends greatly upon drawings and instructions which are readily understandable by the layman, and sufficiently detailed so as not to leave him in the position of working it out for himself at any stage of the construction, and this applies whatever building material is chosen. The situation will plainly vary a bit from one designer to another and from one supplier to another, from the handsome brochure describing the construction of the Mirror dinghy to a few pages of Roneod instructions, but it really does not matter what sort of paper it comes on as long as it is all there.

Apart from some necessary restriction on building methods there appears to be little limitation nowadays on either the type or size of boat which may be offered; indeed, the only restriction is likely to be the prospective builder's nerve. Suitably designed vessels, not just adaptations, are now obtainable for every aspect of the pastime. Pulling, sailing and powered dinghies, inland waterway and estuary craft, sailing cruisers, cruiser/racers, runabouts, weekend cruisers, family power cruisers and express boats petrol and diesel, the range is vast. As a sample one supplier is able to offer a 7ft flattie tender and a 99ft trimaran as the ends of his range, with a large variety of sail and power craft in between.

DESIGN

Thinking first of marine ply craft, basic design generally follows the principle of simplicity to the extent that the assembler is not called upon to steam any members, or put a big amount of warp into the ply sheets or make any but the simplest of carpentry joints.

In so far as sailing performance is concerned, or performance under power, hard chine and double chined boats have shown themselves to be as able as most craft with older conventional sections. A hard chine in a power craft is no disadvantage if one wants speed and semi-displacement or planing performance, so it is a happy coincidence that this hull form is also the easiest for the amateur to build. A double chine design is not much more trouble for those with a keener eye on sailing ability or those requiring a displacement power boat.

The power enthusiast may take his choice from a variety of hull designs within the basic hard chine principle, shallow, medium vee or deep vee, with constant deadrise or warped plane bottom. If he buys his kit at not less than the built frame and bulkhead stage he has no need to worry about it coming out the right shape. These remarks apply of course to marine ply boats but the hard chine design will also be offered as well as round-bilge by the suppliers of GRP shells, and of course there are no. restrictions on shape with ferro-cement construction.

Most marine ply designs depend upon one of the modern wood glues as their principal fastening, supplemented as necessary by bronze screws and nails. An interesting and successful departure from this was adopted by the designers of the Mirror dinghy who employed a stitch and tape method of joining the panels using soft copper wire, glassfibre tape and resin. The thousands of Mirror dinghies now afloat prove that the method is sound for craft of this size or even larger. The chief advantage of the system appears to be that little skill is required, and apart from drilling some small holes, the panels to be joined do not need any edge preparation or any piece at keel or chine to land on. Suitable cutting of the panels at the factory ensures that the right shape emerges when they are drawn up together with the wire stitches, and glass tape inside and out ensures a strong and neat finish.

Although marine ply is pre-eminent for building in timber it is not exclusive for wood kit boats. Some frame kits are perfectly suitable for planking by more than one method and hot press moulded ply hulls are also available.

Since the amateur builder is not involved in the construction of a GRP hull, design in glassfibre has no necessity to consider kit boat requirements as far as basic shape is concerned, although there may be good reason for splitting up superstructure and subsidiary mouldings for easier amateur handling, and designing joints which are foolproof in assembly and waterproof thereafter. Some craft appear to have been designed with particular attention to this, but it is appreciated that many moulders of GRP hull shells and superstructures do their biggest business with the trade, and the boats will be finished by professional boatbuilders who have the skills and the tools.

In spite of what might be a general impression about GRP moulded parts they do not necessarily fit together like Meccano. In fact, in some cases there is a good deal of the old heave ho and considerable adjustment before the subsidiary mouldings are in their required positions. Fitment by measurement or jig is alright for the factory, but fitment by positive location with the necessary landings designed and moulded in is a much better bet for the amateur.

The designer in ferro-cement seems to have few restrictions imposed upon him excepting upper and lower limits in size. The upper limit, presumably, will not interest many amateur builders as there are already many designs of 45ft LOA or more for sailing vessels, and up to about 40ft for power craft. The lower limit is more plainly seen as involving a weight penalty against other methods of construction if the vessel is much smaller than 30ft LOA. Someone is bound to leap up now and produce sheaves of figures to the contrary, but that is our impression of the situation, and it suggests that ferro-cement kits would be viable in the range 30 to 50ft for the amateur builder.

There are other means by which amateurs can build boats but we do not know of any kit or instructional assistance, e.g. it has been suggested that the glassfibre sandwich method is suitable for the amateur builder. It may be so, but only at considerable expense for the necessary mould frame, and we would not consider it to be generally viable although it is an excellent method of construction in professional hands. Maybe there is business to be done by hiring out mould frames? The possibility might bring many more vessels by first class designers within the reach of the home builder.

Part 1

TIMBER KITS

Bell Woodworking produce a range of nine boat kits for power and sail besides the popular Mirror dinghy kits. They have a long experience of the home builder's requirements and their book on the subject has clearly evolved from a long experience of the amateur's needs. This book gives reasons as well as methods and instruction and although it is mainly concerned with sailing dinghies it is good value for any prospective amateur builder at its very reasonable price.

Those with power aspirations will be interested in the Bell Sportsman, a 14ft 6in runabout with several power options which is supplied as a basic kit of prefabricated timber parts, and the Bell Basic Hull which can be had in lengths from 19 to 21ft and finished as a runabout, day cruiser, two berth cruiser or canal boat. This vessel is usable with a wide range of outboard power from 4 to 40hp and inboard engines can also be accommodated.

In both of these power boat kits the set of basic parts includes frames already assembled and transom, so that with these set up on the floor no stocks are required and the framing of the boat may be completed in a few hours.

Cousland & Browne Ltd is another company with experience of home builders' requirements and their interest in designs by Peter Blandford and the prolific R. T. Hartley of New Zealand gives them a very big range of boats. The kit end of the business as distinct from the supply of general materials for boatbuilding is handled by R. C. Marine Ltd. As an indication of the number of kits available, ignoring ferro-cement motor cruisers of which there are two designs, and all of the sailing vessels, there are twenty six power craft kits listed for construction from marine plywood to designs by Hartley, and eight by Blandford.

The Hartley designs include ten deep Vee, eleven moderate Vee and four shallow Vee power craft from small runabouts to six berth family cruisers. As examples, Vim, a 20° bottom runabout, length 12ft 6in, is suitable for outboard power and speeds up to 40mph. It is supplied as a frame kit with the rest of the timber and fastenings, or a hull built to the gunwale with the remainder of the material and fastenings included (Fig. 6.1.).

Fig. 6.1 Vim, a small, fast runabout built from a Hartley kit.

New Powerflite, a 15 degree sports weekender with two berths and some 'mod cons' by way of galley and WC, is supplied as a frame kit plus other material needed, or as a hull built to the gunwale and including the remainder of the pieces. This boat is 19ft 5in by 7ft 10in and has a draft of 1ft 1in. She may be powered with one 10hp outboard to give 10mph or anything up to two 40hp jobs which will give a speed of 32mph. The New Flareline is a sister ship intended for inboard power.

The biggest boat in this range is the New Marksman

which is available as either a cabin cruiser or a sports fisherman. This is a good-looking hull with an easy, non-pounding entry and a 13 degree Vee at the transom. Two 150hp diesels will give 27mph but she has been designed to operate on much less power, a single 100hp motor will give about 13mph. The New Marksman has accommodation for seven in three separate cabins and she has a very simple and workable layout.

The Trailer Sailer 18 Mk II is a centreboard or bilge keel sloop weighing only 1200lb. This is a Hartley design which sailing enthusiasts should find easy to tow behind a family car.

The Peter Blandford designs for power craft in the R.C. Marine range go from an 11ft runabout up to a 24ft canal cruiser, and include two power weekenders with two berth layouts and big cockpits. There are several power options for these. The smaller boat, the 16ft Nomad has a double chine and the 17ft 6in. Woodwych is hard chine with the ability to pull a skier on about 35hp, but the boat will plane on 18hp when lightly loaded.

The ability of a company to sell the same boat year after year without significant modification must be the soundest recommendation and assurance for the prospective customer. Wyvern Boats (Wessex) Ltd, have boats in this category and their Widgeon, an all-purpose, hard chine outboard powered boat which is sold mostly to the home builder continues to advertise the reliability of their kits. There are four more power boats in their list which are of interest. The Wizard, Watermaid and Wavemaster are small runabouts of 10ft 9in, 12ft and 14ft LOA and the smallest of these can be powered with any outboard engine between $1\frac{1}{2}$ and 18hp so as to give speeds up to 28mph.

Finally, the Wyvern Witch, biggest boat in the range offers all the usual facilities of a weekend cruiser. She is 17ft in length and has a cabin with room for two 6ft 2in berths plus cooking and toilet facilities. Weighing only 750lb she is easily trailable by the smallest car and with power options between $6\frac{1}{2}$ and 40hp performance can be varied to suit the requirements of most. A basic kit for this includes all timber parts plus windows and glazing strips. A part assembled hull, that is complete up to gunwale level plus all parts to finish, is also supplied.

In common with most suppliers of timber kits, Cruiser Kits Ltd have a range which includes both sailing and power vessels and it is a very wide range indeed covering single and multihull craft. One of the features of a kit from this company, who have specialized in marine ply construction for many years, is that all important angles are cut on the wood when the kit is fabricated, thus with bevels already present and correct the home builder is less dependent upon drawings and some small skill in assembling his boat.

There are eighteen power craft in the Cruiser Kits list including runabouts, express cruisers, family cruisers and diesel motor yachts. The kits available go from a 15ft two berth weekender to a 60ft diesel powered yacht with luxury accommodation for twelve. Inland waterway boats in the lengths 17, 20, 26 and 30ft all with 6ft 10in beam are also supplied.

York Marinecraft besides providing a range of kits to P. W. Blandford's designs are also timber importers with a useful list of woods suitable for boatbuilding. The motor boats in the range start with the 16ft 3in Bosun single chine runabout. A double chine version of this boat called the Venturer can be had. There are cabin dayboats and weekenders, the Woodnymph and the Nomad, both of which have room for berths, cooking facilities and a WC. Some of the York Marinecraft kits are made up into small stages for purchase at a very modest price, e.g. the Commodore, a 13ft runabout is broken down as follows: (1) Plans (2) Frames, Stem and Transom (3) Timbers for hull, deck and seating (4) Marine plywood for hull, deck, bottom boards and seats (5) Screws, nails and glue. If all is purchased together the price of the full kit is reduced. Deck fittings, instruments, wheels, windscreens, etc., are available for all of the power craft offered in this range.

Potter & Bishop offer the complete catalogue of Hartley designs both ferro-cement and marine plywood, they also provide kits for some *Yachting Monthly* designs. They will supply part built boats and complete vessels. Most kits are available in six progressive stages starting with the basic timber and plywood cut and planed to size as the designers cutting list.

Finally, before leaving the timber kit scene, there is the hot press moulded hull built up with ply veneers as exemplified by the Tremletts designs. Tremlett (Skicraft) Ltd supply wood power boat hulls to amateur builders, the trade and they also finish some themselves. They make hulls from 13 to 40ft in length and they all have the distinctive Tremlett entry, full length spray rails and a fairly deep Vee carried through to the transom.

These hulls are obtainable in three stages: 1. A moulded shell with external rails. 2. Ditto with transom, bilge stringers and gunwales. 3. As 2, plus deck beams, deck, rubbing strip and engine well.

Part 2

GRP HULL KITS

A GRP hull, deck, and superstructure makes a good beginning for those who prefer the material and want to cut down their hours of labour. In some stages there may be interior mouldings such as bulkheads, bunk bases and cabin soles available to finish and in other cases it may only be the smaller items of joinery and trim which need to be added. However, the amount of work necessary to complete from a bare GRP shell should not be under-estimated, especially if it is intended to put in all wood bulkheads and joinery. There is the disadvantage that unless one is a fairly skilled operator with wood, the actual fitment of the innards will be much more difficult than with a marine ply kit, where the correct angles are either already on the parts or detailed in the designer's drawings. That being said, it may also be noted that those who make a good job of a GRP boat may feel a little superior because they will have a professionally built hull.

Amongst other things to remember is that the bare inside of a GRP vessel is not quite so good as the bare inside of a wooden one, either to look at or to experience in respect of condensation. Consequently, unless your kit also runs to a moulded liner you will need to line it with a suitable material such as a patterned or quilted PVC cloth or carpet. This applies particularly to cruisers with sleeping and cooking facilities. Unless the job is eased by the provision of cloth covered boards which can be clipped or screwed into position, it is, in our experience, a difficult job for an amateur to complete with a good final appearance and there are few adhesives which do the job well when including a PVC/GRP joint. Those which do tend to be contact adhesives permitting no errors in placement of the lining material.

In putting subsidiary mouldings into a GRP hull shell it should be borne in mind that cured mouldings are not easy to stick together although they may be of similar material. As mentioned in Chapter 4, it is necessary to roughen up the mating surfaces quite ruthlessly for a reliable joint with good strength since the bond appears to be mechanical rather than chemical. The same roughening up procedure should also be followed when applying glass tape or strips of chopped strand mat to secure plywood bulkheads and other joinery to the hull or superstructure. Another thing is that the wood also must be really clean and dry and completely bare of any varnish or paint where the joint is to be made. Preferably one would use an epoxy resin for all these joints but it is expensive and polyester will serve if the job is carefully conducted. In any case your kit supplier will be able to give you the benefit of his experience of the particular task.

W. Wright & Son who produce Charnwood Craft, which include runabouts, weekenders and inland waterway cruisers, sell about half of their production as kits. They have given an impressive amount of design consideration to the needs and limitations of the amateur assembler. The deck and super-structure on their inland cruisers comprise several separate mouldings of easily handleable size and the matting is arranged so as to provide a positive lodgement and a foolproof water-tight joint. In some cases the coachroof mouldings are designed so as to serve more than one craft, e.g. the main cabin coach-roof and coamings on the 20ft Corinth canal cruiser can double as the forward cabin superstructure on the 25ft centre cockpit Charnwood 25 (Fig. 6.2.). These superstructure parts can be bought separately from the basic hull kits if desired.

Most of the furniture in a Charnwood boat is wood and again care has been taken to ensure that the GRP hull provides convenient landings for the joinery. For some cabin and cockpit panels the plywood is bounded to the GRP at the

Class ... and 25. This is an inland waterways cruiser with a GRP hull and mainly marine plywood joinery.

moulding stage so giving a panel with a good finish on both sides and obviating the need for later work in attaching one to the other.

A Charnwood 20 basic hull includes fore and side decks and all-round fendering. The decks are moulded with an upturn at the inner edge which facilitates a good joint whether the builder is going to put on a GRP or a wood superstructure. It all sounds pretty obvious but it is the sort of thinking which makes all the difference when assembly is started.

These hulls have a 6ft 10in inland waterway beam and they are suitable for either inboard or outboard engines. A Stuart Turner 10hp motor suits these boats very well and neat aluminium alloy engine bearers have been evolved to accommodate this unit in the centre cockpit boat.

A complete listing and pricing of the kits in their various stages is available, but this supplier is prepared to be quite flexible towards a customer's requirements and advise him according to the amount of work he feels he can cope with.

The Conway 26 is a sporty looking fast cruiser which is now available as a kit. This boat accommodates four or five people and with twin Volvo Penta 115/110 Aquamatics she will exceed 27 knots. There are two versions of the kit: 1. The hull, deck and coachroof complete with cabin windows. 2. As before, but including moulded interior seating with stowage lockers, half height bulkheads and cockpit floor joists. This boat has a planing ability on very much less power than that given as an example above. A single sterndrive engine of about 120hp will give her a reasonable performance. The inside of a factory finished Conway 26 is very attractive and any amateur builder who managed to complete his boat to similar ideas would have a nice vessel.

Seaglass Ltd make two very sturdy GRP hulls, of 23 and 25ft LOA available as hull only or with deck, etc., up to a full set of shell mouldings including coachroof and wheelhouse top. These are both fast power cruisers.

A lot of boats on offer nowadays tend to be semi-displacement or planing craft and so the Plymouth Pilot produced by the Monachorum Manufacturing Co makes a change and a most solid and traditional entry on the kit boat scene. The hull can be had in two weights, launch and workboat, the latter having extra laminations. The additional kit does not run beyond gunwales, breasthooks and quarter knees, leaving the owner to please himself for the remainder, but it is not suggested that the Plymouth Pilot should be other than an open boat so the amount of work and pieces remaining to be found should not be extensive. The hull is suitable for any inboard of about 10hp petrol or diesel.

Appleyard Lincoln & Co supply the Elysian 27 and 34 hull kits. These basic hulls can be supplied moulded to suit either single or twin screws and a superstructure is available for aft cockpit, centre cockpit, sportsman or super sportsman versions on the 27 hull. The Elysian 34 is offered as a single screw, centre cockpit, river cruiser. A typical kit in this case for the 27ft aft cockpit model is listed: 1. Elysian aft cockpit single screw hull and superstructure complete with gunwales and full length moulded keel. 2. Moulded forecabin interior. 3. Moulded dinette and galley units. 4. Moulded cockpit linings.

An extensive catalogue of minor mouldings and engineering fittings, screens and deck fittings is given for completion of kit boats.

Sunspeed Boats offer a basic hull with a slightly upswept sheerline forward which will give a little more headroom under the foredeck and the option of two superstructures giving either a two berth sports boat or a four berth weekend cabin cruiser. Both versions are suitable for single or twin outboard or sterndrive installations of up to 100hp. The 6 metre basic hull with superstructure bonded on is supplied for the two berth boat, the 602, and for the four berth model, the 604. All of the bulkheads, floors berth bases and fittings, etc., are available for completion.

There is a range of boats available from Senior Marine and all of them may be obtained as bare hulls or with superstructures and furniture (Fig. 6.3.). These cruisers are the Senior 17, 20, 23, 26, 31, the Sheerline 32 and the Dominator. The Sheerline may be had in three versions; after cabin, aft cockpit or aft cockpit sportsman. The Dominator is a husky fisherman built to BOT specification. A complete set of literature covering all of the Senior boats and the kit prices is available.

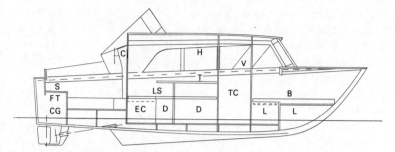

Fig. 6.3 The Senior 23 can be supplied in several stages of completion. It is designed for inland waterways or coastal cruising.

KEY

B	Berth	L	Locker
C	Controls	LS	'L' shaped settee converts to double
CG	Calor Gas bottle		berth
D	Drawer	S	Seat
EC	Engine compartment	T	Table
FT	Fuel Tank	TC	Toilet compartment
H	Hopper window	V	Vent

Express power boat hulls moulded by Powles include High and Low sheer 37ft boats, a 42 for river hull and a 45 for fast cruiser shells.

A type of vessel popular in America but yet to find much acclaim in this country, is the high powered houseboat as typified by the Carribean 45. The hull shape offers tremendous accommodation possibilities but it is capable of 25 knots.

STEEL HULLS

Steel motor cruiser hulls are available for those with sufficient experience to complete, either to suggested plans or their own ideas, and examples in this field are the Arma 26 and 33 for hard chine motor cruisers, and inland waterways boats by Springer Engineering who build the 26 and 37ft hulls for Samson Narrow Boats and others up to 70ft LOA.

Part 3

FERRO-CEMENT BOATS

This method of building, popular for some time 'down under' is now beginning to blossom a bit for kit building over here. It certainly is not everybody's idea of boatbuilding and at first sight 'it don't seem right somehow'. But when one considers the available apertures through six layers of $\frac{1}{2}$in chicken wire tied closely together and clothing fabricated steel frames and longitudinals, then the whole thing becomes not only credible but attractive to those who want a great big boat with the minimum of expense and a reasonable amount of lattitude in the construction.

The success of the job appears to rest upon accurate and well-made frames being purchased and a careful setting up so as to get a complete armature of steel and wire which is as true as may be. Unless one is a plasterer by trade it is not recommended that this part of the job should be DIY. The mixture for this is cement, sand and pozzolan or pozzolith, the material is variously quoted but is present in volcanic ash and its effect is to improve the workability and final strength of the cement mix. In this country it has been found that certain grades of power station ash are usable.

Potter & Bishop provide the Hartley plans for a whole range of ferro-cement boats and they will supply these and the prefabricated frames and any other part of the structure needing professional attention for success. Plans for 30 and 38ft ferro-cement power cruisers are available from Potter & Bishop and also from R. C. Marine Ltd who deal with all Hartley designs.

There are many other vessels obtainable as kits, besides those quoted in this chapter, and if a particular boat appears to suit your requirement it is always worthwhile to enquire whether hull shells are supplied.

It is probable that there are other materials besides marine ply, GRP, steel and ferro-cement which may be offered as the basis of boat kits, but those mentioned cover a major part of the requirement.

chapter 7

Applying the Power

Part 1

CHOOSING AN ENGINE

Nearly all marine engines available for yachts are of the reciprocating internal combustion type. That is to say that they burn fuel in a cylinder and the expansion of the gases moves a piston which drives a crankshaft and so rotary movement is obtained. There are other engines using similar fuels which convert the energy into rotary movement in a different manner, as for instance the gas turbines used in aircraft and some vessels in the Royal Navy, and the Wankel engine currently being developed for use in cars and also suggested for auxiliary use afloat in view of its high power/weight ratio.

Both petrol and diesel engines are built for marine applications and also, amongst them, there are several marine conversions adapted from industrial or vehicle units. In fact, many multi-cylinder diesel engines supplied for motor cruisers and small pleasure craft today are marinized versions of units mass produced for other purposes. It should be noted in passing that the engine which is commonly called a 'diesel' is more correctly a compression ignition (CI) engine since it fires through the heat generated by high compression and not with the aid of a hot bulb or a glow plug. For the sake of clarity and conformity we will continue to call it a diesel.

The horse-power of a marine engine is not given by its capacity as with a car engine, where 1,000cc will rate the car as 10hp, and so on, but by the developed hp known as

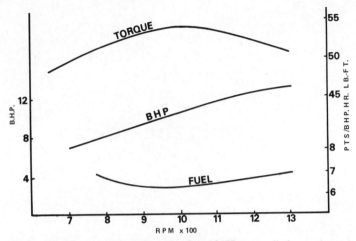

Fig. 7.1 Output curves taken from the Brit 12/55 two cylinder marine petrol engine as an illustration of typical bhp and torque readings. Note that although the bhp continues to rise with rpm and is just beginning to flatten off at 1250, the maximum torque is achieved at about 1000rpm.

'brake horse-power' (bhp). This is of course also quoted for car engines but not as a basic description of engine size. Thus a marine engine which is quoted as 5hp will not necessarily have a cubic capacity of 500cc (it could be less or more), but in view of the fact that it is developed horse-power which is being given, the rpm at which it is achieved will also be quoted, e.g. 5bhp at 1,500rpm. This is because the number of revolutions per minute achieved under a certain load is part of the formulae for the calculation of bhp (Fig. 7.1.).

Torque, which is the turning moment, quoted in lb/ft is a valuable indication of the maximum turning effort which an engine may achieve in relation to rpm. But torque does not continue to rise with bhp although it may be said in general that engines capable of high rpm will produce their maximum torque at somewhat higher rpm.

Another difference vis-à-vis car engines is that whereas a car may be quoted as doing 30 miles to the gallon, it is not practicable to measure the fuel consumption of a marine engine in that way and this will be quoted as fuel by weight or liquid measure used per bhp hour, e.g. .75pt/hp/hour for an engine developing 5hp would indicate a consumption of 3·9 pints or just under ½ gallon per hour.

PETROL ENGINES

Two stroke and four stroke petrol engines are equally popular for marine use. A two stroke engine produces a power impulse every revolution of the crankshaft and a four stroke every other revolution. Very briefly the pros and cons are: Small two stroke units are simple in construction, have less moving parts, are light in weight, compact, and, as single cylinder units versus their four stroke counterparts, probably smoother in operation. As against this, they are not as efficient as four stroke engines in regard to power output and fuel consumption. This arises mostly from the fact that with a two stroke cycle the cylinder has to be scavenged of burnt gases, and charged with a fresh mixture during the course of the same stroke, and some fuel is lost in pushing out the old charge. This is the most critical part of two stroke operation since if old gases are left in the cylinder they will both dilute and reduce the volume of the new charge. Two stroke engines run on a mixture of petrol and oil, necessary because the fuel/air mixture circulates in the crankcase before entering the cylinder. The use of a low octane fuel further reduced by the addition of lubricating oil is another reason why efficient scavenging is so important.

For an equivalent power a two stroke will cost a little more to run in any case since the fuel cost is higher; part of every gallon of fuel will be a lubricant costing perhaps four times as much as petrol. The actual ratio of petrol to oil recommended is varied by every engine manufacturer and can be in the range of 12 : 1 to 100 : 1, the latter being a special lubricant supplied through the engine maker's agents.

Nearly all outboard engines are two stroke units and the power which is now available in such compact packages is an indication of what can be achieved with a motor designed to run at high rpm. Two stroke inboard engines can be either high or low rpm types and one of the most popular and long-standing small inboard engines is in the latter category.

Since acceleration is of little value in a marine unit, but smooth operation and slow running is important, most of the smaller inboard units used for auxiliary purposes, whether two or four stroke, are fitted with a heavy flywheel which helps to smooth out the power pulses at low speed (Fig. 7.2.). Operation at low rpm, so that with or without gearing down the propeller is not turning at much more than 1,000 rpm max, is quite usual and desirable except on very fast vessels. Consequently an engine which produces its maximum torque (turning effort) at low speed is best suited to marine use. This applies particularly to inboard units.

The four stroke cycle enables separate strokes to be utilized for scavenging (exhaust) and charging (induction) and these four strokes in their sequence are induction, compression, power and exhaust. Better breathing, obtained by inducing the fuel mixture into the cylinder with a complete downstroke, results in a bigger charge and higher efficiency. Similarly, more complete scavenging adds to efficiency.

A four stroke unit can have a much higher compression ratio than a two stroke and, although this factor is not exploited to any extent in marine petrol engines, it can contribute to higher outputs for a given engine size.

The valve arrangement for inlet and exhaust on a four

Fig. 7.2 The Brit Sprite 10bhp twin cylinder petrol engine with the large flywheel which is desirable for a small marine engine. The rpm range is 450–2000.

Fig. 7.3   Perkins 6 cylinder turbo-charged T6.354 marine diesel engine developing 175bhp. Maximum rpm is 2400. It has direct injection and a water cooled
inter-cooler in the induction system.

stroke may be either side valve or overhead, and one may
expect that if it is built as a marine auxiliary it will be a low
compression, side valve engine but if it is a marinized car
engine it is likely to be overhead valve and have a much
higher compression ratio.

All reciprocating internal combustion engines may be
either normally aspirated or supercharged. In the first case
the fuel/air mixture enters the cylinder under atmospheric
pressure and in the second it is pressurized so that a bigger
charge can be got into the cylinder. This is effected by a
compressor which may be mechanically driven by the engine
or by a small turbine driven by the engine exhaust gases. Air
gets hot when compressed and takes up a larger volume of
space. Consequently, an intercooler may be used between the
compressor and the engine inlet in order to reduce the
temperature of the charge, and thus get the maximum amount
of air into the cylinder for the volume available. Very few
marine petrol engines are supercharged but it is quite usual
for the larger diesel engines to have an exhaust driven turbo-
blower (Fig. 7.3.).

Most low compression, four stroke, petrol engines will run

Fig. 7.4 A Newage type 4/58 engine fitted with a PRM 100 gearbox. This is based on the Ford 2401E diesel which is a 4 cylinder unit developing 58 bhp at 3650rpm.

on kerosene (also known as vaporizing oil, paraffin, etc.) when they have been warmed up. Some units cater for this with separate fuel tanks so that petrol may be used for starting. The power output is considerably less when using paraffin and however careful one may be in its use, it is almost impossible to avoid the smell which reaches the furthest corners of the ship.

AUXILIARY ENGINES

Excepting the smallest marine engines of less than 5hp a diesel engine alternative is now available and, but for what might be called sprint engines in racing craft and high speed day boats, engines in use of more than 100bhp are, popularly, nearly all diesel. There are several reasons for this, two being the greater economy of the diesel as an engine and the difference in the cost of its fuel both of which make it almost a necessity for a cruising boat. It has been the development of the high speed diesel engine for automotive and industrial purposes which has made these comparatively light and compact high output motors available to boat owners (Fig. 7.4.).

However, whilst there is everything to be said for the multi-cylinder diesel units, the case for the smallest diesel auxiliaries versus petrol is perhaps worthy of more investigation. A lot will depend upon the type of boat but perhaps much more consideration should also be given to the nature of its use. An auxiliary sailing yacht will normally have need of its engine for short periods only, and because of the shape of a sailing hull there will not be unlimited space to install an engine and its fuel tank. Lightness is also an attribute if performance under sail is to be maintained, and furthermore, minimum vibration is important in a light hull. All of these requirements indicate a petrol engine as being far more suitable, but in spite of this and a much higher first cost, many diesel engines are installed in quite small sailing vessels. One of the first reasons given for this is often that of reduced fire risk, but whilst it is certainly true that spilt petrol is much more volatile than spilt diesel oil there is little reason to

Fig. 7.5 Getting near the ultimate in a compact, lightweight auxiliary unit for a sailing boat. The Watermota Shrimp petrol/paraffin engine weighs only 60lbs complete with sterngear and a 12in variable pitch propeller.

suppose that a petrol engine is very much more likely to leak than a diesel. Sensible precautions such as drip trays, flame traps and adequate ventilation should reduce the element of risk to acceptable proportions (Fig. 7.5.).

It is easy to be inconsistent. The owner who opts for a diesel installation purely on grounds of fire risk is quite likely to stow his outboard engine, with fuel running from the carburettor, in the stern locker, plus a can or two of petrol. Perhaps the calor gas cylinder with valve and regulator will also share this accommodation, but because he has a diesel engine he thinks he is fireproof. No plugs, no ignition, no sparks he may think, but what about the starter motor and its relay switch, both capable of producing arcs more than adequate to ignite a gas/air mixture?

DIESEL ENGINES

Whilst one may have room for argument over the claims of small petrol and diesel units there is little doubt that the multi-cylinder diesel engine has most points in its favour. The necessarily high compression ratios needed (more than twice that of most petrol engines) which can give rise to very rough running in single cylinder engines, is ameliorated by multi-cylinder designs, and it will be apparent that the problem is halved at any rate, if the engine is only a two cylinder unit. With three or four in line, six in line and V configurations, the more serious aspects of out of balance are overcome for all practical purposes, and the residual noise and vibration is that which must inevitably result from the nature of the combustion, which is dependent upon extreme cylinder pressures. But even this is amenable to treatment by anti-vibration mountings and noise insulation.

High cylinder pressures call for extra robust design all-round and this makes the difference in weight between petrol and diesel engines of the same horse-power (Fig. 7.6 and 7.6a). For most engines available for marine purposes in pleasure craft, a four stroke cycle is employed. The fundamental difference between the diesel and the petrol unit being that although the strokes have the same purpose, only air is drawn into the cylinder by the diesel and the fuel is injected at high pressure at or near the top of the compression stroke.

Fig. 7.6   The robust Gardner 6LW which develops 94bhp at 1500rpm.

Fig. 7.6a   One of the big range of Lister marine engines, the JW6 MGR producing 138bhp at 2000rpm naturally aspirated or 180bhp when turbo-charged.

The heat engendered by high compression is sufficient to ignite the charge without the aid of a spark. It may be mentioned in passing that there are also petrol engines with fuel injection but these do not have abnormally high compression ratios and they still employ spark ignition. There are also diesel engines fitted with glow plugs to assist starting but they are not in use once the engine is running.

Combustion chamber arrangements in diesels vary and an engine may have direct injection into a conventional cylinder head or indirect injection in which the fuel is directed into an ante chamber with access to the cylinder head, and sometimes, a combination of both. The objective is the highest mean effective pressure combined with a controlled combustion, that is to say burning rather than detonation of the mixture.

Fuel injection arrangements may be either with the use of a multiple fuel injection pump, where there is a cylinder and piston for each injector, or a distributor type pump having

Fig. 7.7 The Kittiwake is an air-cooled 15bhp diesel fitted with the TMP gearbox and marketed as a unit by Nicor Marine.

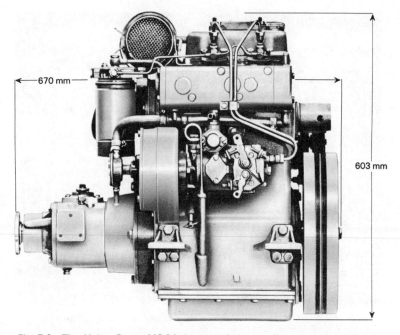

←—670 mm—→

603 mm

Fig. 7.8 The Volvo Penta MD6A is one of the smallest water-cooled twin cylinder diesels. Rated at 10bhp continuous at 2400rpm it is claimed to be very smooth running.

only one pump pressure chamber which supplies all of the cylinders via a distributor head. Engine speed is controlled by metering the fuel to the pump and a governor is usually incorporated to prevent over-speeding of the engine.

Small diesel engines (and petrol engines too) may be either air or water cooled (Figs. 7.7. and 7.8.) but beyond this most are water cooled. Water cooling is a little more troublesome in some respects but engines so cooled are somewhat quieter in operation and most multi-cylinder engines now employ fresh water cooling with a heat exchanger system which keeps the raw sea water away from the water passages in the engine (Fig. 7.9.).

Starting may be either hand or electric for small engines, electric for most engines of pleasure boat horse-powers and compressed air for the largest engines in motor yachts and workboats. Other methods are also employed for the bigger units.

Fig. 7.9 Heat exchangers mounted at the forward end of the Perkins 4.236. This twin installation is in the Apollo 32.

To summarize some points for different means of powering a vessel:

The inboard two stroke petrol engine is simple, low in first cost but available only in the low power range suitable for sailing auxiliaries.

Four stroke petrol engines are available as small auxiliary units and also in sizes suitable for main propulsion on fast dayboats and short range cruisers. They are most efficient in regard to power output for weight and size but the high cost of petrol makes the larger motors very expensive to operate.

Kerosene can be burnt in nearly any low compression four stroke engine with suitable arrangements for the use of petrol for starting and stopping.

Small diesel engines from about 6bhp are available for auxiliaries or for launches and small workboats. The smallest motors are generally single cylinder, frequently with attendant vibration characteristics. Neither this nor the additional weight is of great consequence in a workboat but it can give rise to problems in a small, lightly built vessel.

Multi-cylinder diesel engines are being standardized to an increasing extent for all classes of boats, and apart from the efficiency offered by petrol units for high performance without reference to expense, the diesel is now the most attractive proposition for a motor cruiser owner. A comprehensive power range is available and their economy helps to balance out first cost. This fuel economy is also valuable in that it increases the range of a cruiser without resort to abnormal tankage.

Outboard engines are discussed in greater detail in a later chapter but meantime it should be said that many people prefer them for auxiliary use on small sailing vessels, and they also power the greater proportion of runabouts and weekend cruisers. Horsepowers range from $1\frac{1}{2}$ up to 140 and they are literally the most compact power packs available. In the USA they are used as the main propulsion on sizeable cruisers and big dayboats but in the UK, petrol engines of high horse-power are more likely to be found in conjunction with Z drives as the alternative to diesels on fast, light cruisers.

Part 2

TRANSMISSION

The gearbox in a boat has two main functions: 1. To give a means of changing the direction of rotation of the propeller shaft with an intermediate position where it is stopped. 2. To provide the desired ratio between engine speed and the revolutions of the propeller shaft. Most marine engines suitable for pleasure craft have the gearbox as an integral part of the assembly, but in the largest motor yachts the engines may have gearboxes installed as separate units with a drive shaft between.

Operation of the gearbox may be manual or hydraulic but because hydraulic operation facilitates remote control it is becoming increasingly common for all except the smallest units to be oil operated (Figs. 7.10. and 7.11.). Since, unlike a car, there is no separately operated clutch in the engine/gearbox drive there is no gear changing in the sense of shifting gears in and out of mesh (Figs. 7.10 and 7.11.). Gears for ahead and astern remain in mesh always but they transmit, or are freed from the drive, as required by internal

Fig. 7.10 The type MRF 350 Mk. III gearbox by Self Changing Gears is suitable for an input torque of up to 400lb ft. Coupling to the engine is via a torsionally resilient drive plate.

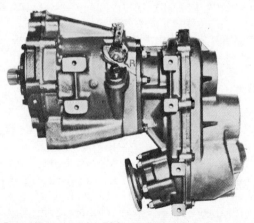

Fig. 7.11 Borg Warner model 72C gearbox which is available with in-line, dropped or V drive as shown. An epicyclic reduction gear enables the complete gear train to be in line if required. This model will take up to 380bhp petrol and 205bhp diesel.

clutches incorporated in the gear train. To make this feasible the transmission is frequently either by bevel gears or by straight cut (spur) gears employed in an epicyclic system. But this is not exclusive and there are examples with helical gear trains in constant mesh operating with and without a separate idler gear for reversing. The gearing for reduction or changing the ratio between input and output shafts can either be a function of the main gear train or a separate gear imposed between the main gearbox and the final drive (Fig. 7.12.).

Dependent upon the type of gearbox chosen, the final drive may either be concentric with the engine shaft, or it may be lower. Other variations are also possible, especially with the fitment of a reduction gear (Fig. 7.12a.).

With a twin engine installation it is generally thought preferable to have opposite rotation of the propellers to cancel out any turning effect on the hull. Outward turning propellers are considered to be best. Sometimes this is achieved with 'handed' engines turning in opposite directions, but opposite rotation may also be obtained by an additional idler gear in

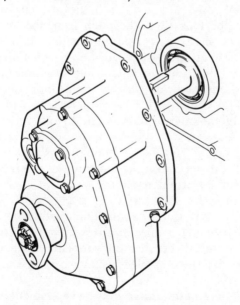

Fig. 7.12   A dropped reduction gear as fitted to the TMP gearbox.

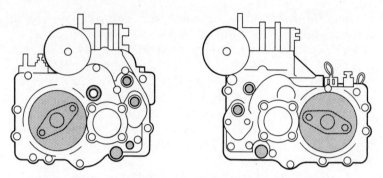

Fig. 7.12a   TMP L.H. and R.H. offset reduction units by Nicor Marine.

the final drive, or the use of both gear and chain type reduction boxes.

Most motor vessels other than large passenger craft, which may have reversing engines, are fitted with gearboxes to give them the facility for ahead and astern movement and also the ability to remain stationary whilst the engine is running. A variable pitch propeller may be fitted as an alternative to a gearbox on some craft and in this case the forward, neutral, reverse facility is provided by blades which rotate in the propeller hub. This alters the pitch from the forward to the reverse angle via a neutral position where the blades will be approximately at right angles to the propeller shaft and thus obtaining no 'bite' on the water. This alteration of pitch can be effected mechanically or by hydraulics, and it will be observed that if the pitch is variable over a wide range, the effect will be the same as that of a multi-ratio gearbox, in that the load on the engine can be adjusted to suit various conditions (Fig. 7.13.). However, although this prospect is attractive, due to the necessary incorporation of mechanics into the propeller hub, restriction on the speed of rotation is more critical than with a solid screw.

This form of transmission may find good use in conjunction with auxiliary engines in sailing vessels, particularly if 'motor sailing' is indulged, because the propeller pitch may also be adjusted to give the best effect when receiving some assistance from the sails.

Some sailing vessels have only very elementary transmissions in which no gearbox or variable pitch propeller is

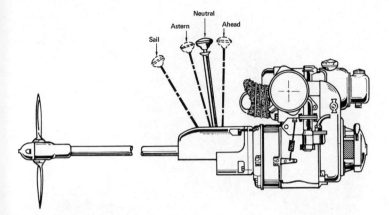

Fig. 7.13 A small, manually operated variable pitch propeller as fitted to the Watermota Shrimp. Movement of the control lever beyond the astern position brings the blades in line fore and aft to reduce resistance and prevent rotation for sailing.

included. The drive from the engine is taken through a sailing clutch which engages only when the engine speed is increased above tickover. The engagement is by centrifugal action on clutch pads attached to the engine shaft which throw out to engage with a drum mounted on the propeller shaft. Many lawnmowers have a similar mechanism. It is simple, inexpensive and entirely automatic. It also enables the propeller to spin when the clutch is disengaged so as to cause less resistance when the boat is under sail, but not everyone believes this to be a good thing and some prefer to have a two bladed propeller which can be stopped in line with the deadwood.

Various hydraulic drives have been available from time to time and one which is particularly noteworthy is the Volvo Hydrostatic Transmission which employs an entirely new hydraulic pump/motor principle. The efficiency of the system is considerably better than that of earlier examples and the potential makes it worthy of description. The basic arrangement for a hydraulic transmission is to have the engine driving an oil pump with the pump transmitting oil at high pressure to an hydraulic motor which is directly coupled to the propeller shaft. This arrangement is followed in the Volvo system but the Volvo pump and motor units are

117

Fig. 7.14 The Volvo Hydrostatic Transmission coupled to an MD2B engine. The motor unit with sterngear is in the foreground; the pump unit is immersed in the oil reservoir seen at the back of the engine.

identical and the same component serves with similar efficiency in both capacities (Fig. 7.14.).

The basic pump/motor consists of a casing enclosing a cylinder drum, pistons and a swash plate mounted on heavy duty bearings. The drum contains five small cylinders with pistons connected by ball joints to the swash plate and the axis of the plate lies at an angle of 40° to the axis of the cylinder drum. The pistons are driven by oil entering the cylinders successively via kidney shaped ports in the base of the drum. The cylinder drum and the swash plate have a meshing bevel gear so that rotation of the swash plate, caused by the successive pressure of the five pistons, also causes rotation of the cylinder drum (Fig. 7.15.). By this means the kidney port in each cylinder head is brought round in turn over the pressure port in the motor housing, which is con-

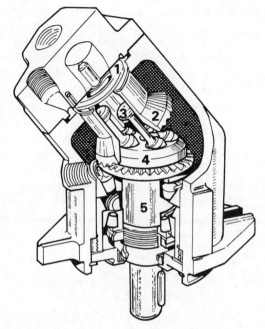

1. Relief Valve
2. Cylinder Barrel
3. Five Pistons
4. Driving Plate
5. Main Drive Shaft.

Fig. 7.15 The principle of the Volvo hydraulic drive showing the cylinder drum, pistons and swashplate.

nected directly to the pressure line from the pump.

There are actually two ports in the motor housing below the cylinder drum sited 180° apart, one for pressure and the other for scavenging, but it will be seen that since the arrangement is symmetrical, a reversal of the flow through these ports will cause the motor to run in the reverse direction but with equal efficiency.

We have of course been describing the operation of the unit as a motor, the description remains the same for the pump but in this case the swash plate journal (which in the motor is the output shaft) becomes a driven member coupled direct to the output shaft of an engine. The power of the engine is transmitted via the pump and high pressure oil lines to the motor, which, within limits, may be put as close to or as far away from the power unit as is convenient. The loss incurred by longer pressure hose is about 1% per metre, the overall loss for the pump/motor system about 13% which compares with

119

E

around 8–10% for a conventional gearbox transmission.

These hydraulic units are made in five sizes to cope with the transmission of from 13 up to 86hp. Size C-19 which is the middle unit in the range and measures only approximately $6\frac{1}{2} \times 5 \times 4\frac{1}{2}$in—it can easily be held in the hand—will manage inputs of up to 34hp as a pump, and a similar unit at the other end working as a motor will deliver a torque of 52·8lb/ft. A measure of the power being handled by such small units is indicated by the size of the bearings required on the input end of the pump or the output end of the motor, whichever way you care to look at it. About one half of the casing, size as above, is taken up by two very big taper roller bearings and the shaft for this size is 1in in diameter. An input oil pressure to the motor of 3,500psi or more, removes the necessity for any kind of mechanical thrust bearing beneath the cylinder drum, the bottom face of which floats in an annulus which is open to the full line pressure.

British hydraulic drives are available for larger engines, the axial piston motors made by Lucas Aerospace Ltd at their Premier Precision Works for 70, 100 (and later) 180bhp are classically simple in design and operation. They employ a fixed swash plate with a maximum of 9 axially disposed pistons in a cylinder drum which is integral with the propeller shaft (it is possible to vary the design by having a lesser number of pistons for lower power requirements). Thus the whole of the mechanism is in line and it is possible to reduce the bearing loads imparted by the propeller by having shaft bearings at both ends of the piston/cylinder assembly. There is a long plain bearing forward and a plain bearing and a heavy duty ball bearing behind which takes both radial loading and the propeller thrust (Figs. 7.16. and 7.16a.).

Provision is made for two basic installations, one with the motor outboard in a streamlined 'thru-the-hull' casing and the other as an inboard unit with conventional sterngear. The outboard unit is naturally cooled by the surrounding water, but it is necessary on the inboard installation to employ waterjacketing around the motor, fed via a bleed-off from the engine freshwater cooling system.

The motor is driven by a Lucas axial piston variable displacement pump working at up to 4,000lb/sq in which

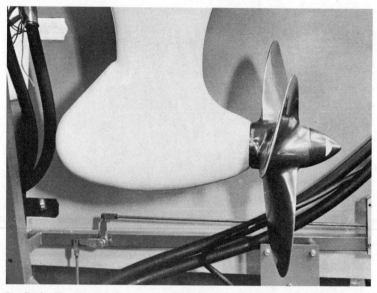

Fig. 7.16 The Lucas, Premier Precision hydraulic drive unit which has a fixed capacity motor and a variable output pump in which the swashplate angle can be varied.

is charged by another smaller pump at 100lb/sq in. Variable delivery is effected by altering the angle of the swash plate in the pump so as to increase or decrease the piston stroke. Due to the use of a charge pump the oil reservoir can be quite small.

The 'gearing' between the pump and the motor depends upon their respective capacities, thus if the capacity of the motor is fixed and that of the pump is variable (and reversible) an infinitely variable ratio is given either ahead or astern.

It is possible to use the pump control regardless of engine speed, and this facility enables propeller speed to be adjusted in order to absorb the engine power available at any rpm. This is one of the advantages of the hydrostatic drive, which tends to cancel out differences of efficiency based upon the optimum performance of a conventional engine/gearbox fixed ratio installation.

It will be apparent that it is also possible to obtain complete variation in boat speed and direction (ahead—astern) when coupled to an engine set to run at a governed speed.

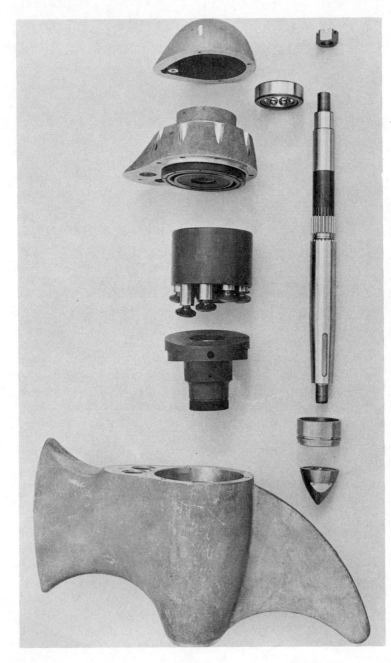

Fig. 7.16a An 'exploded' photograph of the Lucas hydraulic motor and its skeg housing.

Experimenting with the control lever in these circumstances is fascinating since there is no loading on lever in any position, and variation of speed and direction of the propeller is so light and precise as to be near-perfect.

One of the features of these installations is that the power unit may not only be located out of the way, but it can also be mounted so flexibility that the minimum of vibration is transmitted to the hull. Cushioning of this order is barely feasible with mechanical drives.

All forms of transmission, mechanical or hydraulic need to be carefully considered in relation to the characteristics of the engine as well as the kind of vessel involved and the nature of its use. Most manufacturers are very helpful and willing to pass on their experience concerning the use of their product with other equipment, different kinds of craft and conditions. Any owner without knowledge of power installations would be well advised to gather some recommendations prior to the purchase of any part of a proposed installation.

STERNGEAR

Sterngear is the next consideration in the transmission line and under this heading we can include everything aft of the gearbox, i.e. shaft couplings, sterntube, bearings, shaft and propeller. A straightforward in-line drive will have either a rigid, mating flange coupling or it might have one of the cushioned variety joining the gearbox output shaft to the

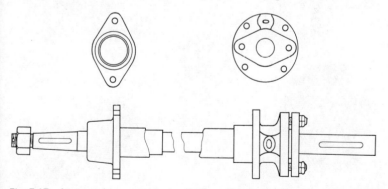

Fig. 7.17 A sterntube assembly by Gaines. This is fitted with white metal bearings and there is a sand excluding gland in the after housing. (See also Fig. 7.17a.)

123

propeller shaft (Fig. 7.17.), in either case the two shafts have to be exactly aligned. The propeller shaft is supported in a sterntube with inner and outer bearings, the inner bearing will incorporate a gland to prevent water seeping in round the shaft, and as a means of lubrication (Fig. 7.17a.). The outer bearing may depend upon lubricant from the forward end of the tube or it can have a water lubricated bearing of plastic or rubber.

If the propeller shaft extends much beyond the outer bearing, as for instance with a twin engine installation where the shafts emerge on either side of the keel, it will have further support by means of a bearing in a bracket bolted or secured by some other means to the hull. The bracket can take the form of a single strut or it may have two legs placed transversely in which case it is called an A bracket, the purpose in either case is to prevent the shaft from whipping. In a normal arrangement none of the bearings on the propeller shaft take any thrust, this being transmitted through to the gearbox or the reduction gear which have bearings suitable for end, as well as radial, loading. It should however be observed that car engine conversions with or without their original gearboxes are not equipped to take the thrust of a propeller, and if a marine gearbox is not fitted, it will be necessary to arrange for a thrust block somewhere along the propeller shaft. The same will apply if a variable pitch propeller is fitted to a car engine conversion.

Fig. 7.17a   Aft bearing housing with sand excluding gland, white metal bearing and forward bearing with gland and greaser. (Gaines.)

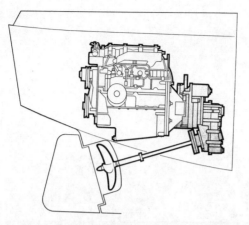

Fig. 7.18   Space saving with a V drive. The gearbox and drive are TMP.

The use of a V drive may sometimes be considered because it can save on the engine/gearbox space requirement, and also, the engines may be located in the stern where they are least likely to make their presence known through noise and vibration. The lower shaft of the V drive box will usually have a bearing to take the propeller thrust. The other attribute of this kind of drive, is that it can enable both the engines and the propeller shafts to lie at reasonable angles, although the fore and aft space may be very limited (Fig. 7.18.).

On lighter, high speed installations there is another form of drive which can claim some of the advantages of the V drive and some of its own. The outdrive, Z drive or inboard/outboard as it may be variously known, is now very popular particularly for use with high performance petrol engines. The engine is installed against the transom through which the drive shaft engages with a bevel gear matched to a similar gear on a vertical shaft. The bottom end of the vertical shaft also has bevel gears with the final horizontal shaft carrying the propeller (Fig. 7.19.). A trimming mechanism is generally incorporated so that the angle of the drive to the horizontal may be adjusted to correct the fore and aft trim of the boat, this is sometimes a manual operation but some units have

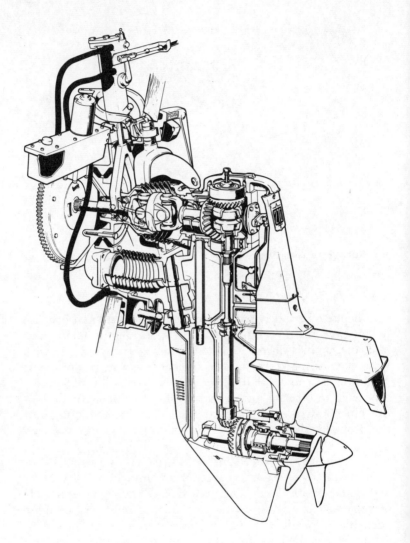

Fig. 7.19 The Volvo model 270 Aquamatic outboard drive with power trim and tilt mechanism.

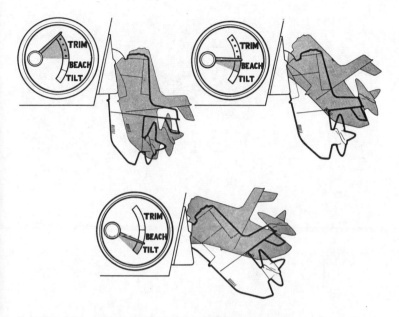

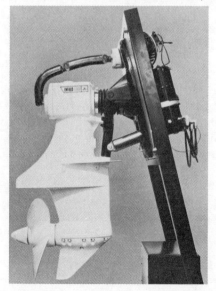

Fig. 7.19a   Inboard indicator for trim and tilt on the 270 Aquamatic outdrive.

Fig. 7.20   Enfield model 130H Z drive with electro-hydraulic trim/tilt. This unit will take petrol power up to 130bhp.

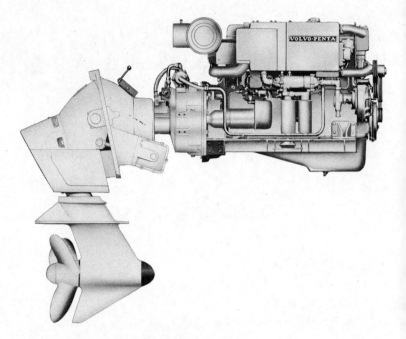

Fig. 7.21 Most outdrives steer via movement of the whole of the outboard unit but this Aquamatic model 750 has a steerable underwater housing and only the lower part of the unit moves.

power trim (Fig. 7.20.). A facility is also provided for retracting the lower part of the drive from the water when the boat is on a mooring, and this is effected by either hinging up the unit as with an outboard engine, or making it rotatable so that it can be turned transversely until the drive unit is clear of the water.

Vessels fitted with Z drives are normally steered by that means also, in the same manner as when outboard engines are used for main propulsion, but the Volvo Aquamatic 750 varies this with a steerable lower unit (Fig. 7.21.) and the Ocean 60 has a separate steering rudder (Fig. 7.21a.).

The arrangement is suitable for either single or twin installations but unless the hull has been built specifically for this form of power it may be necessary to reinforce the transom.

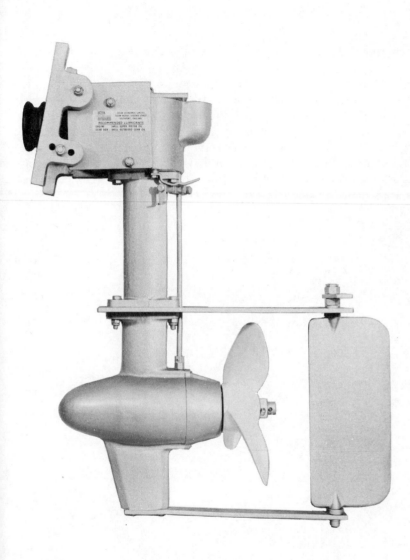

Fig. 7.21a Rugged simplicity gives the Ocean 60 outdrive a non-steering propeller and a rudder blade. Steering at low speeds should be improved by this means.

129

Part 3

PROPELLERS

A great deal of research has been undertaken to extend the knowledge of a propeller's function and give basic data for the choice of screw to give optimum performance. Propeller makers are able to give an indication of the preferred diameter and pitch for most installations, partly from research and partly from what might be called case history or experience. In spite of this, where the installation is completely new in that there has been no fitment to a similar boat and engine combination, it is often found possible to improve performance by trial and error, taking the data recommendation as the starting point of experiment (Fig. 7.22.).

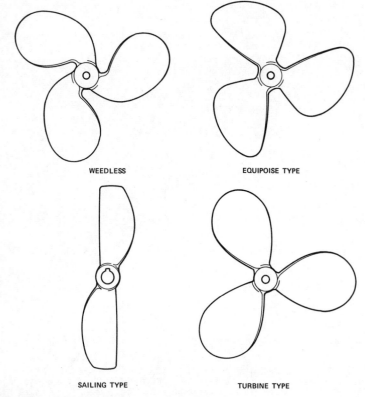

WEEDLESS   EQUIPOISE TYPE

SAILING TYPE   TURBINE TYPE

Fig. 7.22   A selection of propeller types (Gaines.)

With small vessels the loading in normal use is just as important as the basic data such as power, displacement, LOA, beam, etc., which may be provided initially in order to get near to the optimum. If the loading of a boat varies greatly from the original or designer's assessment then a propeller having different characteristics may be an advantage.

Propeller shape can vary considerably and sometimes design inference is varied by practical experience. At one time all aircraft propellers were delicately tapered towards the blade tips, being gradually reduced in both pitch and chord width to account for the higher peripheral speed, but when practical considerations caused the tips to be sawn off they performed just as well, although looking somewhat less elegant. A parallel in the marine field may be seen in the propellers fitted to a well-known range of low hp outboard motors, where, by comparison with contemporaries, they may seem somewhat crude in shape but they perform extremely well.

However, propellers are shaped on the basis that since the speed of the blade increases with diameter, the pitch angle is at its maximum at the root and decreases towards the tip, so that theoretically, the whole length of the blade can make the same rate of progress through the water. The width of the blade is called the chord and the chord thickness, indicated by a section through the blade, may be nearly consistent across the width, or it can have a streamlined or airfoil form, in which case the maximum depth of chord will probably be about one third of the chord width from the leading edge. Clearly a blade rotating at an angle to the water (pitch) will give propulsion without any inherent 'lift' properties in the shaping of the chord section, but the use of a contoured blade can add to propulsive efficiency. It will be apparent though that this will be effective only when the propeller is in forward rotation and efficiency going astern will be proportionately reduced, but for most vessels this will not be important.

Our initial consideration has been of propellers with fixed blades and these constitute the great majority of marine screws in use. The number of blades varies popularly from two up to five but most installations in power boats have three bladed propellers, this compromise allowing the transmission of a lot of power without excessive diameter.

We think of water as a liquid, but for propulsive purposes it may be more helpful and more accurate to think of it as a solid with only a very limited ability to conform with fluid notions. This is the reason why cavitation occurs. As with any foil, efficiency depends upon the maintenance of a flow of the surrounding medium (air or water) across its surface. If the flow breaks down, the foil or blade will lose its grip and become non-effective. Conditions for cavitation can be generated by excessive propeller speed in relation to the type and speed of the craft, or by interrupting the flow of water to the propeller through blanking by the keel, skeg or other part of the hull. In extreme cases it will be recognized by a sudden increase in engine speed accompanied by a slowing down of the boat. Obviously no propeller is 100% efficient and some slip (which may vary between 10% and 30%) must be tolerated, but we may assume that if slip reaches such proportions that the laminar flow of water across the blade breaks down then cavitation will occur. Continued cavitation can cause erosive damage to the faces of propeller blades and the blade section on high speed propellers is often modified to reduce the incidence of this.

Blade profiles may be more or less symmetrical lobes or they are sometimes swept back from the root. Extreme examples of the latter may be known as weedless propellers, since no part of the leading edge of the blade is in advance of the root and they are thus less likely to pick up debris or weed.

Some two bladed propellers used on auxiliary installations have rather long and narrow blades which, with a free shaft, tend to take refuge behind the deadwood and thus reduce resistance when the boat is under sail. This sort of arrangement can give rise to vibration when the engine is running through interruption of the water flow to both blades simultaneously at every revolution of the shaft.

In regard to propeller pitch and speed of rotation it may be said generally that the slower the boat the slower the propeller rpm for satisfactory results. From this it might be assumed that an ideal pitch angle could be chosen and standardized, so that the variation required from boat to boat would only be an enlarged or reduced diameter as required to absorb the power of the engine at the desired rpm. But it will be seen that this has two immediate limitations, first, the notion takes no heed of engine characteristics and second, for obvious reasons, it is impracticable to increase the diameter of a propeller ad lib.

Pitch is measured by the distance the propeller will advance in one revolution without any allowance for slip. The angle of the blade required to achieve this is not usually quoted although the optimum angle, which it is suggested gives maximum efficiency, lies somewhere between 40° and 45° (measured at two thirds the diameter of the blade). However, although this may be a desirable angle there are very few craft which could use it since it implies a pitch/diameter ratio of almost 2 : 1.

A blade angle of about 25° gives an approximately 'square' 1 : 1 ratio and the vast majority of propellers for displacement craft are in this region or below. The approximate figures being 0·75 : 1 to 1 : 1 for pitch/diameter ratio, with propeller speeds of between 600 and 1,200rpm.

Semi-displacement and planing craft, as may be supposed by the general considerations above, can use higher propeller speeds, and with pitch/diameter ratios much the same as for displacement vessels, they can achieve the desired performance. In fact it is only super fast vessels and unconventional craft such as hydroplanes which are able to employ pitch/diameter ratios much exceeding 1 : 1 in conjunction with high propeller speeds.

Selecting a Propeller

The particulars required will include the dimensions, displacement and type of boat, the shape of the stern, the thickness of deadwood in front of the propeller, and the present or expected speed. You will also have to state the rated horse-power of the engine, the corresponding rpm, number of cylinders, bore and the cycle, i.e. two or four stroke. It is also necessary to state whether the propeller required is to be right-handed or left-handed, i.e., whether it rotates in a clockwise or an anti-clockwise direction, when viewed from aft. In this connection it must be borne in mind that a propeller driven through reduction gearing usually rotates in the opposite direction to the engine itself. Other details required include the greatest possible diameter which can be accommodated, allowing for 15% of diameter clearance, the size of the present propeller, if any, with the performance and engine revolutions being stated.

A question which arises is whether a two or three-bladed propeller should be employed. For the average cruiser or launch a three-bladed screw is advised. When the revolutions exceed 3,000rpm a two-bladed propeller is usually to be preferred, as, with a three-bladed screw of large area operating at high revolutions, there is apt to be vibration due to blade interference. By careful design, it is often possible to overcome this when there is a low pitch/diameter ratio.

Measuring Propeller Pitch

As has been mentioned, the common practice when measuring the pitch angle of propeller blades is to refer to the angle at two-thirds diameter.

In order to obtain the pitch the propeller is laid on a flat surface with the boss vertical. The pitch at P (Fig. 7.23.), which represents two-thirds the diameter of the blade, may then be found as shown in the accompanying drawing.

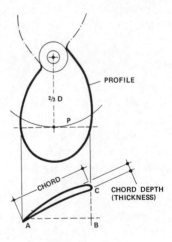

Fig. 7.23   Calculating propeller pitch.

AC is the width of the blade; CB a vertical line from the leading edge, and AB the width projected to a horizontal line. In turning the distance AB the advance neglecting slip is equal to CB.

The circumference of a circle through P is equal to the diameter at P $\times \frac{22}{7}$, and as the pitch is the advance during one revolution, the pitch will bear the proportion to BC that the circumference has to AB, or

$$\text{Pitch} = \frac{\text{BC} \times \text{circumference}}{\text{AB}}$$

Calculating Horse-power

The motor boat owner who puts a converted vehicle or industrial engine in his boat, is often puzzled as to the power output at a given number of revolutions. The following is the formula by means of which the horse-power of a petrol engine can be obtained approximately:

$$\text{Four-stroke} \quad \text{hp} = \frac{\text{B} \times \text{B} \times \text{S} \times \text{C} \times \text{rpm}}{13,440}$$

$$\text{Two-stroke} \quad \text{hp} = \frac{\text{B} \times \text{B} \times \text{S} \times \text{C} \times \text{rpm}}{8,400}$$

where B = bore in inches, S = stroke in inches and C the number of cylinders.

The following formula, on the same basis, gives the approximate horse-power of four stroke high-speed diesel engines:

$$\frac{\text{B} \times \text{B} \times \text{S} \times \text{C} \times \text{rpm}}{11,800}$$

Powers, Speeds and Propeller Sizes

The following formula gives a good idea of the power required to drive planing boats at a given speed, and of the speed likely to be obtained from a given power:

$$\text{Speed in knots} = \text{K} \times \sqrt{\frac{\text{bhp}}{\text{Displacement (tons)}}}$$

Values for the constant K are given in the following table:

Length of boat in feet	16	20	25	30	40	50	60
Very efficient planing forms with small deadrise	2.8	3.0	3.25	3.48	3.95	4.40	4.90
Good modern V-bottom boats	2.5	2.65	2.90	3.15	3.60	4.10	4.55
Old-fashioned, narrow V-bottom boats	2.35	2.55	2.75	3.00	3.50	3.95	4.40
Round-bilge boats	2.10	2.33	2.45	2.60	3.00	3.40	3.80

Bound up with the question of propeller size, is that of selecting a shaft of suitable diameter. From the diameter of propeller suitable for a particular installation it is possible to estimate approximately the size of shaft required, and the graph, (Fig. 7.24.) should prove a useful guide. It will be appreciated that a propeller of heavy pitch imposes a greater load than one of the same diameter, but light pitch, operating at the same speed, and due allowance must be made for this. For diesel installations, tailshafts of slightly greater diameter than those suitable for petrol engine installations of the same power and speed of rotation, are recommended.

For ease of operation and avoidance of any tendency to involuntary pitch change, the blades of variable pitch propellers will preferably have their centres of pressure over the axis of their rotation in the hub. Operation may be effected by longitudinal movement of the propeller shaft or a tube sliding on the shaft. The longitudinal movement being translated into rotary movement in the propeller hub via pegs engaging with slots offset in the blade roots. Alternatively a rack and pinion mechanism may be employed. Some VP propellers have a sufficient range of movement to permit feathering of the blades as well as pitch change from ahead to astern. The use of hydraulics can add considerable refinement to the operation but the final effect is the same.

Another propeller frequently seen on high performance sailing vessels is the clamshell or folding type in which the

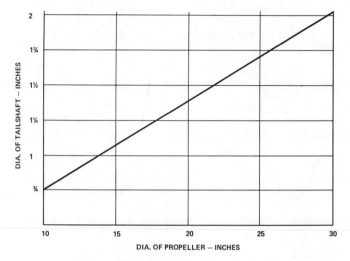

Fig. 7.24   Shaft sizes for propeller diameters.

blades are folded by hinging back in line with the propeller shaft. The two blades are contoured so that they fit neatly together face to face when folded. Centrifugal force causes them to unfold when the engine is started but since the blades are independent there is no guarantee that both will fold completely when the engine is stopped. A later version of the clamshell made in Scandinavia overcomes this problem by gearing the two blades together in the boss so that they both fold or unfold in unison (Fig. 7.25.).

The water jet offers a means of propulsion without external moving parts and from this point of view it becomes attractive for fouled waterways and very shallow conditions. The jet may be ejected either above or below water, and it may be of the type which is purely propulsive or it can have deflectors so as to give directional control also and eliminate the rudder. With this type it is usual to provide too for reversing with the use of another deflector to redirect the flow. The efficiency of these units is somewhat below that of conventional propeller installations, but there are certain savings and benefits. Most jet units can be run at high speed so they are suitable for car engine conversions, and a straight-through drive obviates the need for a gearbox on the deflector type models (Fig. 7.26.).

137

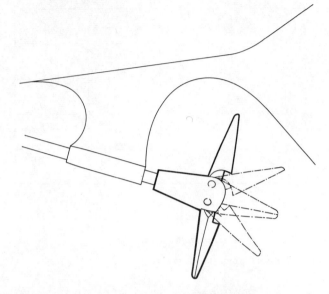

Fig. 7.25 The Menkamatic 'clamshell' folding propeller in which the blades are geared together to work in unison.

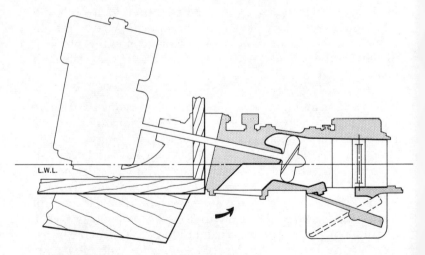

L.W.L.

Fig. 7.26 A simplified diagram showing a section through the Saifjet water jet propulsion unit. These are made in sizes suitable for up to 1100cc engines.

The Hotchkiss cone propeller unit is purely propulsive and requires a gearbox to reverse the rotation for going astern and also needs conventional steering arrangements. This type of unit is very rarely used in yachts but it has a wide range of use in commercial craft. An axial flow model is also produced and reversing on this can be effected either with a gearbox, or a deflector fitted to the jet unit.

Fig. 7.26a   A Bluebird Jetstar runabout fitted with a Castoldi jet unit.

chapter 8

Installation and Installation Equipment

Part 1

THE POWER UNIT

Very few things that we do are forever, and this thought might
be borne in mind with some benefit when installing machinery
and equipment in a boat. Remember when installing anything
that at some time in the future somebody might have to get it
out again, somebody might need to reach that bolt which lack
of consideration has made inaccessible, and it could be you
(Fig. 8.1.). Some of the problems met will be provided
gratuitously by the equipment manufacturers and it is up to
you to spot them and realize their potential for headache
making at a later date.

A case in point is the fact that most engines on offer today,
other than small auxiliaries, are adaptations of industrial
units for marine use. All of the major requirements for the
purpose are normally taken care of very well in the conversion,
but there are some things which may be overlooked because
they only become a problem when the engine is installed.

Since there is generally access to both sides of a single
engine installation, the sump drain plug or a pump facility for
the oil change, plus ability to reach the gearbox and the
sterngear, are probably the major considerations. However, a
similar engine installed as one of a pair in a twin screw boat
will not have the benefit of being 'handed' in so far as its
external components are concerned since such an arrangement
is obviously quite unnecessary for industrial use. Thus it is up
to those who install the unit to ensure that all of those things

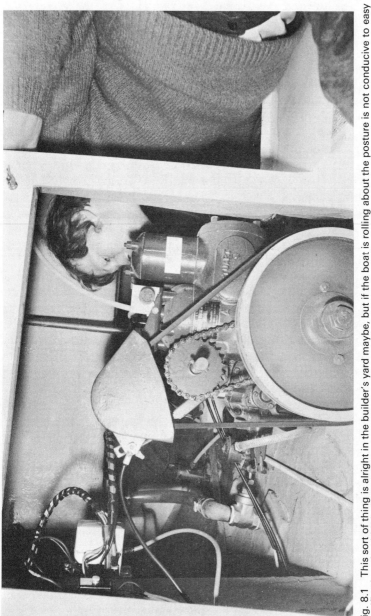

Fig. 8.1 This sort of thing is alright in the builder's yard maybe, but if the boat is rolling about the posture is not conducive to easy rectification should it become necessary.

which need to be reached on *both* sides of the engine are accessible.

Unless there is plenty of lateral space in the engine room one of the engines generally suffers in this respect. It is important therefore to assess how much room is needed between the engine and the ship's side to carry out proper maintenance. An extreme example noted, had been installed with no height to drain the sump and the only access hole (the dipstick), against the ship's side and inaccessible from the top by reason of other equipment.

In regard to basic installation requirements, i.e., boring, engine bearers, etc., information covering single engine installations is given in Chapter 4. The considerations in boring for twin engines are similar excepting, as indicated above, the best spacing between the two sets of bearers needs careful assessment having in mind hull shape, size of propellers, engine inclination and accessibility.

The maximum angle at which the engine may be installed will be given by the makers, the propeller size will be indicated by the supplier from your data, thus, two of the factors governing the installation are available and the height of the final drive will also be known from the gearbox specification. Matching these factors with the others involved will indicate the required fore and aft and thwartships position for the bearers and their inclination.

The bearers for either a wooden or a GRP boat will probably be of wood, but they will be capped with a steel plate or plates of sufficient area to support the metal feet of the engine without crushing the timber. An angle iron on the top of each bearer is one of the best ways of ensuring that the requirement is adequately met. If it is sufficiently stiff it will add considerably to the strength of the bearer and, if necessary, permit some reduction in the bearer cross section, but if in a GRP boat the glassing in of the bearer has made the surface irregular, separate plates under each foot may be used.

The important consideration apart from alignment is the type of attachment used for the engine feet. If the engine is to be on anti-vibration mountings, the makers of these will advise as to attachment. But taking the case of ordinary holding down bolts or studs, these need to have a nut-plate

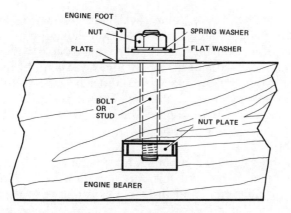

Fig. 8.2 Simple, non-resilient engine mounting.

let into the bearer (Fig. 8.2.) and they should be long enough to go down 2/3rds of the depth of the engine bearer, allowing for the thickness of the engine foot lug and the nuts and washers to go on top. The nut-plate will need to have a thickness of about 2/3rds the diameter of the holding down bolt and be a reasonable fit in the slot in the bearer. This ensures that it cannot turn round, but not so tight that it does not allow some movement in a fore and aft direction as well as sideways, since the hole in the bearer will also be bored so as to give the bolt some clearance. By this means small adjustments in engine alignment can be made.

Unless you are literally using a bolt instead of a stud, the stud should be screwed tight into the plate with the aid of a nut and locknut on the upper thread, so that when the engine is installed it is possible to put on and take off the nuts holding down the engine foot without the stud turning in the plate.

Supposing that you have installed the sterntube as indicated by the notes on shaft line boring, the mating of the two halves of the flange coupling on the engine and the propeller shaft is a matter of commonsense and trial and error. Remember that the engine must be aligned in every plane so that there is absolutely no load on the shaft when the coupling bolts are tightened. A feeler gauge inserted between the two faces of the coupling at 0°, 90°, 180° and 270°, with both shafts remaining stationary, will reveal most things about angular alignment after the initial adjustment for height has been

143

made (Fig. 8.3.). The final check must of course be made with the engine bolted down tight, and later the installation can be given a further check when the boat is waterborne, when some adjustment may be found necessary. In regard to the sterntube, it is necessary to consider its accessibility when the boat is complete, and if direct access to the grease cup will be difficult, an extension pipe from the greaser should be put in with the cup in a position which is handy enough to avoid being overlooked.

A rubber cushion coupling may be used instead of the metal to metal type, but this does not allow any lattitude for initial mis-alignment and the same care must be taken as for fitment of a solid coupling.

Similarly, if a flexible coupling is used to accommodate angular difference in inclination between the engine and the shaft, it should be remembered that it must be at the exact

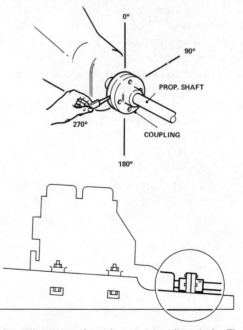

Fig. 8.3 Checking alignment of engine to propeller shaft. The clearance, checked with a feeler gauge, should be the same at all four points. The two halves of the coupling should be kept in the same relationship to each other and further checks made after turning both engine and shaft to other trial positions.

Fig. 8.3a Flexible propeller shaft couplings; this type will also take thrust. (Gaines.)

Fig. 8.3b This thrust bearing by Gaines acts both as a shaft steady bearing as well as taking the propeller thrust. A bearing of this kind is necessary for car engine conversions if not fitted with a marine gearbox, and also where flexible couplings are used unless they are designed to take thrust.

point of interception of the shaft lines, and it will not cater for any differences in height, offset, etc. In view of the difficulties involved, it is usual in such cases to fit two flexible couplings with a cardan shaft between. Thus the engine and propeller shaft alignments can be made independent, but unless the couplings are designed to take end loading, provision must be made for taking the propeller thrust before it reaches the after flexible coupling, by means of a thrust block and bearing on the propeller shaft. If the engine is on flexible mounts it is essential to have two flexible couplings (Figs. 8.3a. and 8.3b.).

Part 2

PIPEWORK

The important thing to remember about the attachment to an engine of any kind of pipework, control rod or linkage is that it must have some flexibility to enable the movement and vibration of the engine to be absorbed without causing strain on the attachment. This applies to engines which are not flexibly mounted and very much more to engines which are.

Sometimes, with small bore pipes, the required flexibility can be given by incorporating a coil or two in the pipe, and this is particularly important if the pipe material is prone to work or age hardening (Fig. 8.4.). Copper and light alloys are cases in point.

With pipes of larger diameter as in exhaust systems some form of flexible steady bracket should be used as an intermediate between the engine and the hull structure or bulk-

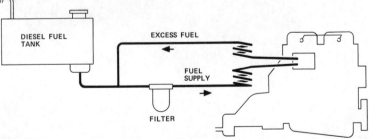

Fig. 8.4 Coils incorporated in fuel pipes to absorb vibration. Note that the excess fuel pipe goes back into the fuel pipeline, not the tank, in order to reduce frothing.

146

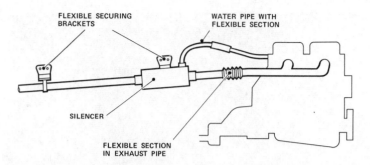

Fig. 8.5   Water-cooled exhaust showing flexible sections and rigid pipework.

head, and also wherever pipework passes through a bulkhead sufficient clearance should be given to permit some movement. It may well be necessary to make a rigid attachment to both the engine and the hull at some final point, but the further apart these points are the better, and a flexible steady bracket in between will prevent undue movement of the pipework, silencer or whatever part of the system is being supported. This applies mainly to engines which are not flexibly mounted. For engines with flexible mountings allowing liberal movement in torsion as well as in the vertical plane, it is essential to have a flexible section in both large and small pipes (Fig. 8.5.), unless in the latter case the solid pipe has an extravagant number of coils put into it.

Coolant system piping is not such a problem because the amount of heat involved is not such as to necessitate solid pipework excepting where it is carried on the engine. Reinforced synthetic rubber hose in a heavy duty grade will give satisfactory service. With a cool diesel exhaust (after water injection) it is possible to have both pipework and silencers of synthetic rubber.

The nature of exhaust systems can be varied considerably but it is an advantage if the gases can be cooled soon after exit from the engine. This may be done by a water jacket around the silencer or by water injection as shown in Fig. 8.5. If the water is injected it must either be on the exit end or a bleed-off from some part of the raw water (sea water) system. Some engines, generally those of the smaller kind as used for launches and in auxiliary yachts, are cooled directly by sea

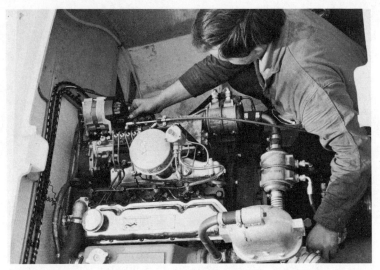

Fig. 8.5a Water-cooled exhaust with flexible exhaust pipe fitted to Mermaid model 236 diesel engine.

water (Fig. 8.6.), but the majority of the larger units fitted nowadays into motor cruisers have a closed circuit fresh water cooling system with a heat exchanger, through which sea water is circulated and then returned to the sea (Fig. 8.7.). The corrosive qualities of sea water make the latter arrangement preferable.

To return briefly to exhaust systems, we have referred to water injection, which besides cooling and contracting the gases also has a silencing effect. This may be used with or without an expansion chamber. The exhaust exit may be above or below the waterline and if it is below then a less elaborate silencing system will be needed. Most water injected systems have their exits just above the waterline, and as indicated in Fig. 8.5 it is necessary that the pipework should have an adequate downwards slope from the engine or that a swan neck be fitted, in which case a draincock must be put in at the lowest point of the system. Again, speaking generally, the engining of a motor cruiser will permit an adequate slope on most installations, whereas with an auxiliary engine in a sailing boat the position is such that a swan neck is frequently necessary.

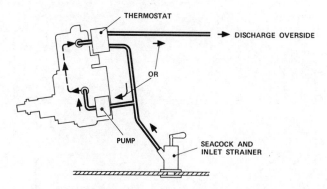

Fig. 8.6 Schematic diagram of direct sea water cooling system.

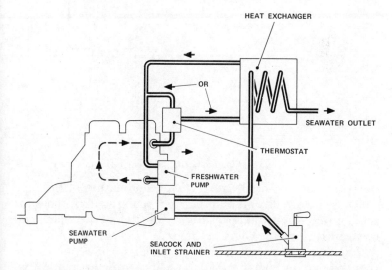

Fig. 8.7 Schematic diagram of fresh water cooling system using a heat exchanger.

Another piece of pipework which may be needed on a big engine will enable the crankcase breather to vent overboard. In this case the pipe will preferably go through the deck, not the topsides, and it should terminate in a swan neck to prevent the ingress of water.

Before leaving exhaust and cooling systems perhaps we should repeat the obvious, and remind you that wherever you make a hole through the skin of the boat below the waterline, a

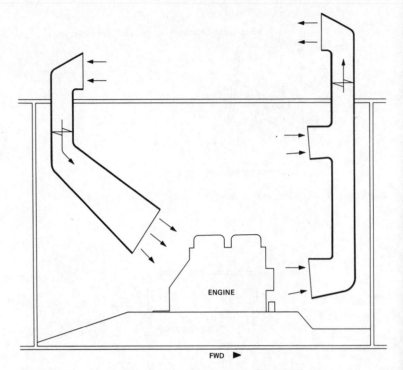

Fig. 8.8   Example ducting and fan arrangement for engine room.

sea cock must be fitted irrespective of the nature of the pipe which is involved. Intake pipes, particularly the intake for cooling water, must have a strainer fitted of a type which can be cleaned when the engine is in use.

Finally, a boat which is big enough to have an engine compartment or engine room, as distinct from an engine box, should have that area properly ventilated by means of a forced draught extractor fan with adequate ducts into the compartment for both entry and exit of air (Fig. 8.8.). As an approximation of the requirement, an internal combustion engine will use about $2\frac{1}{2}$cu ft minimum per bhp and in practical terms this implies an air intake of 1sq in per 2bhp as the minimum area of the duct.

In a small engine room with one or two powerful engines the temperature will rise on shutdown and it can reach 180°F, a temperature sufficient perhaps to embarrass parts of the installation, particularly electrical components. It is wise therefore to leave the engine room fan, or fans, running for a period after shutdown.

Part 3
WIRING

Excluding the starter cables, which are in an entirely separate circuit, the electrical wiring in a boat can be divided into power, for supply to equipment such as anchor winches, boat hoists, radar, etc., and, on the domestic side, refrigerators, ice making machines and the like (cookers too if of the household 240V type), and lighting, for cabins and navigation, chart, compass, etc. Both power and lighting circuits can be divided again if desired, into power for ship working and power for domestic use, and lighting for accommodation and navigation. The distribution board on a modern yacht supplies an extensive and complex installation which could easily merit a manual in its own right.

Generation, storage and distribution are discussed in Chapter 10 and the remarks in this section on installation are general to the requirement.

It should be observed that whereas the provision made for working the ship, starting engines, running winches and so on, may call for the heaviest cables in fact, the total current consumption for the domestic services on a well equipped luxury craft will exceed by far in overall battery demand the very high, but only occasional, drain imposed by engine starting and weighing the anchor. A further point is that most of the domestic load will continue, and can increase, when the engines with their generators are still.

Systems may operate on voltages from 12V right up to the normal domestic 240V enabling standard household equipment, electric cookers, washing machines, etc., to be used aboard. With a high voltage system another means of generation must be provided beyond that given by main engine driven alternators, and although examples are mentioned in Chapter 10, it is not proposed to deal here with other than the low voltage (12V and 24V) systems which are popularly installed in the majority of cruisers. The advantage of using a higher voltage is that battery capacity may be reduced, but

151

F

this is only applicable in reference to low voltage systems, since it is hardly possible to arrange for storage of current at 240V on a small vessel and services at this voltage must be fed on demand by the generator.

The initial choice of 12V or 24V will depend to some extent upon the voltage of the engine system provided as standard; smaller engines tend to have 12V and bigger ones 24V. Apart from lighting, bulbs for which can be obtained in either voltage, most small pieces of navigational equipment needing an electrical service can be supplied in 12V or 24V models or, in the event of the higher voltage system being installed, a tap off at 12V for certain items of equipment is quite feasible.

Excepting only small installations such as auxiliaries, where it may not be feasible because of weight and space, it is advisable, whatever the voltage, to arrange the batteries in two independent banks. For instance, in the case of a 12V system, one 12V battery would cater for engine starting (if necessary, for two engines) and the other 12V battery would serve lighting and other electrical equipment in the vessel. A heavy duty connecting switch should be incorporated so that in emergency the two batteries can be paralleled, i.e., they can be added together to increase the amperage available but at the same voltage (Fig. 8.9. is a schematic diagram for twin charging).

This arrangement ensures that, in ordinary circumstances, engine starting current will always be available whatever extravagant drain may have been made on the battery supplying lighting and other miscellaneous services.

To turn an engine initially for starting requires the full power of the battery and any reduction of the voltage through excessive resistance in the starter motor cables is to be avoided. Therefore the battery should be as close as is convenient to the engine with the cables taking the shortest route. Batteries do not deteriorate from use, in fact they thrive on it, provided it is use and not abuse. Batteries housed in engine rooms should preferably have a canopy over them with a vent to open air.

A starter cable may generate some heat, and therefore its insulation is of a type which will stand a considerable rise in temperature. Much of the lighter wire which is offered for

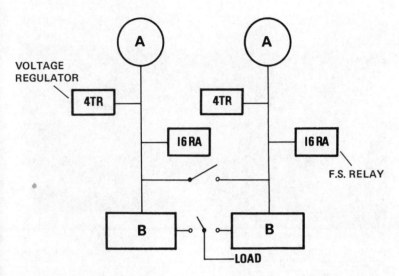

Fig. 8.9 Schematic diagram showing twin charging and paralleling of the alternator-battery circuit (C.A.V.).

general services is insulated with a plastic covering and whilst this is quite suitable in accommodation areas it should be avoided for wiring in the engine room. Here, as noted earlier in this chapter, very high ambient temperatures may be experienced.

It is obviously prudent to keep engine room wiring as far as possible from critical parts of the installation, i.e., hot areas, fuel lines and moving parts such as control rods and cables. All wiring should be firmly secured as high as possible in any compartment being served, and as far as may be colour coded. A fully insulated two wire system is desirable, with entirely separate power and light circuits if there is deck (winches) or other equipment of an important nature in working the boat. Indiscriminate earthing should be avoided and the circuit or circuits should be earthed back to the alternator. Apart from fuses which may be incorporated in individual items of equipment, it is necessary to have a fuse in one side of each main circuit.

Finally, a master switch or switches should be incorporated so that the entire system can be cut off from the batteries (Fig. 8.10.).

153

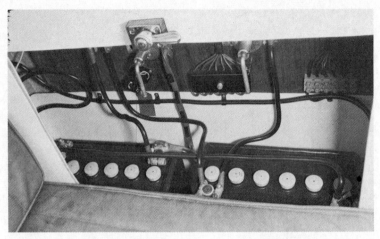

Fig. 8.10 The master battery switch must be capable of taking the full load which may be imposed on the circuit.

Part 4

CONTROLS

The advent of positive control by the use of single unit flexible, push and pull cables has meant that even on the biggest yachts there is now very little control shafting with associated levers, bell cranks, etc., and pull cables. If in an installation it is decided to incorporate any of these the line of their path is important, and it is useful to have a passing acquaintance with the orders of levers otherwise a very stiff and unsatisfactory set up may result. It must also be noted that every time another lever or crank is incorporated so is an extra little bit of backlash. Therefore unless the control envisaged can be reasonably short and direct we would recommend the use of a modern flexible control.

Flexible controls such as Teleflex and Morse are available with 'single lever' operation. This means that the same lever is employed for opening and closing the throttle on the engine and also putting the gearbox into ahead, neutral, astern (Fig. 8.11.). It is a useful and popular method of control particularly in twin engined boats where manoeuvring is somewhat simplified, but for those who prefer it, separate lever arrangement giving independent control of throttle and gearbox is available.

Fig. 8.11 Single lever controls such as the Teleflex permit handling of both throttle and gear change in one movement.

The two important things to observe when installing a flexible control are that the loading is within the makers limits for the cable, and that the cable run has easy curves where it needs to go round obstructions. With a cable of this type it is better to go a little further to reach the objective rather than make a short cut which involves a tight turn.

Part 5
STEERING

There are several options for steering control on a motor vessel. Ignoring the elementary tiller which may be seen on small launches and sailing vessels, there is the choice of cable with either a drum or chain on the wheel, push/pull rods, a rotating system with shafts and universal joints or hydraulic, and on the larger vessels perhaps electro/hydraulic. Whichever method is chosen it is reasonable to have an alternative method of moving the helm should the system fail. On a cruiser of any size the control system will be entirely covered in and mainly inaccessible and it is useful to incorporate some access to the rudder head with provision for an emergency tiller to be inserted. Bigger yachts will have more elaborate provision

155

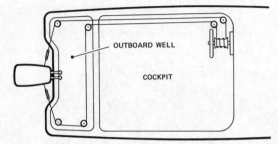

Fig. 8.12 Steering layout for wheel and cable; there are several alternatives for the cable run.

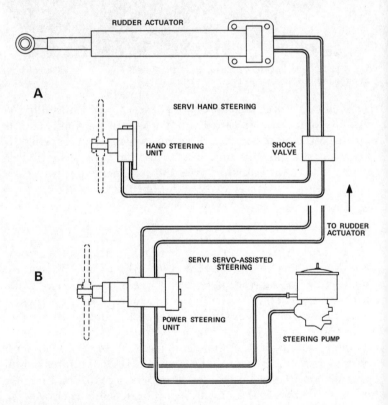

Fig. 8.13 Examples of hydraulic steering using A. a hand steering pump and B. a servo unit for power steering. (Servi. M.G. Duff and Partners).

than this, but a suitable arrangement can be incorporated on most boats if consideration is given during installation of the main steering gear.

A plan for cable steering is given in Fig. 8.12. and two hydraulic layouts as offered by the Servi system are shown in Fig. 8.13. An advantage of hydraulic control is that an additional steering position can be incorporated very easily and it gives a very light helm.

The flexible push/pull cable system as developed for engine control is also employed for steering and, whereas to date, it has had major popularity and use on runabouts and small cruisers fitted with outboard engines, it now appears to be increasingly employed in vessels of somewhat larger size.

Because of its simplicity and comparatively low cost the simple cable system may still be attractive to amateur builders and there are a few points to be observed in installation. All sheave attachments should be through-bolted, the sheaves should be of ample diameter, fifteen times the diameter of the wire is suggested as a guide, and currently these will probably be of tough plastic used in conjunction with stainless steel fully flexible wire. No lubrication will be required for the sheaves. The gearing of the steering will depend upon the size of the drum used on the wheel, but one should not be tempted to make this too small in the interest of light steering. It is suggested that 25D (the wire) would be a safe minimum to ensure a reasonable life for the cable.

Part 6

AUXILIARY EQUIPMENT

This heading can cover a host of equipment but since we are dealing mainly with the engine room and mechanics of the boat in this chapter we may confine ourselves to the essentials in this respect.

Bilge pumps can be manual, engine driven, or electric powered and a sensible boat on which the latter can be afforded will have manual also. It is important that if the pump is electrically driven it is made for a life in the bilges and is not an adaption. It may or may not have a sensing switch for automatic action but it must be either of the submersible type

157

or have sufficient lift to enable it to be well above any likely water level.

Bilge pumps may also be driven from the engine, in which case there can be sufficient pressure for it to double also as a fire and deck wash pump. If an additional power take off from the engine is fitted for this purpose, the bilge pump should have a bleed pipe from the sea water circulating pump so that it does not run dry, or be arranged so that the drive can be disengaged when the pump is not required.

All bilge pumps must be fitted with a strainer on the suction pipe, although hand pumps of the diaphragm type will pass fairly large solids.

Engine room fans are frequently arranged so that they give a forced draught into the engine room as well as extraction, but a minimum for a small vessel is to have intake vents of adequate cross sectional area and employ the fan for extraction (Fig. 8.14.). By this means the vessel will enjoy some advantage from the ram effect of air entering intakes with their openings facing forward (Fig. 8.8.). At one time most intakes were of the conventional cowl vent pattern but a little more thought in the design of modern superstructures generally provides a built-in intake which is unobtrusive and has a good area.

Engine room fans should be of the flameproof variety otherwise their use for clearing fuel vapours and gas leakage (which will find its way to the lowest part of the boat) is obviously dangerous. A good flameproof extractor fan used for a few minutes before starting the engine, if the boat has been left for an extended period, is an insurance against trouble. If there is any doubt about the integrity of any fuel or gas system, or spillage, it is a wise practice in any case.

Fans can be supplied for a 12, 24 or 32V operation and those of general utility, such as may be used in galleys and toilets, are frequently reversible so that they may either extract fumes or draw in fresh air (Fig. 8.15.).

Calor and other gas installations for cooking and heating are convenient in use on a yacht which is too small to enjoy electric cooking, and that will apply to the majority, although there are some vessels of under 40ft with very large output separate generators for that purpose. Alcohol cookers have

Fig. 8.14 Engine room air inlet trunk and extractor fan on the Conway 26.

some vogue on small craft but they are of little use for serious cooking when numbers are involved. The Primus and other paraffin pressure cookers have been popular for many years. The fuel has no storage drawbacks but the preheating required makes it somewhat less convenient than bottled gas.

Part 7
INSTRUMENTS

The instrument requirement will depend upon the type and size of the power unit, from a simple two stroke auxiliary which may have no instrumentation at all, to a multi-cylinder, turbo-charged, twin engine installation which will have a considerable array. In fact the decision as to what

159

Fig. 8.15 A Tannoy ventilation unit with a variable speed fan for either induction or extraction.

instruments are required is taken by the engine manufacturer and they are normally provided by him with the engine. The situation does not therefore arise unless one is making a conversion and fitting a marine gearbox, etc., in which case the provision may be as follows: Tachometer for engine rpm, oil pressure gauge, temperature gauge (these last two items will also be needed for some types of gearbox), ammeter, and warning light. This is about the minimum for essential knowledge of what is happening down below. To the list may be added fuel gauges, engine hour meters and fire and gas warning devices, also telltales for the situation in the electrical circuitry governing bilge pumps, fans and other supplies.

We are of course only discussing here the instruments pertinent to the power installation but there is perhaps a final thing to be said in this connection. Not all of these instruments are weatherproof and they should be fitted in protected places. If you have more than one helm position, as with a flying bridge, it is unwise to elaborate the display at that point and the instrumentation should be minimal and as well protected as possible.

The recommended conditions for the use of petrol and gas installations have been laid down by the Ship and Boat Builders National Federation in a code of practice, parts A and B. Part C adds notes on general construction concerning safety. We quote the recommendations in full here because they cover the whole field of accident prevention in this particular area of the subject.

A. PETROL ENGINED INSTALLATIONS

(1) TANKS may be of terne plate, lead-coated steel, brass or copper, galvanized mild steel or monel metal. Suitable baffles should be fitted in tanks of over 20 gallons capacity leaving not more than 3 cubic feet between baffles. In the case of metal tanks, all joints and seams should be brazed or welded, or rolled and soldered, or rivetted and soldered. A vent pipe to the outside of the boat should be incorporated in tanks of 10 gallons capacity and over; in tanks of less than 10 gallons capacity an adequate vent hole should be provided in the filler cap. The vent pipe should be of adequate size in relation to the bore of the filling pipe, but not less than double the bore of the feed pipe.

Tanks should be rigidly fixed on bearers and installed as low as possible and as far as practicable from the engine. Where tanks have to be fitted in the engine room they should be suitably encased. Tanks and all connections must be readily accessible for inspection.

(2) PETROL FILLER PIPE to be a permanent fixture and led from the deck to the top of the tank. It is good practice to extend an internal pipe to the tank bottom of large tanks. Petrol resisting flexible tubing and good quality clips may be used to connect the deck fitting to the tank, provided the tank is electrically bonded to the engine, but joints must be tested to ensure that they are petrol-tight. Water-tight filler cap to be provided and clearly marked with the type of fuel the tank contains.

(3) PIPING, FITTING AND FLANGES. All fittings and flanges for unions should be brazed or welded or rivetted and

161

soldered. The petrol feed should be carried in softened copper pipes of suitable size so fixed as to minimize vibrations, and with a flexible connection to the engine. Petrol-resisting flexible tubing may be used provided the tank is electrically bonded to the engine. All unions and fittings should have metal-to-metal joints, or be brazed on to the pipe. Soft solder should not in any circumstances be used.

(4) PETROL PUMPS. Where an electrical pump or other suitable mechanical means be employed, petrol should be drawn through the top of the tank by means of a pipe running to the bottom of the tank.

(5) GRAVITY FEED SYSTEMS. Gravity feed is not recommended, particularly where tanks exceed 2 gallons capacity. If gravity feed is employed, a tap must be fitted at the bottom of the tank. If the tank tap is not easily accessible, a second tap should be fitted in an accessible position as near to the tank as possible.

(6) FLAME TRAPS. Should be fitted wherever possible to all except crank case compression engines and a screened drip-tray fitted to all carburetters other than those of downdraught type.

(7) AN ENGINE TRAY wider and longer than the engine should be fitted under each engine to catch any oil or petrol to prevent it from going into the bilge.

B. LIQUIFIED PETROLEUM GAS INSTALLATIONS

(8) INSTALLATIONS. Only experienced persons should install, repair or modifiy a LPG gas installation. Appliances should be of a type designed for the use of LPG gas, and approved by the British Standards Institution. (See British Standard Code of Practice (CP 339: Part 3 (1956)).

(9) CYLINDER VALVES. Cylinders must be equipped with a pressure regulator. The cylinder should be so located to (i) facilitate changing, (ii) facilitate operation of the main gas valve, which should be closed when the installation is not in use, (iii) be easy of access, (iv) be stowed upright.

(10) ALL CYLINDERS AND REGULATING DEVICES below deck should be contained in a separate compartment so located that any escaping vapour cannot reach any enclosed spaces, e.g., cabins, engine compartments or bilges.

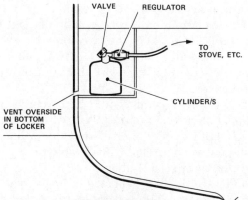

Fig. 8.16 General arrangement of locker for bottled gas with vent overside.

Such separate compartments should be deep enough to cover the cylinder effectively and be vented at top and bottom, and means should be provided for any escaping vapour to flow overboard (Fig. 8.16.). It is appreciated that in small craft with low freeboard it may not be practicable to comply with this recommendation, in which case bottled gas should not be used.

Cylinders and regulating devices on deck should be protected from the weather and spray, and should be so placed that escaping gas cannot flow into compartments.

If the cylinder is in a well it should be treated as if below deck.

(11) SECURING OF CYLINDERS AND EQUIPMENT. Cylinders and stoves must be fastened down securely to avoid any possibility of movement when the ship is rolling, pitching, etc.

(12) PIPING. All piping should be made with virgin seamless copper (preferably $\frac{1}{4}$in to $\frac{3}{8}$in outside diameter 20 gauge semi-soft annealed) and compression type fittings, carried as high as possible in the ship. Pipe lines should be rigidly secured at intervals of not more than 2ft and protected against mechanical damage. Where it is impracticable to use copper piping (e.g. with a gymbal stove), flexible piping may be adopted provided it is of the armoured, fire and petrol-resisting type to a standard not less than BS 3212. Rubber

piping must in no circumstances be used.

(13) JOINTS. A minimum number of joints on all installations is desirable, but where joints cannot be avoided they should be in accessible positions. A fixing clip should be provided not less than 4in or more than 6in on each side of the joint connector.

(14) BENDS. Copper piping should be carefully bent round corners instead of cutting and installing connections.

(15) FLEXIBILITY. The end of the pipe adjacent to the regulator should be connected with flexible piping of the type stipulated in paragraph (12) above.

(16) CONTROL TAPS. Where the main valve on the cylinder is not reasonably accessible from the galley it is advisable to fit a controlling tap adjacent to any cooker or hot plate which can be turned off when the cooker or hot plate is not in use. This tap should be of the special type provided for bottled gas installations.

(17) AVOIDANCE OF DRAUGHTS. Care should be exercised when siting cooking stoves, hot water geysers, refrigerators, etc., to preclude the possibility of a current of air blowing out the ignited gas and thus permitting gas to escape. While it is appreciated that a completely draught free position might not be possible of arrangement in a pleasure craft, it should be borne in mind that this should be carried out as far as is practical. On petrol engined boats gas operated refrigerators with a continuous burning flame shall be approved only when the refrigerator is fitted with an approved safety unit or when the continuous burning flame is at least 3ft above the hob, in order to remove the hazard of explosion caused by the ignition of accumulated gas or fuel fumes.

(18) VENTILATION. Adequate through ventilation of a type that cannot be closed must be provided in all cabins, galleys, etc., where bottled gas appliances are used.

(19) INSULATION. Woodwork adjacent to all appliances must be suitably insulated with non-combustible materials against excess heat and all flues where they pass near woodwork be lagged with asbestos. Where permanent appliances are fitted, suitable means should be adopted to prevent adjacent bulkheads, supports, the deckhead or furnishings from attaining a temperature of more than 120 degrees F.

Particular care should be taken in mounting gas brackets and water storage heaters to allow sufficient headroom to observe the foregoing recommendations.

(20) PRESSURE REGULATOR. The pressure regulator should be screwed securely to the outlet of the cylinder valve (left-hand thread). It is very essential that the washer in the union nut on the pressure regulator is in good condition and makes an absolutely gas-tight connection. Where craft are let out on hire charterers should ensure that these washers are inspected at frequent intervals and replaced when necessary. On privately owned boats spare regulator washers should be provided.

(21) LEAKAGE TEST. The regulator should be checked by an experienced person to ensure that it is supplying gas at the correct pressure and the whole system checked for leaks by means of a water gauge or similar satisfactory method.

C. GENERAL CONSTRUCTIONAL RECOMMENDATIONS

(22) MEANS OF ESCAPE. Where the normal exit from living accommodation leads over an enclosed engine space an alternative means of escape should be provided.

(23) FIRE EXTINGUISHERS. Sufficient fire extinguishers according to size of the boat, type of fuel and fuel capacity, should be carried and placed outside the compartments they are intended to serve. At least one dry-powder (gas pressure) type or CO_2 or foam type hand extinguisher to be installed on every cabin yacht or mechanically-propelled boat. Dry powder extinguishers of the canister or pistol type are not recommended for marine use. Methyl bromide extinguishers should in no circumstances be used and CTC and chloro-bromomethane (CB) extinguishers should not be carried where danger exists of their being used in confined or badly ventilated spaces, because under certain conditions the fumes given off are liable to be dangerous.

(24) VENTILATION. Thorough ventilation of engine, fuel tank and bilge spaces is essential. In each such separate space there should be a minimum of two air trunks, one of these extending to the lower part of the space. As an alternative one or more extractor fans may be fitted, but these should be

165

of explosion-proof type. All accommodation spaces to be provided with permanent ventilation of a type that cannot be closed.

(25) INSULATION. The exhaust pipes and silencer should be efficiently water-cooled or lagged.

(26) BATTERIES. To be adequately secured and compartment well ventilated. No battery to be fitted under any petrol tank, cock or filter.

(27) ELECTRICAL WIRING. The battery should be as near to the starter as is compatible with safe stowage arrangements. Adequately sized leads to be taken direct to the starter via the starting relay contacts. The relay should be mounted direct on the starter or adjacent to it.

Wiring, with the necessary fuses, should be taken through the appropriate junction boxes to the various point fittings, cleated at intervals of not more than 12in and installed sufficiently high as to remove the probability of it being washed by bilge water. Cable connectors should be sited in positions where there is no possibility of contamination by bilge water.

Wiring to be preferably of the stranded cable type (not solid conductor), and it is recommended that PVC covering, being impervious to petrol, oil and water, should be used.

Care should be taken to keep wiring from running near exhaust pipes or other forms of heat and clear of places where loose objects may knock against it.

Where the installation load is in excess of 15 amperes the main fuse should be capable of taking the full load and be further broken down by a fuse splitter immediately following it, so that each separate circuit is protected by its own fuse.

chapter 9

Outboard Power

OUTBOARDS FOR MAIN PROPULSION

With the availability of outboard engines approaching 150hp
there is clearly no difficulty in obtaining units to drive either
very fast or quite sizeable craft. Runabouts and weekenders
employ either single or twin units to an extent that shows a
decided preference over an inboard installation, and larger
craft, such as small to medium size fast cruisers, are obviously
also suitable for this kind of power. Fig. 9.1. is a cutaway
drawing of a 65bhp Evinrude. This is a very compact 3
cylinder unit.

Development of these engines has now reached a stage
where reliability with continuous running over long periods
need not be questioned. But there are other considerations
related to the use of outboards in cruising boats which are
intended to have a reasonable range and some seagoing ability,
and the principal of these is probably the vulnerability of
outboards to swamping in adverse, open sea conditions.
Consequently whereas larger craft on lakes and estuaries may
enjoy portable power for main propulsion, one would not
make it first choice for a coastal cruiser, unless it was intended
to restrict the use to the kind of range enjoyed by the smaller,
power weekender.

Having said that, it is necessary to acknowledge the fact
that most modern outboard engines appear to be able to
run under almost any conditions except complete immersion,
and there are a number of reasons why this flexible approach
to powering a boat may be preferred.

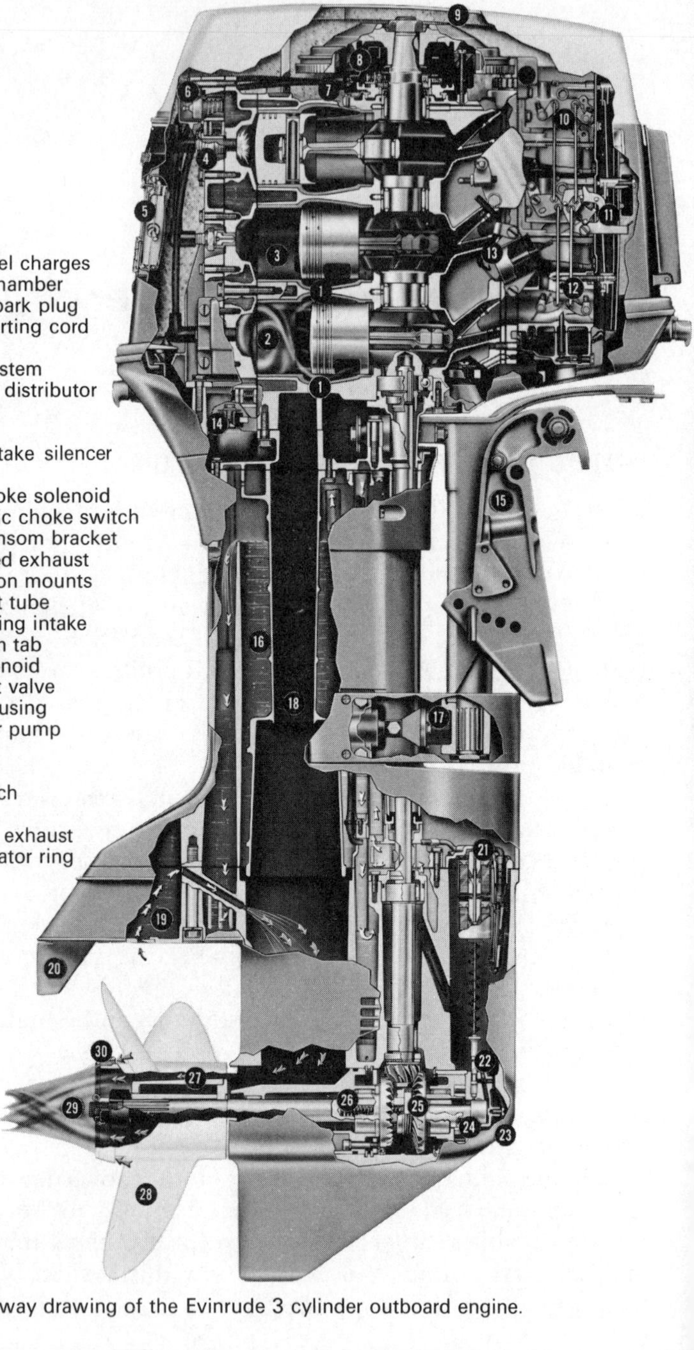

1. Intake ports
2. Converging fuel charges
3. Combustion chamber
4. Surface gap spark plug
5. Emergency starting cord
6. Thermostat
7. CD ignition system
8. Alternator and distributor
9. Motor shroud
10. Carburettor
11. Carburettor intake silencer
12. Fuel linkages
13. Two-stage choke solenoid
14. Thermo-electric choke switch
15. Adjustable transom bracket
16. Water curtained exhaust
17. Rubber isolation mounts
18. Tuned exhaust tube
19. Gearcase cooling intake
20. Adjustable trim tab
21. Gear shift solenoid
22. Hydraulic shift valve
23. Lower unit housing
24. Hydraulic gear pump
25. Shift gears
26. Clutch dog
27. Safti-grip clutch
28. Propeller
29. Through-prop exhaust
30. Thrust accelerator ring

Fig. 9.1   Cutaway drawing of the Evinrude 3 cylinder outboard engine.

168

The first and obvious advantage is to be able to avoid installation problems. The 'package' nature of the unit also gives advantages in transport and maintenance, and beyond this it is possible to change one's ideas about the power requirement at any time, without making any alterations to the boat. Steering and other control arrangements now available, provide the same sort of facilities as one might expect with an inboard installation, including electric starting, and many motors are fitted with a generator (Fig. 9.2.).

The runabout is typical of the vast majority of these small craft which use outboard power and the power weekender in Fig. 9.3. indicates the very small amount of boat which is taken up by the power department, most of which overhangs the transom so giving more room for the cockpit and cabin space.

Main propulsion for canal craft is another field, particularly for low hp outboards which, because of the modest speed

Fig. 9.2 Powerhead of the Johnson 125hp V 4 cylinder engine.

Fig. 9.3 The Shetland 570 powered by a Chrysler unit.

Fig. 9.4 A Crescent 18 pushes this Charnwood Corinth inland waterways cruiser. Note lifting outboard bracket. (Yachts International.)

requirement, are able to provide suitable power from the smaller units plus the advantage of low first cost. Fig. 9.4. is an example.

OUTDRIVES
These are referred to in Chapter 7 and some examples are illustrated.

SMALL OUTBOARD ENGINES FOR TENDERS
Anyone shopping for a small outboard nowadays has a very wide choice ranging from the rugged Seagull units which, externally, appear to change little with the years, to the rather smoother looking imported units which take their style from their bigger brothers. Incidentally, there are no indigenous high power outboard engines, any engine offered of over 8hp will be imported. Until the so-called boating boom and the advent of large numbers of light runabouts and small cabin powerboats the demand in this country for medium and high power outboard motors was very small.

It is advisable that when getting an outboard for either a small rigid or an inflatable dinghy that you enquire of the makers of the boat their recommendation for the maximum power to be used. Failure to observe this may cause you to be overpowered in more than one sense. However, with a power range starting at $1\frac{1}{2}$hp there should be no difficulty in acquiring a suitable unit. The smaller units tend to have integral fuel tanks whilst others, and particularly imported engines may have separate tanks for quite low hp motors. A bigger range is given by a separate tank which can be of larger capacity than an integral supply, but this is hardly important in view of the general nature of the task required of them and the self-contained job is probably handier for tenders (Fig. 9.5.).

THE LARGER INFLATABLES
Development in this field has provided boats of sufficient size and rigidity to accomplish a variety of tasks besides that of acting as a tender to a larger vessel. The RNLI inshore rescue craft are a case in point and most makers of inflatables now have a range of models, several of which command attention as motor craft in their own right, suitable for high speed launches, workboats and runabouts. Because these craft are

Fig. 9.5   The ever-ready Seagull at its customary task.

Fig 9.6   One of the bigger inflatables. A 13ft 6in. C craft.

usually much lighter than their rigid counterparts the power requirement is somewhat lower and high speeds can be achieved without resort to very high powered outboard units (Fig. 9.6.).

AUXILIARY USE

Sailing boats, cruisers particularly, have the need for auxiliary power and the smaller vessel of about 18 to 25ft LOA may use outboard power of from 5 to 9hp with advantage in relation to the first cost of powering the boat. Longshaft units are frequently necessary for this purpose, the Johnson 6hp Fisherman is typical, and so is the Seagull Silver Century Plus of 5½hp. They can be mounted in a variety of ways, in trunks built in at the stern of the hull and on a number of either rigid or retracting outboard brackets. Unless the engine can be tilted sufficiently on a rigid bracket to be well clear of the water when sailing, it is advisable to get a bracket which enables the engine to be retracted or lifted clear without recourse to dismounting the unit. Two types of these are shown in Figs. 9.4. and 9.7/7a.).

Fig. 9.8. shows a selection of inflatables as tenders for larger vessels.

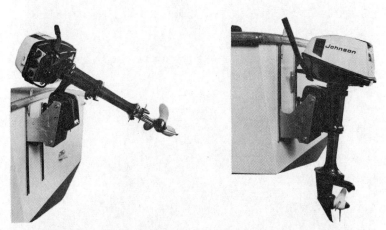

Fig. 9.7 and 9.7a   A sliding outboard bracket which gives the proper immersion but enables the propeller to be lifted clear for sailing. (Buck Marine). See also Fig. 9.4.

Fig. 9.8 A clutch of small inflatables. Clockwise from the Avon, Sportboat, left foreground : Hutchinson Nautisport 30, Astral XX, Zodiac Cadet and Campari Marina.

chapter 10

Electrical Equipment

GENERATION AND STORAGE

The dynamo which produces direct current, and with which we have been familiar for many years on boat and car engines has largely given way to the Alternator. This generates alternating current, and a rectifier has to be incorporated in the system so that the function of battery charging and supply to DC equipment can be met.

Alternators have the advantage of being able to cater for heavy current demands and they will generate at very low rpm. They are also rather more compact than DC generators of similar current capacity. Engine mounted alternators are now standard on most marine engines, excepting only very small motors suitable for auxiliary use, where the provision of a generator may be optional.

The advantage of being able to produce a significant charging current at tickover rpm means that battery charging when tied up is rather more easily accomplished, and in many cases a separate small charging unit may be dispensed with except for standby.

Bigger boats using 240V systems employ separate generator sets and a typical unit such as the GM Power Plant Marine Dieselite (Fig. 10.1.) is driven by a 12bhp diesel engine and produces 6KW at 240V or 120V. A generating set of this kind besides powering the ship's domestic equipment direct, e.g., mains type 240V cooker, deep freeze, etc., can also be used to charge a battery bank at say 24V, via a converter (Fig. 10.2.). Also, since the system is arranged, suitably insulated, and fused for 240V it becomes possible to utilize a shore supply

Fig. 10.1 The G. & M. Power Plant series MDL 6 kilowatt diesel driven generator.

Fig. 10.2 Galley equipment in a luxury yacht; 4 burner electric hob on the left with a Tricity double oven opposite. The equipment in this all-electric galley also includes a deep freeze and two refrigerators. (Camper and Nicholson.)

whenever it is available, and this similarly, can be used for battery charging via a converter.

The storage batteries in a boat may be either of the lead/acid or nickel-cadmium alkali type. The former are less expensive and have a higher output per cell, whilst the latter, besides costing a lot more also, have a very much longer life and will stand more neglect and abuse in the way of crash charging and long periods out of use.

The voltage on a 24V lead/acid battery may vary from 20V to 27·5V, according to its state of charge and any equipment in the circuit must be able to accommodate the higher voltage. The battery state can be checked with either a voltmeter or a hydrometer. In the latter case it is the specific gravity of the battery acid which is recorded and a fully charged battery cell should read 1.250–1.270.

A lead/acid battery which has become badly sulphated through disuse can sometimes be revived by a very long, slow charge. Never top up the cells with anything other than distilled water and keep this just above the top of the plates.

All batteries should be properly secured and stand in trays. Since one or more 24V banks of batteries of ample capacity will weigh a considerable amount, they should be located as low as possible in the boat consistent with being clear of bilge water. Some thought should also be given to their athwartships position since a heavy battery bank can cause a list on a vessel of considerable size if it is placed against the ship's side on the maximum beam. It is particularly important to keep nickel cadmium battery cases clear of bilge water and a rubber or pitch-lined wood tray is indicated, which is also good for lead/acid batteries.

The minimum voltage from a single lead/acid battery cell will be 1·8V and the maximum about 2·2V, thus for a 24V battery 12 cells are required, but a nickel-cadmium battery produces only approximately 1·4V per cell and therefore 18 or 19 cells will be needed to make up a 24V battery.

Battery charging is governed by an automatic voltage control regulator between the alternator and the battery, so that the charging current is reduced as the battery regains its power. The alternator is well able to cope with the higher outputs required by this method of charging, which has the

Fig. 10.3 A neat Petter AB1W battery charging set of 2.5Kw. with remote control panel. Output is at 32 volts DC.

advantage of bringing the battery up fairly quickly in the early period of the charge when its internal resistance is low. But DC charging sets are still much in use and the compact Petter ABIW can produce up to 2·5KW at 32V (Fig. 10.3.).

For a proper study of electricity, a suitable handbook may be acquired, and for the purpose of this manual it is not intended to provide cable sizes, charging rates, etc., but Appendix 14 gives a table of current and ratings for cables and there is some information which is basic to the subject and which can help you to work out a requirement. In consideration of volts and amperes, volts is the 'pressure', amperes is the 'quantity' and watts, which is merely volts multiplied by amperes, is the power available or required. It will be readily seen that if we know two of these figures we can find the other one, e.g., if a generator is said to produce 40 amperes at 24V then the output is 40 × 24 which is 960 watts. Similarly an electric fire, which is rated at 1,000 watts (1 Kilowatt) at 240 volts, will have a current requirement of just over 4 amperes, that is 1,000 divided by 240.

It will be understood from the foregoing that the higher

the voltage the lower the current requirement can be to produce the same wattage or power. Thus an electric motor which has a power requirement of 100 watts and runs on 12 volts will have a current consumption of just over 8 amperes, but a motor of the same power which is wound for 24 volts will consume only 4 amperes. This is the advantage of using the higher voltage system as it enables the battery capacity to be reduced and reduces the current load in connecting cables.

There is however another consideration in regard to the supply of current and that is the resistance of the electrical conductor through which the current passes in order to reach any piece of equipment in the system. This resistance is measured in ohms and it has the effect of reducing the voltage (pressure) at which the current is supplied. Naturally the longer the wire or cable, the higher the resistance, and the thicker the cable the less will be the resistance.

There is a law about this which says that 1 volt is the pressure required to supply a current of 1 ampere through a resistance of 1 ohm. This, however, need not exercise the mind to any extent, since if you know the voltage and the current consumption of any piece of equipment you can ask your supplier to provide you with suitable wire to make the connection. Wires are made with different current ratings, e.g., you could require a 5amp or a 10amp cable as the case may be. Remember though the length involved, and that if your cable is to supply a number of pieces of equipment by having connections made to it along the line, it will need to have a current rating equivalent to the combined current consumption of all of the items of equipment.

With the advent of alternators the requirement for battery capacity has altered somewhat, but the basis of its assessment remains the same, i.e., it must be in relation to the total current consumption of all of the equipment that you are likely to have in use simultaneously, excepting only the engine starter motor or motors. In the past, with the use of dynamos and slower charging facility, it was suggested that the battery capacity reckoned in ampere hours should be four times the figure given by totalling the equipment requirement. Of course, the installation of electrically powered equipment has increased in recent years and this, to some extent, cancels out the alternator's advantage. But one is hardly likely to have an ice-making machine producing continuously, whereas the cabin and other lighting will involve a considerable drain over a long period when the boat is tied up. Consequently the maximum load becomes a matter of intelligent assessment, and when you have come to a conclusion about this, it is suggested that your required battery capacity can be calculated by multiplying by three if you have an alternator or by four, as before, if you have a dynamo.

The situation will be secured if the batteries are split into two banks as indicated in Chapter 8. By this means one is unlikely to be bereft of starting power for the engines, and if you can start the engines you can charge the batteries.

Fuses must obviously bear close relationship to the load being passed, and the cable carrying it, otherwise they will not do their job of protecting the equipment and the supply. Apart from the main fusing of any major circuit which may be effected with either a fuse or a circuit breaker, separate fusing of subsidiary circuits is also necessary, otherwise a tiresome number of things may go out of action through an unimportant piece of equipment being damaged, e.g., a smashed light bulb causing a short circuit.

DISTRIBUTION

It may be helpful to think of distribution wiring as a river system in reverse, that is, starting with the main estuary and devolving through its major tributaries and finally to the minor streams which run into the major rivers (Fig. 10.4.). The ship load or total current demand must feed first into the mouth of the estuary then into the major rivers which are the supply routes for the different areas of demand, e.g., navigation lighting, cabin lighting, deck equipment (winches, etc.) domestic equipment, navigation aids and so on. To take the last as an example, equipment in this field could now include depth sounder, RT, speed and distance log, radar etc. Each of these minor streams needing supply will, as far as possible, retain its integrity within the major branch, e.g., it is not good practice to tap off the wiring supplying the radar because it runs conveniently near to the refrigerator.

Keep an orderly notion of supply arrangements along the

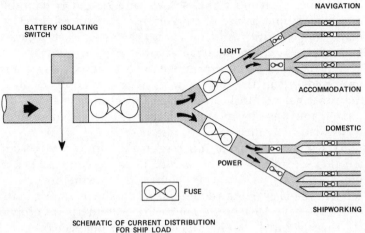

Fig. 10.4   Schematic electrical distribution diagram ; return leads not shown, but all insulated.

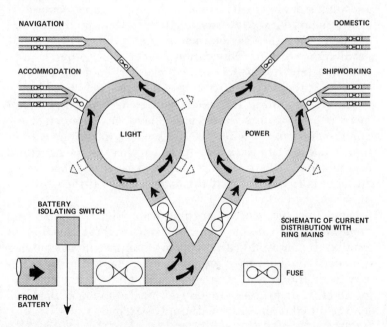

Fig. 10.5   Schematic electrical distribution diagram employing ring mains. Return leads not shown, but all insulated.

above lines, remember that a two wire system is desirable everywhere, and a fuse of suitable size is required on every major supply branch. Also, as far as possible, on each separate item of equipment or the tributary that feeds it.

The basis of the arrangement with a fully isolated and protected system does not vary if a ring main is installed, since the major branch supplies can be taken from this in the same manner as they are taken from our earlier main estuary which had only one end (Fig. 10.5.).

It will be seen that the ring main supply has certain advantages since with the use of an adequate number of junction boxes at strategic points, the wiring for major branches can be facilitated and shortened. Furthermore, in the event of a severance of the main wiring at any point around the ring the supply to all branches remains unaffected.

The actual detail of wiring is something which will not be assisted by anything we may say here, excepting that all wires should be adequately supported by cable clips, and all joints and junctions should be made with proper cable connectors and junction boxes. Ready made distribution boards are available and the use of one of these will facilitate new installation wiring. Navigation lights and other equipment needing supply in exposed places should be fed from waterproof sockets or wired so that the cable does not provide a convenient lead-in for water. Supposing a piece of equipment is fitted with a water-tight gland or grommet at the point of entry of the wire, it is still sensible to run the wire *up* into it rather than *down* into it, and if, because of structural arrangements, your wiring approaches from the wrong altitude, take it down past the component and then bring it up to the point of entry.

Some of the electrical equipment, ship working and domestic now available for small craft is illustrated in this manual. If you would care to make a dummy run at equiping a modern family cruiser with the things you feel to be necessary or desirable, and then add up the total current demand for all of the items chosen, you will have a notion of the work load required of the electrical supply system.

chapter 11

Making a Better Boat

Most vessels are amenable to a good deal of improvement in their various functional areas, and whereas with unlimited money and a great amount of thought many of the 'extra' features can be incorporated in the boat whilst building, there is considerable scope for those who take interest in advancing the specification of a well-tried boat which has already given much pleasure.

Many may think that the first criterion of performance in a power boat is the manner in which the engine does its work. Even on new craft, installations come in varying degrees of satisfaction and although one would think that by this time there would be some universally recognized standards, it is in fact, an area worthy of more attention. The situation does not lend itself to universal solutions, and, excepting flow production boats, radically different solutions may be found for similar ailments in different craft. For example, in one boat, vibration may be claimed to be low because the engine is solidly mounted, in another it will be found that the answer rested in anti-vibration mountings. It is necessary therefore to point out that those who already have a reasonably satisfactory installation, re vibration with solid mountings, will not with certainty make improvement by re-ordering things, but for those who suffer unduly with a solidly mounted engine, some carefully chosen anti-vibration mountings could reduce both vibration and noise levels through the ship.

Engine makers can often provide cushion mounts as an alternative when the engine is supplied, and there are also firms who specialize in noise and vibration problems who have

183

a wide range of mountings and data from which they will help you make the right choice. Some of these products are illustrated in Fig. 11.1. and 11.1a.

Supposing that you do put your engine on cushion mountings it will of course be necessary for you to incorporate flexible couplings at both ends of the propeller shaft, that is, if you have an integral gearbox you will need one coupling immediately behind this and another just forward of the stern-tube bearing. We have said 'of course' but we have seen an installation with the engine flexibly mounted and only one rubber muff coupling connecting it to the rigid propeller shaft. It seemed to work alright and the builder insisted that the method was always satisfactory in his experience but we would not recommend it as being generally acceptable.

Noise seems to arise in two forms, that which is generated by vibration in bulkheads, etc., and that which is a part of the general mechanical noise from the engine and its transmission. The former will be alleviated by reducing vibration, but the latter requires a different kind of treatment involving both hard and soft shields between the area where the noise is produced and the rest of the vessel. Various methods may be employed including the use of laminated panels and sound-damped bulkheads and cabin soles, which have a layer of non-resonant material, such as one of the foamed plastics, either secured to a plywood panel or sandwiched between two sheets of plywood.

Other materials which are employed in this connection include aluminium sheet to which synthetic rubber has been bonded. Lead, in conjunction with glass wool and plywood and also GRP which is used for moulding nacelles for complete engine enclosure. This is quite an attractive approach to the problem but consideration must be given to the manner in which the engine is to be vented.

It should be noted in connection with noise transmission, that however thick and efficient the shielding of soles and bulkheads may be, most of the effect will be lost unless the integrity of the physical barrier is maintained. Even the smallest hole will permit passage of noise out of all proportion to its size. A dramatic demonstration of this effect was given on the yawl Nylanni which had received special attention to

Fig. 11.1 Barrymount cup-type shock mounts fitted to the engine feet on a Mercedes OM 636 diesel. Cementation (Muffelite) Ltd.

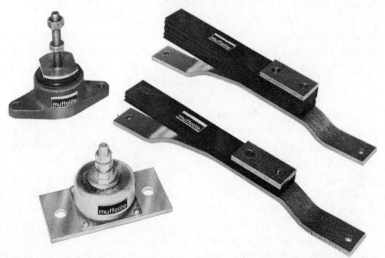

Fig. 11.1a A selection of anti-vibration mountings marketed by Cementation (Muffelite) Ltd.

reduce noise and vibration from its large diesel auxiliary engine. The engine hatches were sealed with a magnetic tape on the edges which made intimate contact with a metal strip around the hatch opening. With the hatch opened only a crack, as it were, the noise was still appreciable, but when the tape was permitted to seal down it was like turning off the noise with a tap.

Condensation was at one time a great problem on GRP boats but, by using methods very similar to that employed in cutting down noise, i.e., by insulating the inside panel from the outside panel, most modern craft are freed from this particular nuisance. There are several approaches. On a steel vessel the hull may be sprayed internally with a considerable thickness of foamed plastic (Fig. 11.2.). GRP craft are more likely to have either a separate internal coachroof moulding which leaves a small insulating air space or a vinyl cloth headlining backed with foam plastic. The latter is quite a feasible operation for the amateur improver, but it is not absolutely simple, and besides getting the right adhesive it is advisable to cut paper patterns first of the areas it is intended to cover. Adequate ventilation is of course another means of keeping down condensation and suitably located vents will help to keep the boat sweet and dry (Fig. 11.3.).

A point about comfort down below in hot weather is that it is not sufficiently appreciated that the colour of the coachroof and deck can affect the temperature in the cabin to a considerable degree. This one can prove by touching a pure white hull surface with the hand when it is in hot sunshine and then transferring the hand to a pigmented area such as the deck. Even slight colour tints such as ivory, pale grey or light blue will have an appreciably higher temperature than the pure white surface. So although your coachproof may be insulated a boat intended for sunny climes is better off with a pure white top.

For comfort of another kind we would draw attention to the known movement of all things that float and suggest that many bruised shoulders, hips and thighs could be prevented if a sufficiency of handholds and grab rails were provided through the ship, both below as well as on deck. Besides being more secure from bodily harm, it is rather more elegant to

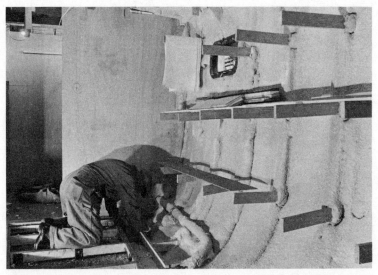

Fig. 11.2 Anti-condensation and sound damping with polyurethane foam sprayed onto steel hull plating and frames. (Camper and Nicholson.)

Fig. 11.3 A group of Tannoy vents on the coachroof of the Dervaig 38.

187

make progress through the vessel upright instead of lurching violently from one piece of cabin joinery to the next.

For very small vessels, both sail and power, sundry other small precautions are advisable notably in reference to cooking and toilet arrangements. Stoves must be fitted with a fiddle, preferably of the adjustable type which enables the saucepan or kettle to be held securely in position. You may think that you are never going to expose yourself to conditions requiring this safeguard, but a vessel passing at speed whilst you are moored quietly against the river bank can slide the whole lot into your lap, or worse still, endanger a child nearby. If you frequent open waters and you still wish to have hot meals then your stove must be gimballed (Fig. 11.4.), as well as sporting a fiddle. Also, if things are so bad that you can only heat up soup, you will want some sort of rack in which the mugs can stand securely whilst you fill them.

In the matter of toilets, there is the choice between a proper marine WC and the chemical type. In practice you will need to have a chemical job if you intend to sail mainly on inland waterways, whilst if you are an open water man the flushing, marine WC is much to be preferred. The disadvantages in taking a conventional chemical toilet to sea are fairly obvious, but those of the flushing type may be suitable if absolutely spill free (Fig. 11.5.). Marine WC's can be installed so as to discharge optionally into a holding tank whilst on inland waters, but this facility depends upon the size of the boat and the willingness to spend a good deal more on installation.

In some vessels rain may add more depth to the bilge water than any hull leakage, and fresh water in the bottom of a wooden boat is an enemy. It is important then to ensure that if your boat is to remain unattended over long periods that the deck and superstructure are free from leaks, but beyond this, continuous movement of the boat on a mooring will cause the bilge water to surge about, particularly athwartships. In a shallow draft boat which is open below the cabin sole, the water may be able to roll up the sides of the hull until it reaches the berth cushions. Improvement can be made by fitting baffle boards on edge on both sides of the bottom in the cabin area. They can be sited roughly where the bilge stringer is fitted and can in fact be attached to this if

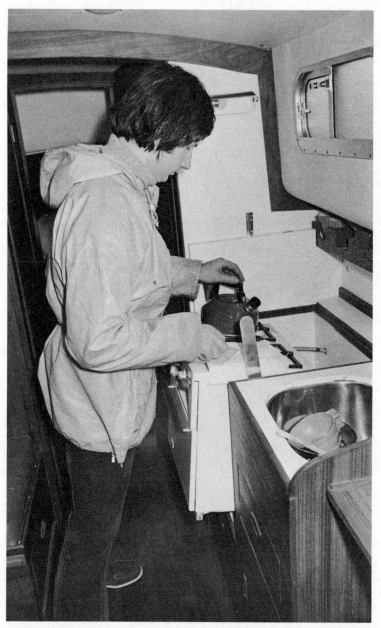

Fig. 11.4   Gimballed cooker with oven in the Fairways Fisher. Alas, no fiddle!

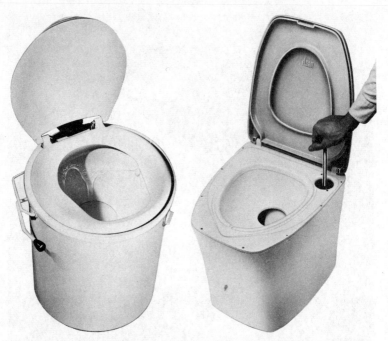

Fig. 11.5 (Left) The Jetflush Cadet by Perdisan which is claimed to be odour-tight and spillproof. The flush is electrically operated and it will work on a 12 volt system or a dry cell battery. (Right) The Elsan Superflush chemical toilet with bowl seal and hand flush.

convenient. They need to be only about 3 to 4in high and freeing slots must be cut in the bottom edge before fitting so that water which goes over can drain back towards the keel.

Owners of medium size and larger cruisers can update their galley and toilet arrangements, and get something for nothing by incorporating a small heat exchanger on one engine. These are available for the supply of domestic hot water, they use what would otherwise be wasted heat, and they are surprisingly efficient (Fig. 11.6.). A good installation will supply gallons of hot water hours after the engine has been stopped. Another modernization which may be appreciated is a pressurized water system, which may also permit the installation of a shower if space can be found in the toilet compartment (Fig. 11.7.).

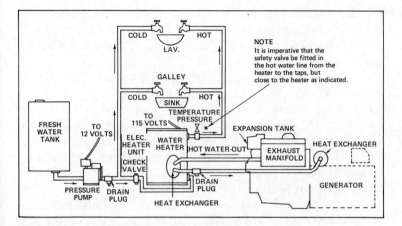

Fig. 11.6 The G. & M. Aquaheat hot water system working from a heat exchanger on a G. & M. Dieselite generator in conjunction with a water pressure pump.

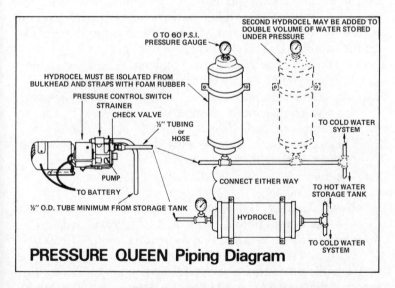

Fig. 11.7 The Crowell 'Pressure Queen' water pressure system, this will provide up to 5gpm and operates on 12, 24 or 32 volts DC.

The lighting in many vessels could be improved and current saved by the wider use of fluorescent fittings. These now have a good appearance and some are rustproofed with a plastic coat over the metal.

Continuing the theme of comfort below decks, there is now a wider choice of means of cabin heating, and the small charcoal or anthracite stove although practical and simple is no longer the automatic choice for heating in small vessels. There are fuel-gas heaters both conventional and catalytic, and also oil fueled heaters used in conjunction with a warm air distribution system. A warm, dry atmosphere will tend to keep both boat and crew in better condition.

Returning to the needs of the boat as distinct from those of the crew, one hardly needs to be reminded of the old enemy—corrosion. You will no doubt, be taking the obvious precautions to delay its onset already, and in a later chapter dealing with fitting out several aspects of the problem are touched upon, but the area to which we would draw attention is that where substantial improvement can be made by cathodic protection, 'properly applied'. It is one thing to attach a zinc waster plate hopefully somewhere near the propeller, and another thing entirely to obtain one of the correct bulk and alloy, and wire it back into the sterngear so that it can do its work properly.

The types of corrosion most common to small craft are:

1. Galvanic action due to the use of dissimilar metals.
2. Impingement attack due to water velocity, sometimes aggravated by contained impurities.
3. Cavitation erosion. (Closely allied to the previous item).
4. Crevice corrosion. Pitting started by oxygen starvation. (Most common in stainless steels).
5. Weld decay.
6. Fatigue cracking.
7. Dezincification. (Of brass and some other copper alloys).
8. Corrosion from impressed current. (Electrical leakage.)
9. Corrosion due to sulphate reducing bacteria. (Affects steel boats and steel fittings when laid up in mud berths.)

Cathodic protection is an established method of controlling many of the above forms of corrosive attack, besides straight-forward galvanic effects due to unlike metals or stress differential. In nearly all cases mentioned there arises a potential difference which helps in the breakdown of the material, sometimes by initiating side effects.

The trouble is that what one may think of as a simple hull built of apparently inert materials, actually becomes dynamic in association with sea water, and cells of varying small voltages are trying to equalize their potentials by breaking down the less noble material which happens to form the anode. The situation has some interesting if doleful aspects, for instance, and touching again on our first example. A boat of wood, conventionally fastened and treated with an anti-fouling composition of high copper content is entirely dependent on the priming under the anti-fouling to prevent every nail and rivet from becoming part of a large battery, the effect of which can either deteriorate the fastenings in the case of some metals and/or the wood. Any galvanized or plain iron fastenings would be open to attack and brass would be liable to dezincification and failure.

A possibility which is not generally considered is that these conditions can also arise inside the hull, if paint is lacking and the bilges hold any amount of sea water or brackish water. Similarly, a high copper anti-fouling will be prone to attack any below-water fitting whose metallic make up makes it vulnerable unless it is properly primed and insulated. As an example of this, galvanized bilge keels can be very badly pitted if copper anti-fouling is applied direct or the priming coat is insufficient. The degree of attack can be affected by temperature and also depth, and whether immersion is continuous or intermittent, but the possibilities for trouble are all there unless suitable protection is given.

The foregoing are examples arising from galvanic action involving two dissimilar metals and an electrolyte (sea water) but there are other ways of generating or adding to the effect. When the propeller is rotating, the sterngear of a vessel can be subject to higher potential differences than would come about purely in the proximity of dissimilar metals. Current leakage from electrical equipment in the boat can also cause rapid corrosion, something to which perhaps more thought should be given, and earthing plates for radios can simulate conditions capable of the destruction of steel plate. Blocking condensers should be used to prevent the passage of direct current. Ill considered bonding of electrical equipment can aggravate galvanic corrosion to an undesirable degree.

Apart from the wastage of components and materials which is caused by electrolytic corrosion, it contributes significantly to falling off in efficiency in the case of propellers, even slight roughening by erosion can require a ten per cent or more increase in the power necessary to develop the same thrust. In addition to roughening as a general case, fast running propellers are often victims of cavitation erosion, which is a breakdown of the surface metal, initiated, it is thought, by excessive water velocity (impingement) with or without water-borne impurities, and electrolytic action.

There are some complaints currently about corrosion of stainless steel, including pitting. Some of this may be due to a lower specification than is suitable, but very severe pitting can be shown on stainless steel propeller shafts made from what was assumed to be the correct material, where the shaft has suffered oxygen starvation in a water lubricated bearing. This pitting or crevice corrosion can, as witnessed, result in cavities $\frac{1}{4}$in in depth on a $\frac{7}{8}$in diameter shaft. It is noted that the appearance of these cavities is frequently very similar to those on the faces of propellers rendered unserviceable by cavitation erosion.

In some cases of propeller face erosion the erosive agency explores in greater width, partly beneath the surface metal, after initial entry, apparently making a preferential attack on the softer metal below the skin. Surface oxidation provides protection for many metals by being harder and more resistant to attack from the elements than the base material. Presumably destruction of the oxide film can lead to an increasingly rapid erosion of the raw metal beneath by one or other of the agencies which are at work.

Things are frequently not what they seem to be when galvanic action has been accelerating the normal corrosive process on fastenings, through bolts, etc., in wet timber. A $\frac{3}{8}$in diameter steel coachbolt, with a perfectly respectable looking head and an apparently sound nut and washer at the other end, might prove to have nothing in between except a thin strand of corroded metal. Necking of bolts from diameters as above down to $\frac{1}{16}$in or less is not unusual, and if the head has remained in fairly good condition, the knowledge of where to expect this kind of deterioration becomes highly important.

The purpose of cathodic protection is to neutralize electrolytically initiated or assisted corrosive effects. This can be done by either accepting the potential differences which cause the trouble and diverting the attack to a sacraficial anode, which can be replaced when necessary, or by providing an electric current via inert, non-consumable anodes to depress the potential difference by a calculated amount. Sacrificial anodes are the chosen method on small craft and they can be made of zinc, magnesium or aluminium alloy according to use. Just as important as their use, however, is their number, size and location. Consequently, unless the builder has already made a satisfactory job of incorporating the anodes it is best to ask the suppliers to give a recommendation based on the details of the vessel.

The first essential for the protection of metal fittings on wood or glassfibre craft is for the anode (or anodes) to be in electrical contact with the metal which is corroding. For example, in the case of a propeller, the anode, situated on the outside of the hull, must be bonded through to the sterntube and gearbox. This establishes a simple galvanic cell with the current leaving the anode (which corrodes), passing through the sea water electrolyte and returning via the propeller and shaft, which are protected. Zinc anodes properly applied will give protection until about 80 per cent of the sacrificial metal has been consumed. In comparison with the components they are protecting, the anodes needed for a small vessel are not expensive.

For vessels with cast iron propellers, magnesium anodes which have a much higher potential can be supplied for fitment to the propeller hub. Special aluminium alloy anodes (Galvalum) can be substituted for zinc but the Guardion range of zinc alloy anodes and their associated fittings as developed by M. G. Duff and Partners are recommended by them for most general applications in yachts and small craft.

chapter 12

Sailing Cruisers and Motor Sailers

A sailing cruiser or a motor sailer sometimes becomes the final choice of the power boat man, especially if his inclinations are more towards the essential and elemental aspects of seafaring, as distinct from speed and penthouse luxury, although many of the larger sailing cruisers yield nothing to power when it comes to comfortable living.

Certainly there is more to do about a sailing boat when voyaging, and again it depends whether one is inclined to welcome such tasks and distractions, or whether the sole desire is to arrive as quickly as possible and with the least amount of effort. Clearly, if one undertakes to learn the tasks and acquire the extra skill, then it is also vastly more rewarding.

The first division of craft types is monohull and multihull. The former is self explanatory, the latter includes catamarans and trimarans, and also any other vessel which has more than one hull in the water. The single hull vessel is still the most popular and in ultimate conditions it is also the safest, although multihulled vessels have been cruised and raced across the world.

The multihull has many attractions for family cruising, notably, large deck areas, shallow draft and high speed. The accommodation down below is also generally impressively big for the overall length. In regard to hull configuration there are ardent supporters in both camps, i.e., cat-men and tri-men will each declare that their's is the logical choice. It is an argument we would not care to enter, except to say that unless the question of choice is sharpened by the need to consider respective merits in ocean conditions, one could acquire either, with equal satisfaction, dependent upon ones notions as to accommodation layout.

Rigs on multihulls are generally kept to simple sloop or cutter, frequently in conjunction with a fully battened mainsail and with the mast stepped well back in the boat. Auxiliary power depends mainly upon outboard engines mounted on the after end of the bridge deck, in the case of the catamaran, and in a trunk in the centre hull for a trimaran. The arrangement leaves something to be desired, particularly in the case of the catamaran. It will be seen that for those who are prepared to have a propeller permanently in the water the trimaran lends itself to an inboard engine installation.

There are catamarans with two inboard engines, one in each hull, but excepting that one is primarily intending a power vessel or a motor sailer multihull, it is rather an extravagant approach to the question of auxiliary power. However, recent developments indicate that there can be a fairly elegant solution with the use of one of the later hydraulic drives which have many virtues. These include acceptable efficiency and unit construction of the drive, sterntube assembly, and propeller which makes them very easy to install, and further permits two drives to be taken from one engine, which may be placed anywhere in the boat.

Catamarans may be fitted either with shallow, fixed keels or with centreboards but for a cruising boat the fixed keel appears to be more attractive.

In single hull vessels the keel configuration is probably the first choice an owner makes before that of size, rig, etc. Some of the choices are as seen in Fig. 12.1–3; each has its merits. For a cruising boat a long keel will give better directional stability and require less work at the helm, whereas a cruiser-racer will no doubt benefit from the lower wetted area of the fin keel. The higher the aspect ratio of the keel, the more necessary it is to achieve a balanced hull and rig, otherwise steering becomes a chore and the helm cannot be left for a moment without the boat going off course. One sees a large number of vessels these days fitted with wind vane self-steering gear. So many in fact, and some on very unlikely hulls, that one gets the impression that it may in some cases be a 'keeping

197

up' exercise rather than a useful addition to the vessel. One also hears of the undue wear which has taken place in the bearings, etc., on gear which has been used on long crossings. There is no doubt however that these gears can work well and save a lot of time at the helm. It does seem that many would work much better if some effort were made to balance the boat before fitting the self-steering so that there might be somewhat less strain upon it.

For many years the standard arrangement for the shoal draft boat was to have a shallow ballast keel and a centreboard, and there is no doubt that for estuary conditions it is still near-ideal, but in recent years bilge keels or twin keels have taken over the territory. The question of efficiency vis-à-vis fin keel or twin keels is always fogged by the fact that twin keels are never expected to have anything like the depth of a fin keel. If they are given half a chance in this direction the results might be rather better than current opinion would allow.

Experience tends to show that there is a significant difference in performance between a true twin keel arrangement and vessels with a shallow, centre ballast keel and two plate bilge keels. The latter is often accompanied by a skeg of some length preceding the rudder and the total wetted area of all the protuberances down below adds up to something which is better avoided (Fig. 12.1.).

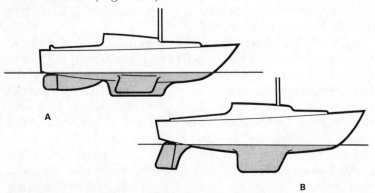

Fig. 12.1 A. Shallow centre ballast keel, plate bilge keels and a long skeg results in a considerable wetted area. B. Solidly ballasted twin keels of thin section going deeper, and a narrow skeg gives a better grip on the water but the wetted area is reduced.

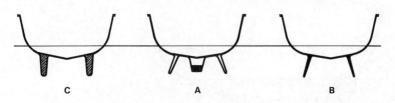

Fig. 12.2 Section showing frontal aspect of different twin keel and bilge keel configurations. A and B correspond with Fig. 12.1.

There are of course good and bad examples of the twin keel arrangement. Some vessels are fitted with great big boots of considerable width and frontal area, all of which needs to be pushed through the water. Others fail to take advantage of the fact that by angling the keels to the vertical efficiency is maintained when the boat heels. It would seem that a twin keel boat with slim, ballasted keels of reasonable depth, set at an angle to the vertical of about 10° to 15°, would be taking advantage of most possibilities for the type (C in Fig. 12.2.).

In regard to skegs, huge ones, fitted to make up for deficiencies in hull and rig, seem to have little to recommend them but small high aspect ratio skegs for hanging rudders thereto can do much to improve helm balance. Spade rudders do not seem to be necessary to cruiser performance and those of the balanced type may cause some sailing vessels to have undesirable steering characteristics. Rudder characteristics will depend a lot upon what precedes that component. A transom hung rudder on a long keel boat, e.g., Folkboat, may be expected to have some directional stability. A transom hung rudder, sans skeg, on a small, fin keel cruiser may not have any inherent directional stability, although it will provide quick and accurate steering when attended. However, this kind of dinghy helm which is undoubtedly of value in racing round marks, does not seem to have any particular merit for a cruiser excepting that for centreboard boats the rudder blade can be made retractable (Fig. 12.3.).

The Bermudian sloop rig is perhaps the most efficient sail plan for sailing cruisers but because of the large single sail areas involved, this, from necessity, is amended on larger vessels and hence there are cutters, yawls, ketches and schooners. Multiple sail arrangements are drawn so that a

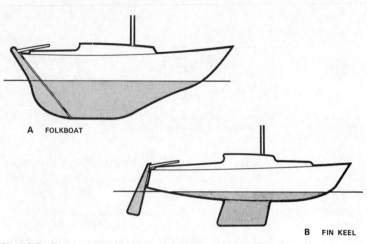

A FOLKBOAT

B FIN KEEL

Fig. 12.3 Transom hung rudders with different characteristics.

reduction in area may be made without affecting the balance of the vessel although the effect may be to alter substantially the sail plan. For example a ketch might reduce its headsails and reef the main and mizzen, or it might take down the main and sail on only headsails and mizzen, there are obviously several permutations when the sail area is divided up.

It is necessary to the safety of sailing boats that they carry some weather helm, so that the vessel has an inherent tendency to come up towards the wind rather than fall away from it, but excessive weather helm can ruin performance and make a hard and tiring boat to steer. Nobody appears to have worked out exactly why, but it is a fact that the centre of lateral resistance on a hull, about which the boat pivots, moves forward as speed increases, and in consequence weather helm is accentuated. Another contributary characteristic on small, beamy, and particularly hard chine hulls is that as the vessel heels the large curvature on the topsides tends to steer the boat up into the wind. Thus the boat may not react to small movements on the helm and excessive rudder angle is required to hold the boat off the wind. In consequence the rudder acts as a brake upon progress and the boat may make as much leeway as headway.

Because of the foregoing, two thoughts may be offered to

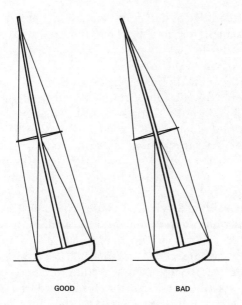

GOOD   BAD

Fig. 12.4 Setting up the standing rigging.

those with short, beamy boats when the wind stiffens. First, they will go faster if allowed to sail with the minimum heel. Second, reef the main before reducing the headsails. If you have a really efficient genoa it will pull you up to windward on its own anyway, but the circumstances we have in mind will keep the genoa in its sailbag.

Most modern sailing vessels have metal masts. These are of light alloy, although in the dinghy field it is possible that a thin-wall steel mast may be fitted. Mast sections can vary from round to pear shape, almost square, and plank type (as fitted to catamarans). Rectangular sections with rounded corners have been made in GRP for cruisers in Scandinavia but at present they have no vogue here. Generally speaking, the situation is that a GRP mast gives ample strength but it is difficult to get the required rigidity within reasonable limits of size and weight.

The staying of a metal mast will be recommended by the makers and it is unwise to depart too far from this. A point to watch is that whilst the mast will accommodate a fair amount of bending athwartships and aft (a characteristic which can

201

be taken advantage of in rigging for racing), it will stand very little when bent forward towards the bows. It is desirable therefore either to have a pair of lower forward shrouds or a centre stay down to the foredeck.

A general indication for the setting up of rigging on a small cruiser is that the cap shrouds should be set up absolutely taut, also the forestay and backstay (or stays). The lower forward shrouds should have sufficient tension to prevent the centre of the mast from going aft, and the lower after shrouds need be given very little tension, so that under pressure the mast will bow at its mid height athwartships and not at the top (Fig. 12.4.).

Efficient sailing to windward demands both a taut forestay and adequate tension on the luff of the sail so that there are no pockets between the hanks. In regard to headsails, this will apply whatever the weather but the tension on the luff of a mainsail may be adjusted according to wind strength, the lighter the weather the less the tension so that the sail is enabled to take a full shape. Similarly the boom outhaul may also be slackened to promote fullness in the sail, but hard weather demands flat sails with tension on luff and foot. (For sail measurements see Fig. 12.5.).

In regard to halyards these can be of wire or terylene and on many small cruisers the latter is preferred, if so, it is important to get pre-stretched cordage otherwise continued adjustment will be needed during sailing. Sheets, particularly headsail sheets, should similarly be of minimum stretch material. However, some of the cordage and cables on a boat benefit from having some stretch capability, e.g., warps and soft anchor cables.

The tension on the headsail sheets of even small cruisers is considerable and if they are to be brought in properly taut, as for instance being hard on the wind with some wind strength to contend with, then however small the boat, it is not sufficient to have just fairleads and cleats; winches are a necessity.

Self-steering devices dependent upon a large wind vane for sensing, and mechanical linkage to the tiller, sometimes via a paddle operated servo as in the Hasler gear, have been available for some time and more compact systems are now

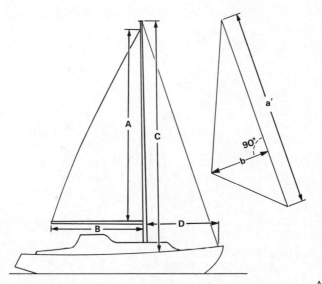

Fig. 12.5 Measuring sail area: A and B, also a and b. Sail area is $\frac{A \times B}{2}$
Measuring fore triangle: dimensions C and D.

available with either an electronic wind vane and actuator or a terrestial compass as the sensing device. We have already mentioned some considerations in this connection.

For those who are new to sailing, the handling of cruisers and a general understanding of the requirement, will be greatly facilitated by some time spent in sailing dinghies. Not only can the basic points of sailing be more quickly understood and practised by this means but also, since a dinghy is far more sensitive than a larger vessel, the benefits or otherwise of adjustment to sail setting and trim are more easily recognized (Fig. 12.6.). For the cruiser owner however, there is the additional necessity to become competent in handling his boat under conditions which are additional to proficiency in dinghy manoeuvres. Nearly all of the boobs which one makes in a cruiser, and who has not made a few, are made when close to the shore, picking up and dropping moorings, coming alongside, warping out of a berth, etc. These are the times when the wind appears to stiffen or change its direction, orders become ambiguous, lines tangle and spectators foregather.

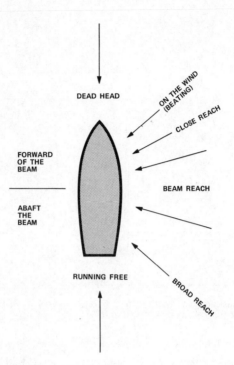

Fig. 12.6 The wind and points of sailing.

You will no doubt study diagrams showing what to do when the wind is here and the tide is there. Indeed we have incorporated a few in the next chapter, but beyond this the thing is to know the characteristics of one's boat in different manoeuvres. Perhaps the least painful way of doing this is to take it well out in the bay and either put the dinghy at anchor, or drop some floatable object over the side which you can use as a target, approaching from all directions and finding out what happens under various angles to wind and tide. Try it under different sail arrangements, under main, under jib and with both up, and try it with your auxiliary running. There is no need to be a purist in these things, better a touch of motor in a crowded anchorage than general acrimony. In extremes remember that your anchor is useful for emergency as well as planned mooring, so have it ready for use if you think you may need it.

Fig. 12.7 The Alacrity 22 has a shallow ballast keel and a drop plate so that she may increase her draft from 1ft 8in to 5ft 0in.

Fig. 12.8 At 30ft LOA the Fairways Fisher is still one of the smaller motor sailers but as one would expect from a boat of this size she has good accommodation.

Fig. 12.9 Suomi is a Nauticat 33 motor sailer with a big wheelhouse and good all-weather family accommodation.

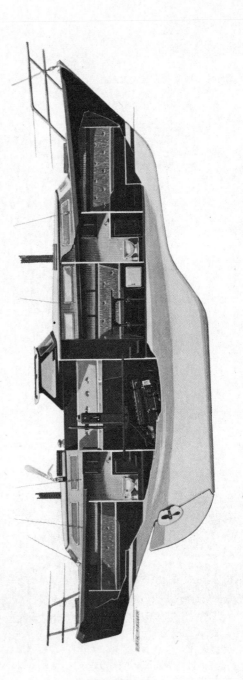

Fig. 12.10 The MS 40 by John Teale is 41ft LOA and has a 106bhp diesel engine but also sufficient depth of keel to give her a sailing performance.

Fig. 12.11 A good-looking 48ft ketch rigged motor sailer by Camper and Nicholson.

209

chapter 13

Handling Power Boats

Supposing that your boat is lying out at moorings, and that preparations are complete for getting under way. Do not simply drop the mooring buoy overboard and engage gear. With luck you may get away with it, but it is an even chance that the buoy rope will foul the propeller, which, having wound a few feet of the rope tightly round its boss, will cease to revolve, and you will find yourself up against a real job of work at the start.

Wait, after slipping the buoy, until wind or tide has drifted you clear, so that you can go ahead without running over it. Possibly they will not do this, and your boat may even tend to drive up over the buoy. In this case, reverse the engine, but if the dinghy is made fast astern, see that the painter does not foul the propeller. It is advisable to keep the dinghy on a very short painter when getting under way, as not only is it then impossible to foul the propeller, but the rope cannot hang up across the bows of an anchored vessel when you have just managed to pass clear. The painter must, of course, be slacked away later.

THE TURNING EFFECT OF THE PROPELLER

Once in open water you will find, unless you are fortunate enough to own a twin screw vessel with engines rotating in opposite directions, that your craft tends to turn one way, and needs a certain amount of helm to keep her on a straight course. This, in a more or less marked degree, is found in all single screw vessels, and is due to the fact that the lower part of the propeller turns in more 'solid' water than the upper part.

For instance, with a right-hand propeller, which revolves in the direction of the hands of a clock, when observed from aft, the tendency is for the bow to turn to port when going ahead and the stern to port when going astern.

Do not rely too much on your reverse until you thoroughly know your craft. Many boats will not steer well when going astern, and some refuse to answer the helm at all until a good speed has been worked up, so at the start, it is better to look on the reverse as little more than a brake.

When going astern in an obstinate vessel and you wish to turn against the throw of the propeller, declutch as soon as she has gathered way. She will then respond to the helm.

Always slow down in good time when returning to moorings. To dash up at full speed and stop suddenly with a boil of water under the quarter may be spectacular, but such behaviour is not for the novice. Even if you find that your boat has too little way to reach the buoy, you can easily engage gear again for a few moments to gain the extra distance.

PICKING UP THE BUOY

If possible, always come to moorings against the tide, as you then have more control and, in a fresh breeze, aim a little to windward of the buoy, for, as the vessel loses way, the wind tends to blow her head off, and will then blow it in the right direction.

If you are coming in with the tide and have to turn round in order to pick up the buoy head to tide, make a wide circle and straighten up a little beyond the buoy so that you approach it on a straight course. If you try a sharp turn at the exact spot you may find yourself circling round the buoy with it hopelessly out of reach on the inner side of the circle.

APPROACHING AND LEAVING A QUAY

In going alongside a quay the same procedure holds good. Run in head to tide and slow down in good time. Many novices make the mistake of attempting actually to run in alongside. This may pan out all right with an experienced skipper in, say, a ferry launch, the sides of which are padded with old motor tyres, but the novice, if he wishes to preserve the beauty of his paint, should try to come to a standstill a few

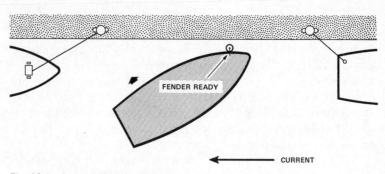

Fig. 13.1 Approaching the quay.

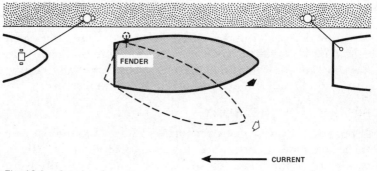

Fig. 13.1a Leaving the quay.

feet clear of the quay wall and then, giving his boat helm, let the tide sheer her gently alongside.

In a manoeuvre of this sort, the fact that the propeller turns the boat one way may be utilized. Suppose your yacht has reached the position shown in Fig. 13.1. and is stopped. 'A kick ahead', the few revolutions will not be sufficient to give her way, with a left-handed propeller will swing her stern in alongside the wall, while a kick astern with a right-handed propeller will have just the same effect on the boat. Ensure you have a fender in position at the bow.

In making fast your vessel, do not forget to allow for the tide, otherwise, if you go ashore at high water, you may return to find that the warps have parted, that whatever you made them fast to has pulled out of the deck, and that everything having held, your vessel is suspended in mid-air.

If moored alongside and you find you will have a strong tide to contend with when you wish to leave, it is well to take the chance of the previous slack water to swing your craft so that she heads in the desired direction. It is easier to get away against the stream.

Cast off the bow rope and let her bow swing out. The tide will probably do this for you, but, if not, a push with a boat-hook will help. When heading clear, slip in the clutch, and if you know that the throw of the propeller will tend to swing your quarter against the wall, protect it with a fender (Fig. 13.1a.).

If it is necessary to leave stern first, swing the stern off and go astern. In boats that handle badly when in reverse, however, this is a manoeuvre that may lead to trouble, and is better avoided.

MANOEUVRING IN A NARROW SPACE

Suppose the harbour is narrow. Your vessel having a left-handed propeller, turns more readily to starboard than to port. She is heading up harbour against the ebb and you wish to proceed to sea. How will you get away?

There are two courses open to you. If the crew are aboard the next vessel ahead, you may hand them a warp and, having gone ahead, heading out into the stream as just described, make the warp fast on your quarter and hold on, letting the tide swing you round until you are heading in the right direction down stream and it is safe to let go. Do not, in the excitement of the moment, let go your end. It is your warp, so hail the other fellow to cast off and see you do not let it foul your propeller when hauling it in.

If getting away unaided, do not try to turn sharply to port. Your boat responds sluggishly to the helm in that direction, and you will probably find yourself broadside across the stream. Instead, you must stand boldly across to the other side and make your turn to starboard. If the harbour is very narrow, it may be necessary to go into reverse, but when you put her ahead again you will find she swings very readily to starboard.

With a twin screw craft, manoeuvring is simplified by putting one engine ahead and the other astern, balancing their effect by the throttles, the vessel can be pivoted around almost in its own length.

With outboard craft, and those having inboard/outboard installations, steering is usually effected by changing the direction of thrust of the propeller(s). This gives much quicker response to the helm than with fixed-propeller craft and facilitates manoeuvring. Those used to handling boats without this 'power steering' must be careful at first when they change over, especially with high-power installations, and should go easy until they get the feel of it.

SPRINGS

The use of springs is of the greatest assistance in coming away from a berth alongside and it is often of equal value in getting the stern in under awkward circumstances. Their function may be summarized as (a) preventing a ship ranging (moving back and forth) in her berth; (b) providing a means of bringing the bows in to the quay, and thus swinging the stern clear, or vice versa; and (c) causing the vessel to pivot about a given point.

There is more than one opinion as to the correct naming of the two principal springs. To avoid confusion, we will call the spring leading aft from the bows to quay the fore spring and that leading forward from the quarter the after spring.

Usually, it is easier to bring a vessel's stern away from a berth by going ahead against a fore spring than to bring her bows out by going astern against an after spring. This is due to two causes. First, the rudder is effective when the engine is moving ahead and shooting a jet of water on to the rudder blade, which, put over towards the quay, materially assists in swinging the stern out. Secondly, in nearly all ships the lateral distance between the forward fairlead and the quay is greater than the distance between quarter fairlead and quay. So if we steam ahead against a fore spring, the first effect is to bring the bows in to the quay and swing the stern out, whereas bringing the stern in with an after spring would not swing the bows out so far, owing to the shorter distance between stern and quay (Fig. 13.2–A/B.).

Fig. 13.2–C/D. shows how the current can be used to swing the stern out.

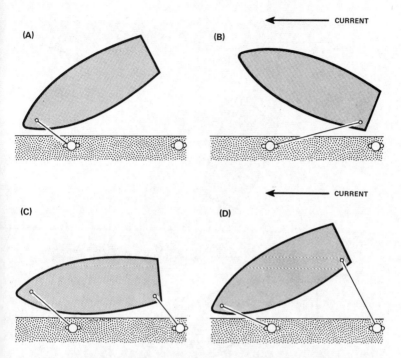

Fig. 13.2 A and B. Springing in the bow or the stern. C. and D. Using the current to get the stern out.

In a strong off-shore wind, you can berth your ship in the following way. Come in at nearly 90 degrees. It is then easy to get the bows in. A stern line may be passed outside all obstructions from quarter to forecastle, so that it can be sent ashore together with a head line. With both of these lines fast to the quay where the bows will lie the head line will be a breast rope and the other an after spring. Slack out the former a little with the engine astern, and the stern will approach the quay until an after breast rope can be passed ashore. Then haul in forward (Fig. 13.3.).

ANCHORING

To anchor with a single anchor, come to a stop in the desired berth heading against the current, if any, and go gently astern, letting go the anchor as the boat gathers way. Never let go when stationary, as if the chain falls on top of the anchor it

H

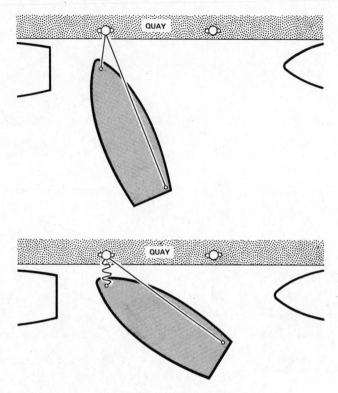

Fig. 13.3 Berthing between other vessels in an offshore wind.

may foul it and the vessel will very probably drag.

Except in a tideless anchorage, or possibly for a short time on a tide, it is unsafe to leave a vessel riding to a single anchor. Sooner or later she will sweep round it and foul it. The only safe way is to moor with two anchors.

In small yachts it is common practice to let go the bower anchor from the vessel and to run the kedge anchor away in the dinghy, but in a vessel of any size the following is a better plan.

Let us suppose that you are going to bring up in an anchorage where the depth will be three fathoms at high water, which means that you must have not less than nine fathoms of chain, at least three times the depth of water, on each anchor. Let go the first anchor under foot while the

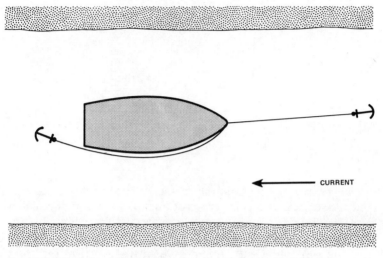

CURRENT

Fig. 13.4 Anchoring in a tideway.

vessel is still running slowly ahead and slack away on the chain, checking it slightly at intervals to make sure it is stretched out, until 18 fathoms are in the water. Check the vessel, give the engine a kick astern and let go the second anchor.

Now haul in on the first anchor, slacking away the chain on the second, until you are midway between the two. You are now properly moored.

In anchoring in a tideway you must remember to let go your anchors, as Fig. 13.4. i.e. up and down the stream so that you are always riding fairly astream on one anchor or the other.

It is a good plan to lash the two chains together and lower away until the lashing is below the forefoot, since this will keep the chains clear of the bow to a great extent.

ANCHOR WEIGHTS

The weights of anchors to be carried should really be based on displacement, but the table overleaf, based on Thames Tonnage (see Appendix 16), will serve as a rough guide for yachts used for serious cruising.

Thames tonnage	Bower Anchor lb	Diam. of Chain in	Length of chain fathoms	Weight of chain in lb
3–4	30	$\frac{1}{4}$	25	112
5	40	$\frac{5}{16}$	30	225
7–8	50	$\frac{5}{16}$	35	262
10	60	$\frac{3}{8}$	35	350
15	75	$\frac{3}{8}$	45	450
20	90	$\frac{7}{16}$	50	675
25	100	$\frac{7}{16}$	55	742
30	120	$\frac{1}{2}$	60	1050

The kedge is usually about two-thirds the weight of the bower anchor.

These recommendations are for fisherman-type anchors. There are several special types of anchor available for which superior holding powers are claimed and for which lighter weights are recommended.

Danforth and CQR anchors illustrated in Fig. 13.5. are both popular with yachtsmen for their compactness and holding power.

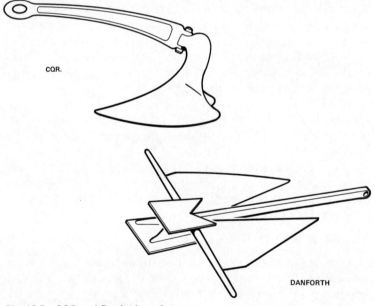

CQR.

DANFORTH

Fig. 13.5 CQR and Danforth anchors.

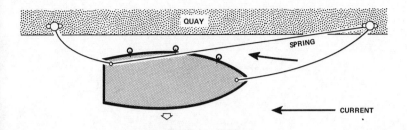

Fig. 13.6 Temporary berthing in a tideway; use of a spring to keep boat away from quay.

If you are tying up alongside a quay for a short spell it is sufficient to use bow and stern warps. Remember to keep them long enough to cater for any rise or fall in water level if you are in tidal conditions, but if the boat is to be left unattended and for long periods, you should put on a spring fore and aft as well as bow and stern warps, and breast ropes. These will allow the boat a considerable latitude in rise and fall but restrict her movement fore and aft. Wherever possible the warps should be taken as far ahead and astern of the vessel as conditions, bollards, other boats, etc., will allow, since this also restricts the boat fore and aft without limiting her ability to rise and fall with the tide.

Where you may be tied up alongside temporarily, and there is a strong current, the use of a spring can still be worthwhile since it can be used so as to keep the boat clear of the quay wall (Fig. 13.6.). You should of course be properly equipped with fenders disposed between your topsides and the quay but if, as in many cases, the quay has projecting timbers or buttresses you will also need a spar or a plank of wood, as shown in Fig. 13.7. otherwise your fenders will be useless. A long, sausage fender is good for these occasions if slung horizontally. In fact this type of fender and the flat, cushion shape are more generally useful than the cylindrical fenders with which most vessels seem to be equipped, and which have the habit of never staying where you put them. Hence the popularity of old car tyres which, apart from several dis-advantages in handling, are nevertheless much better suited to the job than many of the purpose designed offerings.

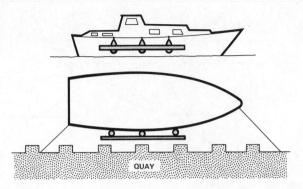

Fig. 13.7   Use of spar or plank over fenders where quay has projections.

Nowadays, laying a mooring is liable to prove much easier than finding a place to lay it, but for those who are fortunate, the job is fairly simple although there are a few basic rules which are important. Supposing that you have not got a screw picket or a big old anchor which you can dig in, the popular method for a single boat is to cast a mooring block or sinker in concrete, complete with a steel eye, the metal of which should be of larger gauge than the chain which is to go upon it. A mould for the block is easily made from a few planks so that when the concrete is poured it makes a rectangular slab.

The actual dimensions will depend a lot upon local experience, but as an example, a slab some 2ft 6in square and 8in in thickness dug into the Thames estuary mud held a 5 ton TM sloop satisfactorily in summer gales and winter storms (Fig. 13.8.). There are several similar moorings in the same area, all very exposed, and although boats have gone adrift occasionally it has never been anything to do with the mooring block. Common causes of trouble are, failure to observe wear which has taken place on the chain, and jumping of the mooring chain from the bow roller. The latter is not so fraught with disaster if the samson post is well forward in the boat but, if it is set back on the foredeck, so that when the chain is free from the eye the bows of the vessel can swing off, then trouble will follow. The weight of the seas on the exposed bow will put a tremendous strain on the mooring and on the boat and one or the other will eventually give way.

The length of the chain cable should be something over

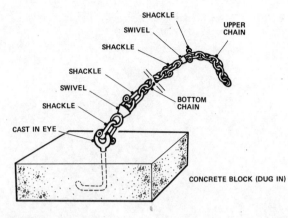

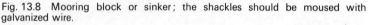

Fig. 13.8 Mooring block or sinker; the shackles should be moused with galvanized wire.

three times the maximum depth of water for a permanent mooring of this type. It should be connected to the cast-in mooring eye via a large swivel and the top quarter of the chain length, which can be of lighter gauge should be connected to the bottom length with a swivel also. In regard to size of chain, a reasonable guide for the piece at the top is that it should be one size up on that recommended, for the bower anchor of your boat and the bottom chain can be a size or two up on this. In fact, the heavier the better from two points of view. First, a heavier chain will reduce the amount of 'snatch' and act as a shock absorber in heavy weather. Second, dependent upon the ground, the bottom chain will get a lot of abrasion through being dragged around at every tide, hence the thicker it is the better. Only the top quarter length of the chain which is exposed to wind and water needs to be galvanized.

The final requirement is a buoy of visible proportions secured to the upper chain with a few fathoms of grass rope or light-bulk synthetic line. The loop of chain which goes over the samson post should be made with a galvanized or stainless steel shackle or appropriate gauge. Never under any circumstances use a yellow metal shackle on any part of a mooring.

In protected areas somewhat less stringent arrangements can apply. Sometimes a nylon rope yoke and two bow fairleads is used instead of the upper length of chain cable.

221

Fig. 13.9 The Fairey Spearfish, a light, fast weekend boat capable of 29 knots with two Perkins 6·354 diesels.

Fig. 13.10 Maclan 22, a four berth GRP boat with an unusual recessed chine hull form.

Fig. 13.11 The Souter 50, a cold moulded express cruiser with flying bridge and a speed of 25 knots.

Fig. 13.12 A handsome Dagless 88ft motor yacht with a cruising speed of about 11 knots. Accommodation is on three decks.

223

chapter 14

Navigation Equipment

The equipment you acquire for navigation is more likely to depend upon your pocket than your needs. That is not to say that an ocean racer equipped with all the latest electronic navigational aids would not have more than a moral superiority over the competition, but that unless you are ambitious in your voyages your equipment need not be extensive. You will probably not have essential use for more than a reliable compass, a log, your watch, plus charts, tide tables and Admiralty pilot for the area. You will of course also need a few small tools such as parallel rules, dividers and pencils, and no doubt you will already have a portable radio upon which you can get the weather forecasts.

If one wished to improve on the above list then we could suggest, in order of merit, a depth sounder, a hand bearing compass and a direction finding radio set (DF). The priority of the hand bearing compass will depend upon whether your steering compass is 'wooded', i.e., it is placed where you cannot get a sight across it.

The reliability of small radios has largely removed the necessity for an accurate clock and a barometer when in UK waters. Good marine versions of these are expensive but they are much more robust than the ordinary domestic kind. A clock with a sweep second hand and an alarm is most useful. It will help you to identify lights and also give a reminder that the weather forecast is due. It is in any case advisable not to venture far with only one timepiece, e.g., your watch. Also radios have been know to have flat batteries—so a cruising boat should have both a ship's clock and a barometer.

After this, one enters the higher flights of electronic navigation and communication aids with auto-pilots, radar, radio telephone, wind speed and direction indicators, etc. An auto-pilot is a great help on long passages and in confused seas it will frequently helm the boat more satisfactorily than any member of the crew. Radar is a tremendous boon for coastal work in thick weather and the installations which are now available for small craft are thoroughly practical and give a very good presentation. Incidentally, because of the increasing dependence upon radar in merchant vessels a radar reflector is essential now for small craft in estuary and coastal waters. It will add to peace of mind when the traffic is heavy, and especially in poor visibility (Figs. 14.1 and 14.1a.).

Celestial navigation requires, not more, but different equipment, principally, the sextant, an accurate chronometer and the appropriate tables. We would recommend that navigation, both coastal and deep sea is more easily assimilated by instruction rather than by reading alone. Most areas now have winter evening classes for the subject, valuable both for

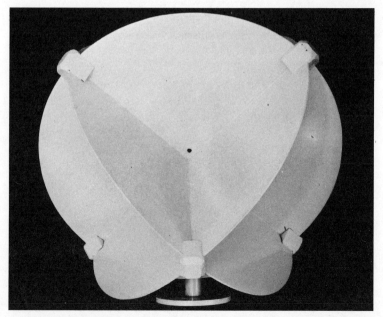

Fig. 14.1   SC4 Reflector by Radar Reflectors Ltd.

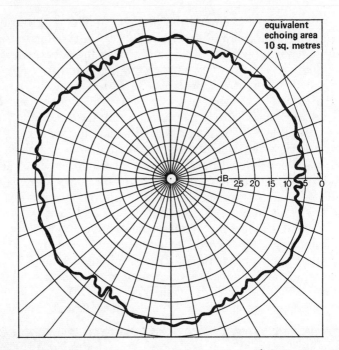

Fig. 14.1a Polar diagram showing effective coverage by the SC4 reflector.

initiation and brushing up.

It occurs to us that navigation and communication for the amateur boat owner are attractive fields where it is possible to acquire considerably more equipment than practice, and unless one wishes to have the equipment for decorative purposes, an array of radio, RT medium range, VHF, etc., is an expensive way of obtaining Radio 2. Captain Slocum made his way around the world with only a sextant and a battered alarm clock, and whilst he was a master, and better than his tools, which few of us can aspire to be, at least he was unlikely to be confused by his array of instruments. For those who wish to keep it simple there could be a lesson in this.

In considering the compass, there are three card notations available, Points, Quadrant and the Circular or full 360° marking. The points marking is traditional but, together with the quadrant, it has largely fallen out of use in favour of the circular notation which goes from 001° to 360° and

226

has less possibilities of error in use. Some cards are marked with both circular and points notation and these perhaps are the most useful, since whilst most working can depend upon the degree marking, any reference to a points bearing can be quickly related.

The compass may be arranged with a vertical lubber line against which the rim of the card can be read, or it may be of the grid type where a North-South line on the card is maintained between two parallel lines on the face glass, the latter being rotatable with a degree marking on the bezel on which the course may be set. A grid compass is only helpful if it is placed where the helmsman can look down into it, and a considerable error in reading can occur due to parallax if it is situated at a height which prevents a good downward view. This can be particularly difficult at night when only luminous marks may be visible and the relationship is hard to determine.

Compasses are also made with a vertical rim marking as on a drum, sometimes the card is open or it can be enclosed with an aperture making only a segment of the rim visible. The latter certainly removes most possibility of mis-reading, but one cannot sight across it, and it is useful only for steering.

Whatever the make or type of compass you obtain, it will need to be adjusted and the deviation on different headings recorded when it is fitted in the boat. The deviation card is your permanent reference for corrections so long as the situation of the compass and any nearby metalwork remains unchanged.

The hand bearing compass (Fig. 14.2.). is useful for taking bearings and it is simple to use but it will have its deviation, which may be changed considerably or multiplied by adjacent metalwork. An alternative, worthy of consideration when the steering compass is inconveniently situated for taking a bearing, is the pelorus, which is a simple instrument incapable of deviation. It consists of a compass card or face engraved with the circular, degree notation and a pointer centrally pivoted upon this so that it can be turned through the full 360°. The pointer has a sighting arrangement on top so that it can be directed with accuracy on any object of which one wishes to take a bearing. Provided the pelorus has been fixed so that it is on the fore and aft line of the boat no correction is

Fig. 14.2 'Seapoint', a typical hand-bearing compass fitted with a prismatic magnifier.

required before referring the degree reading indicated to the compass, to obtain a bearing. Thus one is dealing only with the known deviation of the fixed steering compass. Relative bearings (to the boat) can of course be read straight off the pelorus. A bearing obtained on radar similarly requires no correction for a relative angle.

Parallel rules may be of the opening or the roller type, the latter are more expensive but rather easier to use on a small chart table. Dividers can be had either straight or bowed, the latter can be used with one hand which is a useful asset.

There are several patent course calculators which may be used in conjunction with the chart and these have various means by which the variables may be accommodated so that the user avoids the usual small calculations required in course laying. The method is not important, but the answer is, so it really depends upon what one finds easiest in use.

The depth sounder is a most useful instrument which brings a traditional navigation aid within the use and understanding of the most amateur. It is probable that large numbers of boat owners tended to ignore soundings, by investigation with the lead line, and the inexpensive electronic sounder has given them a valuable aid against which other findings can frequently be checked. There are various forms of presentation, neon, needle gauge and digital, the latter reserved for large yachts with repeaters. If they are properly fitted they are all surprisingly sensitive and accurate. Most makers also do a recording model.

Speed logs may be mechanical, pressure difference or electronically operated or combinations of these. The tendency today is away from the mechanical trailing log to a more compact system which requires no handling. The operating end of these is a small through-the-hull fitting and the instrument head can be put almost anywhere in the boat. The situation of the operating head is generally important and most of these instruments need to be adjusted precisely to get the necessary accuracy.

A radio DF set can have many useful functions besides that of homing on the short range coastal radio beacons. It can give reception on the ordinary broadcast bands including VHF and Marine shortwave and also be tuned to the Consol long range radio beacons on LW. Modern RDF sets incorporate a 180° error sensing device which obviates the possibility of using the reciprocal bearing. As with some other small electronic navigational equipment, e.g., depth sounders, these sets can usually be operated from internal batteries or low voltage ship's current. This feature makes such equipment very suitable for small cruisers including sailing vessels which may have only a very limited main battery capacity.

Radio telephones for small craft may be either medium range, working on a frequency of 2182kHz or short range VHF. The Post Office radio stations working on the medium range can communicate in an area of up to about 200 miles radius, although the overlap between each station along the coast is considerable, and an RT set fitted into a boat would rarely be on extreme range for communication. However, there are changes taking place in regard to the nature of the transmission which until recently has been double sideband (DSB). The changeover, which will be mandatory for all vessels by 1981, when DSB transmissions will cease, is to the single sideband (SSB) system which has a narrower bandwidth and thus takes up less room in the ether, which is getting rather congested. It is therefore important that when a medium range RT installation is under consideration, the suitability of the equipment for SSB working is ascertained, since SSB equipment is mandatory now for new installations.

VHF radiotelephony operates over a much shorter range but it is adequate for inshore coastal communication. The equipment is somewhat more compact than the medium range sets working on the international distress frequency of 2182kHz and it will be unaffected by the arrangements for SSB working on medium range.

The latter part of this chapter is devoted to a description of some of the modern electronic navigational aids, but there is one inexpensive item of navigational equipment which we would suggest every UK cruiser man should possess as soon as he starts to equip his boat, and that is the annual edition of *Reed's Nautical Almanac* which is the best value for money of any of his navigational aids. This together with the appropriate charts and pilots will be the foundation of his navigating ability around these coasts and the near Continent. Fortunately the textual side of navigational assistance is the least expensive to acquire, albeit it provides the most secure groundwork for the operation.

ELECTRONIC NAVIGATION AIDS

While marine electronic navigation aids have been used in ships for many years, it is only comparatively recently that suitable equipment has been produced for yachts and smaller commercial vessels. While the economically priced echo sounder has already become as much a part of the yacht's equipment as the compass, trends indicate that owners will soon expect to have also the more sophisticated aids such as radar and auto-pilot. Racing helmsmen can also have wind speed and direction and boat performance information computerized and presented at the steering position.

Electronic navigation instruments group under certain categories, within each of which there are various manufacturers' instruments. The basic requirements for navigation are direction finding and a means of determining the depth of water, a useful addition being an ability to identify the type of bottom, i.e., rock, sand or mud. These aids, used in conjunction with up-dated charts and an accurate steering compass, provide for safe navigation of any craft. To these may now be added speed and distance logs, auto-pilots and radar.

A brief look at these groups of instruments will give an idea of their function and use.

ECHO SOUNDERS (DEPTH FINDERS IN USA)

The echo sounder is an electro mechanical device for creating electrical energy, converting this to sound energy capable of making a vibrating wave motion in water by transmission from beneath the vessel, measuring the time lapse between the signal and receipt of an echo, and presenting this information visually on a calibrated dial (Fig. 14.3.).

The electrical energy to sound energy conversion is done by the transducer which, fitted in the bottom of the boat, contains a piece of piezo electric material, i.e., a compound of ceramics, which deforms when an electric field is applied across it and in so doing creates sound energy. The pulse, repeated as a vibrationary wave motion in the water, is at ultra sonic speeds of some 10,000 to 200,000 cycles per second.

Thus far the operation is straightforward. But when it comes to presentation there are different schools of thought, some people opting for a neon light, others for a needle. Either must indicate against a scale calibrated in feet, fathoms or metres, but the neon system provides more information than the needle which suffers from random movement, is erratic and can record only a single echo. The neon, on the other hand, because it is carried on a continuously rotating arm driven by a high accuracy electric motor, can light up more than once anywhere on the circuit. It can therefore record intermediate echoes (such as a school of fish) in addition to that of the bottom and by showing a hard, thin, or broader

Fig. 14.3 A selection of echo sounders: A. The Hecta with dial indicator by Brookes & Gatehouse. B. The Seafarer with neon indicator and C. The Seascribe with chart recording, both by Electronic Laboratories. D. The Electradepth II neon indicating by EMI Marine.

'fuzzed' appearance, can give guidance as to the type of bottom. In contrast the needle cannot interpret bottom characteristics and if mid-depth echoes occur can only jump around the dial. An additional advantage of the neon indicating instrument is that chart recording can be added. This is a system in which echoes are recorded continuously on electro sensitive paper by an electronically actuated stylus which responds to echo interpretation. This has many advantages such as course recording, bottom identification and location of bottom feeding fish.

A point to remember for owners of deep keel sailing craft, is that a transducer transmits its signal downwards through an angle of approximately 45 degrees and so its effectiveness can be reduced by the banking effect of the keel, particularly when the yacht is heeled over on a tack. It is therefore advisable to fit two transducers on this type of craft, one each side of the keel, with an automatic changeover switch incorporated in the installation.

RADIO DIRECTION FINDERS

The radio direction finder (RDF) is an electronic device consisting of a receiving aerial, a radio receiver tunable to various frequencies and an amplifier. The simplest and easiest to use equipment for a yacht is the self contained RDF, incorporating aerial, receiver, amplifier and precision prismatic compass in one hand held unit. This enables bearings to be taken direct without relation to ship's head and the necessary subsequent re-calculations.

In operation the RDF is tuned to a selected radio beacon and then the loop aerial (in a fixed installation) or the whole unit is rotated until the signal is received at weakest strength, known as the 'null'. The bearing is then read off relative to magnetic north.

A radio direction finder is as good or bad as its signal-to-noise ratio measured at one microvolt. That is the ratio of received signal to inherent background noise at high levels of sensitivity. If the noise level is high bearings will be inaccurate and the instrument unreliable as a navigation aid. In this connection it is worth remembering that 1 degree error 60 miles offshore will give one nautical mile error at landfall, and

Fig. 14.4 The navigator with the very sophisticated tools of his trade. Equipment by Brookes & Gatehouse.

a poor performance instrument can be anything up to 5 degrees out. This is because the signal-to-noise ratio determines the width of the null, which must always be as narrow as possible for accurate bearings.

In the hand held instrument the compass, too, must be a precision job, accurate to not less than $\pm\frac{1}{2}°$, with well damped card readable to 1° and graduated every 2° with two scales for direct and prismatic viewing.

All RDF equipment is affected by quadrantal errors due to local distortion in the path of the beacon signal such as may be caused by metal structures on the yacht, and 'loops' formed by shrouds, metal deck, stanchions and safety wires. These problems can be countered by the insertion of an insulator somewhere in the 'loop'. If the errors persist a quadrantal deviation card must be drawn up by swinging the RDF compass against the ship's compass. If possible the hand held RDF should always be used in the same position in the craft.

Other errors affecting RDF are coast line refraction which occurs when a signal makes an oblique angle with a coast line, and sky wave interference, due to atmospheric conditions at dawn and dusk, which can cause problems with long range beacons, but is not of particular significance generally (Fig. 14.4.).

LOGS

A vital factor in navigation is knowledge of the distance the vessel has travelled through the water when making a passage. Although not quite so important from the navigational point of view, indication of speed through the water is also useful. These two requirements are handled by the ship's log.

For the smaller and medium size craft electronic logs have now largely replaced the towed line and propeller type, because of their advantages in economy, ease of installation and accuracy (Fig. 14.5.).

While there are several systems available the principle of operation is the same. The water flowing along the vessel's hull activates a flow measuring device, or sensing element, which in turn, by means of polarized magnet and static coil, produces electrical impulses. The rate at which the impulses occur is proportional to the rate of water flow and so to the vessel's speed. Electronic processing then presents the information on a dial and digital counter.

The sensing meter may be a small impeller, a trailing arm or lever, or a pitot head, which is another form of pressure sensitive equipment. A more sophisticated system incorporates an electrical field to measure water flow rate. By far the most universal method is the small impeller. But this, like the pitot, suffers the risk of being put out of action by weed, and for this reason some installations allow for retraction of the unit to inside the hull for cleaning while the vessel is under way.

AUTO-PILOT

Although not widely used in small craft as yet an electronic auto-pilot is available to yachts. The system is new in application rather than principle, which basically consists of the use of an electronic compass to activate an electro hydraulic system operating the rudder. In this way deviation from a set course is automatically corrected (Fig. 14.6.).

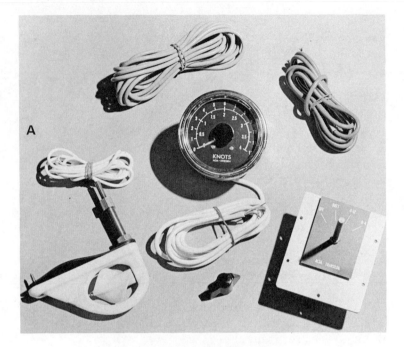

Fig. 14.5 Two electronic logs, one with its associated equipment. A. The AGA Transilog supplied by Mansell & Fisher and B. The Electralog by EMI Marine.

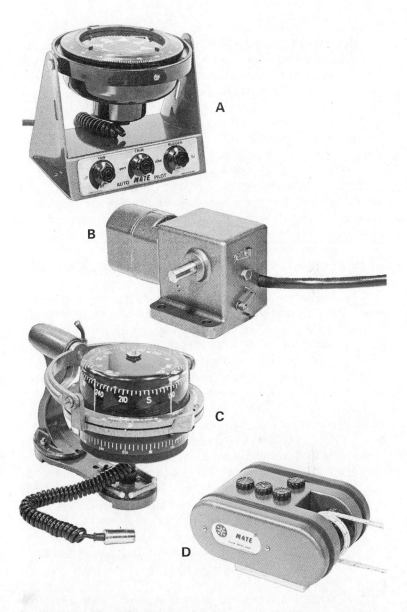

Fig. 14.6 The 'Mate' Grid Steering Compass Automatic Pilot (A) with rudder actuator (B) suitable for torques up to 500lbs. (C) shows a course detector attached to a Sestrel compass which controls the tiller power unit (D). The power unit (D) can also be controlled by an electronic wind vane. (Sharp & Company.)

RADAR

By far the most significant developments in radar during the past few years have been in equipment specifically designed for smaller craft rather than ships. The yachtsman now has a choice of instruments ranging in price from a little over £500 ($1200) to within £1500 ($3700), power outputs in the region of 3kW, and current consumption as low as 48 watts, less than that of a 60W domestic light bulb. Weight, too, has been kept low and installation costs reduced by, in the smaller sets, two unit equipment (Fig. 14.7.).

Radar works on much the same principle as the echo sounder except that there is no conversion of electrical energy to sound energy. Electrical energy only, in the form of very high frequency radar radio waves being used to create an electronic echo from a target. Because of the very high speed of the waves, in the region of 162,000 nautical miles a second, the echo is virtually instantaneous.

The equipment consists of a generator for the power supply, a transmitter, a receiver, a revolving scanner and a cathode ray tube (Fig. 14.8.). Waves emitted as rapidly repeated short duration pulses of radio frequency energy return as echoes and are electronically processed to appear as light blobs on the screen. Distances are obtained by the time lapse between emission of the pulse and its return as an echo.

For small craft radar, performance should still be up to professional standards with good picture clarity and definition, full controls, which include at least anti sea clutter, with preferably anti rain clutter as well, grouped close to the display. A 6in diameter screen is adequate as is a range of, say, 16 miles, for radar cannot 'see' over the horizon which, in a small craft is only four to five miles distant. It is more important to look for accuracy at short range, up to two miles.

Because of its ability to give bearing and distance of a target, and operate equally well at night and in poor weather, radar is one of the most effective electronic aids to safe navigation (Fig. 14.9.).

A radar development, at present intended only for ships, but which may well be adaptable for yachts and smaller professional craft in the not too distant future, is the 'Situation Display' introduced by Kelvin Hughes. Here the picture is

Fig. 14.7 The Display end of three small boat radars: A. The Decca 050.
B. The Seascan by Electronic Laboratories. C. The Electrascan by EMI Marine.

presented on a special television screen and so is viewable from wider angles and greater distances by, if necessary, several people at the same time. The system gives a 'retained' situation picture of the whole area in range, on which moving targets have 'tails' from which the operator can determine their course and speed.

Fig. 14.8   The enclosed scanner units employed with small craft radars facilitate fitment to sailing boats as well as power cruisers. This is the radome for the Decca 050.

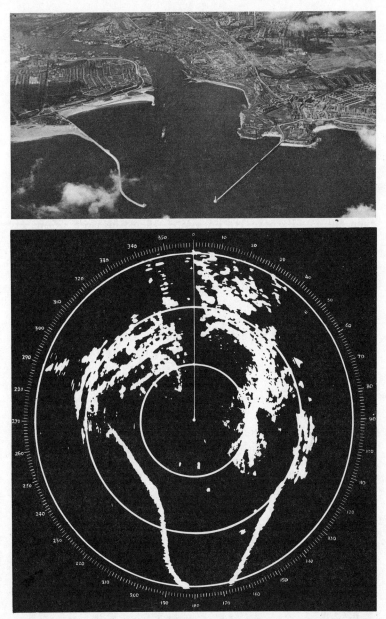

Fig. 14.9   Photograph of a harbour entrance with, below, the radar presentation of the scene.

chapter 15

Emergencies and Equipment

Lifelines are now accepted as almost standard equipment on even the smallest boats. They are a sensible precaution but not too much should be expected of them and there are certain considerations in fitment. First, it should be made clear that in rough conditions one does not advisably make journeys along the deck clutching the lifelines for support. They will add little to personal stability and the requirement is good, continuous handholds on the coachroof, etc., a non-slip deck surface and a sensible toe rail. Thus, although the lifelines might give you some feeling of security, their function is mainly for emergency and it is clear that if you get hurled against them they will have to be very strongly attached.

It is to the attachments that one should look, for the lines themselves and the stanchions will normally stand a good deal more than their fixings. In every case the stanchions or their sockets must be bolted down to the deck and the bolts should have plates under to spread the load so that the nuts and washers cannot pull through the deck. It is as important that a stanchion should be stiff in a fore and aft direction as well as athwartships since if you put a load on them the tendency will be to draw them towards each other.

Another thing to note is that if on a very small cruiser you are unable to fit stanchions of reasonable height you may be better off without them. A lifeline not much higher than a tripwire has no obvious advantages and you might do better to improve the handholds, deck surface and toe rail. If it gets really nasty put on a harness when on deck and shackle yourself to something solid.

Liferafts are obtainable in sizes to accommodate from four people upwards and your decision to acquire one, or to hire one, will depend somewhat on the size of your vessel. Many midget cruisers both sail and power have very little deck space where such an item might be stowed. It is clearly of little use poking it away in some stowage where it is not easily accessible. A solution for very small boats, which has more than one virtue, is one of the smaller inflatable dinghies which can be carried, perhaps partially inflated, on deck, and this will also give service as a tender (Fig. 15.1.). In passing, it should be mentioned that although rubber dinghies are light in weight they do not tow easily, in fact the drag on the painter can be out of all proportion to their size, so it is generally better to carry them aboard on even the slowest vessels.

In regard to the towing of tenders of the rigid kind, it should be said that with vessels capable of only a few knots, it may be satisfactory to tow the tender in sheltered conditions,

Fig. 15.1 The Avon Redstart in use as a tender—but you should have more freeboard than this in open water.

but it is most unwise to tow a tender at sea even for coast hopping. Given conditions which, although rough, your boat can cope with, the dinghy can become a real menace and it may charge at you with sufficient force to cause serious damage. If this occurs the only answer is to cut it loose, which is both galling and expensive, but rather better than losing your rudder or a few fingers.

Flares come in a variety of patterns, so please find out how to use them before you need them, but the ones most useful for emergency are the orange smoke float, the red star distress signal, which must be capable of reaching a height of not less than 150ft, and the parachute distress signal. Any of these will bring immediate attention from shore stations or any vessels which are in the vicinity. But remember that distress signals do not promise to perform irrespective of age. Look at the date printed on them and if in doubt renew and use the others on firework night.

The Department of Trade and Industry regulations for ships in Class XII, which includes pleasure craft of over 45ft, state that they shall carry not less than six pyrotechnic distress signals and that these shall be packed in a water-tight container indelibly labelled to indicate their purpose. You will be well advised to follow this instruction for coastal cruising and ventures further afield, even supposing your boat is smaller than the length at which it becomes mandatory.

An audible warning device is essential for navigation in poor visibility and it may also be used to advise other vessels of your intentions (see Chapter 19). Boats under 40ft are not compelled to have a whistle or a foghorn but they must carry some means of giving audible warning, e.g., an electric or manually operated horn, or even a hand blown trumpet. Small portable horns, operated by pressure from throwaway containers, may not be effective in very foggy conditions since the emission of gas or air under pressure can lower the temperature at the vent to cause any moisture therein to freeze, and so the horn becomes mute.

One or more lifebuoys with buoyant lines attached should be part of the standard equipment of the boat and, if you cruise at night, one of these should be fitted with a self-igniting light. Your crew might have their own personal buoyancy but whatever the size of boat sufficient lifejackets (to BS 3595.1969) for a normal crew should be carried as part of the ship's stores.

Fire and gas risks aboard are frequently generated by lack of attention to installation details which may have a danger potential, and in an engine room which is out of sight and largely out of mind, it is obviously worthwhile to have continuous monitoring of the conditions by fire and gas detection devices. Some of the modern detector systems have multiple roles and will give audible and visual warning of fire, gas, immersion (bilge water) and illegal entry. Automatic switching of bilge pumps and cut out trigger switching for electrical circuits can also be incorporated. Smothering systems for engine room fires can of course be built-in (Figs. 15.2/3.), but there is a recommendation that a warning system may be better than automatic extinguisher operation, since it enables action to be taken in shutting down the engines, closing vents and stopping fans so that the situation is not aggravated by a forced draught.

Gas may be difficult to dispel according to its origin, since some, such as petrol vapour, will rise, and if it escapes ignition it will eventually disperse, whereas bottled fuel gases are heavier than air and will continue to lie in the lowest parts of the vessel. Hence it is of value if one of the engine room extractor vents has its intake low down so as to capture any heavier mixtures that might have crept into that area. Bottled gases should in any case be kept in a separate stowage and preferably at a height which permits leakage to drain overside (Fig. 15.4.).

Fires from most sources can be dealt with by extinguishers containing Dry Powder, CO_2, BCF, or Freon FE 1301.

There are some things worth observing in regard to extinguishers. First, make sure that the extinguisher is of a type recommended for the various kinds of fire it might meet on a boat and is not likely to generate dangerously toxic fumes in use on certain materials, etc. Second, the recommended life of the contents must be observed and if no date is quoted for renewal then you must be sure to obtain a recommendation from the supplier or the maker. Thirdly, do not be mean with extinguishers. It is probably better to have several small ones

Fig. 15.2 The Sowester automatic marine fire extinguisher fitted into a Conway 26.

Fig. 15.3 Another automatic extinguisher which can be installed on the deckhead in the engine room or elsewhere. This Noxfire model is fitted with a micro switch which can be used to trigger an alarm or other electrical circuitry.

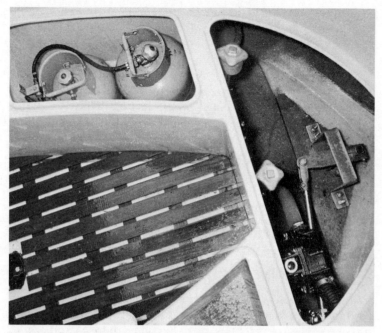

Fig. 15.4 Cockpit lockers in the Fairways Fisher; note bottled gas stowage isolated from remainder of vessel and with easily accessible valves; diaphragm bilge pump; access to rudder head which is squared and could be used with an emergency tiller.

at strategic points, e.g., engine room entrance, galley, distributor board, etc., than one mighty container which is unwieldy and which all depends upon. The Department of Trade & Industry list their recommendations on fire-fighting equipment as follows:

For vessels over 9 metres (30 feet) in length and those with powerful engines, carrying quantities of fuel—two fire extinguishers should be carried, each of not less than 1·4 kilos (3lb) capacity, dry powder, or equivalent, and one or more additional extinguisher of not less than 2·3 kilos (5lb) capacity, dry powder, or equivalent. A fixed installation may be necessary.

For vessels of up to 9 metres (30 feet) in length, with cooking facilities and engines—two fire extinguishers should be carried, each of not less than 1·4 kilos (3lb) capacity, dry powder, or equivalent.

For vessels of up to 9 metres (30ft) in length, with cooking facilities only or with engine only—one fire extinguisher should be carried, of not less than 1·4 kilos (3lb) capacity, dry powder, or equivalent.

Carbon dioxide (CO_2) or foam extinguishers of equal extinguishing capacity are alternatives to dry powder appliances. BCF (bromo-chlorodifluoro-methane) or BTM (bromo-trifluoromethane) may be carried, but people on the boat should be warned that the fumes given off are toxic and dangerous in a confined space, and a similar notice should be posted at each extinguisher point.

Additionally for all craft:

Buckets—two, with lanyards.

Bag of sand—useful in containing and extinguishing burning spillage of fuel or lubricant.

YACHT MEDICINE

Serious accidents aboard boats are fortunately rare. The assistance of a doctor should be sought as soon as possible, but even when a yacht is in a harbour there is sometimes considerable delay, and the very life of the injured or sick person may depend on some knowledge of first aid. Hence the advice given here, but it should in no way take the place of medical assistance in serious illness.

Many of the accidents on board are due to living in small and close confinement, and are particularly common around the galley associated with burns and scalds from the stove. It is important that the cook should have supreme right of way and consideration when he or she is working.

Fatigue

Arthur Ransome once said that yachting should be pleasurable. Too many people rush down to their small cruisers after a sedentary life and proceed to treat themselves as if they were on a commando assault course. Perhaps the first night of a cruising holiday should be spent in port so that everybody could have a good night's sleep. Sleep is all important in combating fatigue. It must be remembered that a whole day spent in invigorating air is in itself extremely tiring after town life. Children get tired and fractious and should be bedded down early. Sleep can be encouraged by giving them one or two junior Aspirins or Disprin, and a very useful sedative for children is to have on board a bottle of Gees Linctus, which is a cough linctus with some sedative action. A teaspoonful of this often helps a child to sleep. Sleeplessness, cold, over exertion and lack of food all contribute to fatigue. If cooking or sea-sickness has made eating difficult, it is often helpful to have an easily digestible form of sugar available and tablets of Dextrosol can be obtained from any chemist. They now have various flavours and they are composed of the correct sugar for human beings and are absorbed very quickly. They should always be aboard and if sudden extra energy is needed a tablet will often suffice and give the necessary added boost.

Sea-Sickness
This is a form of travel sickness and some people are affected more severely than others. Those people who experience a feeling of nausea just by seeing a picture of a boat afloat should never go near the sea and should certainly not be allowed aboard. It is the most common ailment of all afloat. Luckily for most of us it is only temporary, and rarely do people become completely incapacitated. It is important before a cruise starts, to be fairly kind to one's stomach, do not take too much highly spiced food and keep off excess of alcohol. There are various types of anti-sea-sickness tablets on the market. Nearly all of them have some side effect such as dryness of the mouth, or drowsiness. In our experience the best of these remedies is tablets of Meclozine, the dose being 12·5 milligram tablet. These are sold as 'Sea-legs' and it is better to start taking the first tablet the night before the cruise starts. Some years ago a very experienced cruising friend gave this tip. He makes all members of his crew take a 12·5 milligram Meclozine tablet the night before going aboard and every eight hours for the next twenty-four hours whether they feel sea-sick or not, and this has kept his boat free of this complaint over many years.

Bed rest and warmth are very important. Sea-sickness is not an illness but does produce considerable depression which can be contagious. Often people are kept from being sick by being given a job to do. It is important that they do not become fatigued by insisting on being on deck all the time and it is essential that they should get an adequate amount of rest and warmth. Coldness, fatigue and hunger all increase the symptoms. The patient should drink little, eat nothing but dry biscuits or nuts or whatever they feel they can keep down. Their energy requirements can be kept up by Dextrosol tablets. Most of us get over the nausea of this condition after about twenty-four hours. The worst thing before starting a cruise is to have a really good nosh up the night before with lots of alcohol and spiced foods. This should obviously be avoided.

Drowning and Artificial Respiration
Drowning may cause the breathing to stop before the heart stops beating. The heart beats may be so weak as to make the pulse undetectable. Lack of oxygen in the blood supply to the brain causes irreparable damage to the brain cells in a matter of some three minutes. Resuscitation, by whatever method, must therefore be given as quickly as possible. Seconds count. The best method nowadays is that known as the expired air resuscitation or 'kiss of life'. Small mouth masks can be obtained from life saving societies, but it is important to get over one's own squeamishness as quickly as possible, and to start the method without too much notice being paid to the condition of the patient's mouth.

Method
When a patient has been saved from the water his air passages and lungs are filled with water. The first thing to do therefore is called inversion. The patient is turned face downwards, preferably with the head lower than the feet and is yanked up by his feet or stomach so that the air passages and lungs are cleared of water. The patient should then be turned on his back. Make sure that there is an air-way, that the mouth and nose are clear of obstruction, pull the chin upwards and remain supporting the chin throughout the period of un-consciousness. Take several deep breaths, pinch the patient's nose and apply your mouth wide open over the mouth of the patient and blow into the victim's lungs. After exhaling, take your mouth away from the patient, turn your head to watch

the chest movement and replace your mouth on his and repeat. The rate of respiration is dictated by the emptying of the patient's chest, about ten respirations a minute for an adult, and twenty for a child are needed. No more force than is needed to fill his lungs should be used and particular care should be taken with children. This action should be continued for at least an hour before hope is abandoned. If the patient starts to breath, he should be rolled over on his side so that he will not choke if he vomits. Until consciousness is regained, the chin should be supported and every breath watched. As soon as the patient is breathing on his own, his wet clothes should be stripped off and substituted by warm dry garments. When he can swallow or cough a little warm tea or coffee should be given. He should be carefully watched for twenty-four hours but as soon as possible he should be taken to hospital.

Shock
Shock follows all accidents and may be serious. The symptoms are a combination of a pale face, lips pale, nails may be blue, pulse fast and weak, cold sweat on the forehead, and palms of the hands and a feeling of exhaustion, shaking, nausea or vomiting. The patient should be laid with his head down low, wrapped up warmly but not over heated. Give hot sweet tea or coffee provided there is no head injury or abdominal pain. Do not give alcohol before recovery is complete. The odd drink is better given to the attendant than to the patient.

For a fainting fit, sit with the head between the knees, loosen clothing around the neck and treat for shock, give hot stimulants.

Wounds
All wounds are liable to infection. They should be bathed with antiseptic solution, such as Cetablex cream or Savlon and covered with a firm crepe bandage dressing. Wounds with bleeding should be carefully inspected. Bleeding is of two kinds, the more important is arterial which comes in spurts. The blood is bright red and can be stopped by firm pressure over the bleeding point. If the blood loss is intense, occasionally a tourniquet may have to be applied around the limb above the point of injury. This is a tight bandage tightened

with a stick or marlin spike and twisted round tightly. If this has to be applied and it is very rare, it must be released every fifteen minutes otherwise gangrene or death of the limb will set in. Usually bleeding stops on firm pressure over the artery and the wound that is bleeding with arterial bleeding can often be stopped by using tiny strips of adhesive dressing which bring the skin edges together firmly. These strips are placed across the wound and take the place of stitches. Firm dressings, wool and a firm crepe bandage over should stop the bleeding in time, or until further assistance can be obtained.

Venous bleeding is more of an ooze or welling up into the wound of bluish looking blood, and this can always be stopped by firm pressure over the wound and elevation of the limb.

Nose Bleeds
The patient should be sat up and cold compresses placed over the base of the nose. They should be encouraged to lie quietly and on most occasions the nose bleeding will stop.

Burns
The patient must be treated for shock. Cut away any clothing which is not adherent to the burnt area and apply burn dressing. If burn dressings are not on board, it is best to clean the area with some antiseptic cream such as Savlon and apply tulle gras if possible. Fucidin inter tulle is the best of these and then a clean dressing such as a clean handkerchief. Cover with a crepe bandage fairly firmly but very well covering the burnt area. Make sure that the area above and below the burn is covered. It is important never to put cotton wool directly onto a burn, as the fragments of the wool adhere to the burnt area and can cause trouble in the treatment of the wound, and subsequently produce more scarring.

Sunburn and Heat-Stroke
For sunburn, calamine lotion applied night and morning gives considerable relief. Keep covered away from the sun's rays, using a protective cream before further exposure.

In sun-stroke the head aches, the face is red, the skin is hot and dry, the pulse is strong and rapid, the temperature is high. Sometimes the patient becomes unconscious. If possible lay down with his head elevated, cool the head and body with cold water, sponging and do not give stimulants. Heat exhaustion as opposed to sun-stroke is due to exposure to great heat and loss of salt from the body. In this case the face is pale, the skin is moist and cool, the pulse is weak and the temperature is low. The patient should go to bed, external heat should be applied and stimulants given including fluids with added salt. Salt tablets can be obtained.

Rope burns caused by ropes running through the hands are extremely painful and should be treated as for ordinary burns or scalds.

Food Poisoning and Tummy Pains
When cruising in foreign parts, care should be taken about drinking unboiled water and eating salad stuffs without carefully washing them using a very mild antiseptic, such as a few potassium crystals in the water. Water should be boiled.

Stomach upsets with diarrhoea and perhaps vomiting are caused by eating and drinking things to which one is not accustomed and which have become infected by bacteria which one is not used to. Tincture of Chlorodeine is very useful in settling these upsets and should always be carried in the boat. If the diarrhoea is serious, then dosage with Kaolin and morphia several times a day may be required. The diet should be kept strictly to bland fluids and glucose until the condition gets better. If necessary, Sulphonomide or anti-biotic tablets should be taken.

Abdominal Pain
If the tummy pain is coming in waves or that is to say is colicky in nature this should be taken seriously, especially in children. If this pain goes on for six hours, it is an indication of very severe trouble and a doctor's advice should be obtained as soon as possible. It may be an appendicitis or in the case of an adult a ruptured ulcer. The abdominal pain becomes more intense and there is usually some guarding, that is to say when the tummy is carefully touched the muscles in the tender area become very tense. A doctor's advice should be obtained as quickly as possible in these cases and until this can be obtained, the patient should be given nothing to eat or drink.

Boils

These are common in long distance cruising particularly in hot climates. Boils or septic spots around the face should never be squeezed. They should be dressed repeatedly with an antiseptic cream or lotion and an antibiotic taken.

Antibiotics

Very many people nowadays are sensitive to antibiotics, but those carried in the first-aid box should be carefully screened by the patient's doctor to make sure that the patient is not made much more uncomfortable by being given an antibiotic which does not suit him. Before a cruise starts for a family, the family physician should be consulted and his advice sought as to the most useful antibiotic to be carried.

Head Injury

The boom is a common source of injury to the head or sometimes a deck hand slips and strikes his head. Any slight period of unconsciousness, even of a few seconds, means that the patient has suffered concussion. He should be laid down and if unconscious make sure his airway is clear by turning the head to the side and extending the neck, if necessary, propping the mouth open. The patient should have his head slightly higher than his feet. If the patient is conscious keep him quiet and comfortable for a few hours. Pain-killing drugs such as Panadol (Paracetamol) can be given. If some time after apparent recovery the patient becomes irritable, the headache becomes worse or there is nausea and vomiting, the pupils of the eyes should be carefully inspected and if one pupil is larger than the other, urgent medical advice should be obtained.

Fractures and Joint Injuries

Fractures and dislocations of joints need professional care as soon as possible. Temporary relief can be obtained by making the part look as normal as you can, that is to say, see that the line of the limb is more or less normal and the joint pulled into a straight position. There is swelling, pain and discolouration around the area and deformity. The patient may well have felt or heard a bone break. Cold bathing of the part helps as does elevation but the area of injury should be immobilized by splinting. Cover the injured part with wool and splint the joint above and below the injury. Sail battens are extremely useful splints and they should be put outside the woollen dressing and bandaged in position. The limb should be elevated.

Sprains of Ankles and Wrists
Sprains of ankles and wrists should be bathed in cold water for half an hour and bound firmly with adhesive tape or crepe bandage. The colour of the fingers or toes should be carefully watched. If they are white or blue, the bandages are too tight and should be loosened.

Fractures of the Toes and Fingers
Fractures of the toes should be left alone, bathed and elevated for a short time and pain killers given. If the fingers are broken, one finger can be strapped to the other and splinted in this way with $\frac{1}{2}$in to 1in elastoplast tape.

Insect Bites and Stings
There is a very good aerosol spray called Wasp-eze which should be applied to the sting or bite as soon as it is noticed. This relieves the swelling, pain and itch. Calamine lotion is also useful. The wasp bite is acid and ammonia should be applied. In the case of a bee, the bee-sting is alkaline and vinegar should be applied.

Toothache
If due to a cavity this can be relieved by a temporary dressing to the cavity, and filling it with a little cement made of a few drops of oil of cloves on some powdered zinc oxide. This applied to the cavity and allowed to set is a very good temporary dressing and is pain-relieving. The gum can be bathed with whisky or other preferable spirit, or failing this, with iodine. Aspirin or Panadol or other pain relieving drugs will also be useful.

Alcohol, Whisky, Brandy and other Spirits
These have a useful place in the medicine chest as pain relievers and are excellent to use after being chilled by exposure to cold, but they should not be used unless the person is able to be in the warm for some time afterwards. It is no good giving alcohol and then going out on deck on watch as the

alcohol dilates the blood vessels of the limbs and increases the cold effect.

Pregnancy
It is unwise for pregnant ladies to go cruising any distance off shore. The first three months of pregnancy are the most dangerous as far as miscarriage is concerned, and the patient can lose terrifying amounts of blood very quickly. It is therefore advisable to leave pregnant ladies ashore.

Foreign Bodies in Eyes
These should be carefully removed with a wisp of cotton wool or edge of a clean handkerchief and the eye bathed with suitable eye lotion. If the eye is irritable and inflamed, Chloromyecetin eye-lotion should be applied and a pad and bandage placed over the eye. Keep it closed until expert opinion can be obtained.

The Medicine Chest
Various approved dressings and burn dressings.
Assorted band-aids and elastoplast including small strip band-aids for holding the edges of wounds together.
Two each of 2, 4 and 6in crepe bandages.
Sea-sickness tablets such as Qwells, Avermine or preferably Sea-legs.
Antiseptics such as Acriflavene, Catablex or Savlon cream.
Anti-histamine cream for burns and bites.
Wasp-eze.
Eye lotion and eye lotion applicator.
A roll of adhesive tape 3in wide which can be torn into strips of whatever size one requires.
Scissors.
Safety pins.
Splinter forceps.
A pair of eyebrow tweezers.
A thermometer.
Ammonia for insect bites.
Oil of cloves.
Zinc oxide powder.
Sunburn ointment or oil.

Sedatives such as Disprin, Soluble Asprin or Paracetemol (Panadol), Codis or Veganin.

A laxative, e.g., Senakot granules.

Antibiotic tablets (see doctor).

Tincture of Chlorodeine for tummy pains and diarrhoea.

A bottle of mixed Kaolin and morphia, obtainable from doctor.

8oz bottle of Gee's linctus.

A bottle of tulle gras or Fucidin inter tulle.

Antibiotic spray such as Poly Bactrin or Cicatrin powder for application to wounds.

A bottle of tincture of iodine.

FIRST AID FOR THE BOAT

A tool kit for a boat may be anything from a pair of pliers and a screwdriver to an elaborate inventory which permits almost complete engine overhaul and major repairs on the hull. It is largely a case of state of mind and although traditionally sailors are supposed to be self-sufficient it may be difficult to draw the line if this notion is taken too literally, unless of course one is undertaking an ocean crossing, in which case we would not care to advise!

It seems that the real requirement is to be able to make things serviceable in an emergency, rather than do a boatyard job, and regarded in this light one may get some indication of the extent of the equipment.

Engine tools: Plug spanner, feeler gauges, wire brush, side cutting pliers, points file and fine grade abrasive paper, screwdriver, ring or set spanners to suit engine, cross-headed adjustable spanner, small stilson wrench, small hand or table vice, 10in rat tail file, 10in medium cut flat file, hacksaw and spare blades, hand-drill with small set of twist drills, centre punch.

Hull and rigging tools: Large screwdriver, hammer, half round rasp, bradawl, small saw, pincers, two chisels, ½in and 1¼in, oilstone, mallet, two carpentry clamps, brace and two bits, say ⅜in and ¾in, pinepunch, 1in cold chisel, mild steel block about 6 × 2 × 1in or bolt cutters in lieu of the last two items.

Engine spares and stores: The instruction book, plugs, contact breaker points, condenser (for petrol engines), alternator or dynamo drive belt, fuses, piece of flat gasket material, liquid joining, assortment of fibre washers, spare filter elements, reserve engine oil and stern tube grease.

General: One or two good torches, a small assortment of nuts, bolts and washers, ditto wood screws and nails (galvanized), split pins, bulldog grips to suit rigging wire, small reel of copper wire, length of electric cable, insulating tape, codline, two hardwood wedges, a few assorted short lengths of timber, assorted shackles and a couple of spare blocks, length of polythene tubing, funnel, bulbs for lights, equipment fuses, tube of sealastic. A fairly comprehensive kit which should cater for most running repairs aboard.

Engine failure should be approached with reason rather than speed and the possible sources of trouble should be eliminated one at a time, unless of course you have a clear idea of what has gone wrong. A sudden failure is very likely to be ignition and a slightly slower cessation of power may indicate a fuel supply problem. A gradual falling off in power without complete failure could indicate overheating. Be systematic in your approach, check all the gauge readings, or those which are still functioning, first, and see if they give a lead.

With a petrol engine, check down the ignition system from its origins for a spark, starting at the magneto or coil and working down through the distributor to each plug. A spark can be induced at any point by flicking the contact breaker points open, but another check is to see that these have the recommended gap when opened by the cam. Lack of a little lubricant can cause the fibre pad that lifts the points to wear down quite rapidly, in which case the gap will decrease until it fails to break the low tension field and no spark will be generated. Condenser trouble is more likely to cause poor starting and a bad fall-off in performance rather than a complete failure.

Diesel engines are obviously not prone to these problems but both petrol and diesel, and especially the latter, are sensitive in regard to fuel both as regards quantity and quality. Again the thing is to start at the source if possible and work one's way down the line. If you work from the other direction you might find that you have to take everything down from the engine back before finding the source of the trouble. This should be qualified by noting that of course the very first thing to check before becoming involved in any dismantling is the fuel filter.

Diesel engines are particular about the cleanliness of their fuel and apart from this there is very little to go wrong with them as far as sudden breakdown is concerned. So if in trouble with a diesel, look first to the fuel supply to ensure that there is no dirt, scale or water in the system. If you need to do any draining, whatever fuel is put back should go through a filter, and in an emergency this can be a piece of non-fluffy material such as a nylon stocking or a silk scarf.

The first check for overheating is to see if water is being ejected whether with the exhaust or other means according to the installation. Again, the strainer is the first check and if the inlet strainer is blameless then the pump output should be next for investigation and so on down the line. Air cooled engines with the proper environment are unlikely to overheat through any sudden fault in the cooling system, although air screens and cylinder fins may become somewhat bunged up in the course of time, and thus prevent an adequate passage of cool air. Petrol engines can overheat through maladjustment of the ignition timing (retarded) but it is not likely to happen suddenly unless the clamp bolt on the drive casing has worked loose or a magneto coupling has developed play.

Contrary to the recommended approach to engine problems, hull difficulties such as sudden leakage should be attended, if not without reason, at any rate with all speed. The first snag is generally to find out where, and if you have no indication, such as a sudden crunch on any part of the hull, then the places to look first are those where a hole has been made through the hull by design, and that includes all skin fittings, sea cocks for engines, lavatories, etc., the stern gland, pitot and other actuating heads for logs, sounders and so on. In the event that you have good reason to believe that you have been holed, the first thing is to locate the damage by tearing away everything obstructing approach and then stuff a cushion over the hole. If you have time to insert an oilskin between the cushion and the hole so much the better. The cushion can be covered with a flat surface according to the size of the damage and its accessibility, e.g., a plate, the frying pan, or a locker hatch, and the whole lot braced back against whatever is convenient. Meanwhile another crew member will have been pumping, and will go on pumping until relieved. If subsequently you are able to get something temporarily over the hole outside the hull it might enable you to make a more effective patch inside, but the difficulty of one-sided operation on a GRP hull is obvious, and although it would be possible to do something with self-tapping screws it would be no easy task.

Wire rigging can be repaired temporarily by doubling back from the break and securing it with bulldog clips. You will afterwards need to extend the length to reach its original attachment point either with an extra rigging screw or a lashing. If the stay has parted further up you will need to double back both broken ends with clips so that they are looped together. Lashings can be strong and effective, and one never need be worried about using them for setting up rigging provided they are kept short (long lashings will alter their length according to whether wet or dry), and the eyes they pass through are of large enough diameter and smooth enough not to cause the lashing to be cut.

The remedies for broken tillers are also a bit obvious but it is to the point, that irrespective of the type of steering, whether wheel or tiller, some part of the system should be viable for emergency operation, e.g., with wheel steering it is sensible to have access to the rudder head so that some jury helm can be arranged. Many vessels have the rudder head squared off or a socket welded on so that an emergency tiller can be accommodated (Fig. 15.4.).

A final word is offered in regard to all emergency equipment, whether lifejackets, flares, fire extinguishers, inflatable liferafts or any other gear which may be needed urgently: KNOW HOW TO OPERATE EVERYTHING AND MAKE SURE THAT ALL CREW MEMBERS ARE SIMILARLY INFORMED.

chapter 16

Fitting Out

The amount of labour which goes into this annual task depends greatly upon what has gone before. It is very much easier to keep a boat in good condition, doing a little bit at a time as it becomes necessary, than it is to leave things until a major refit is required. This, like many other truths is self-evident, but that does not mean that anyone acts upon it. The boathook carelessly dropped sharp end down on the brightwork in the Autumn may cause a small scar, but by Spring, after exposure to months of moist air and some frost, you might be scraping down and re-varnishing the whole of one side of the coachroof coaming. The end of your forefinger dipped into the varnish tin and applied immediately to the scratch would have saved all that labour.

Having started with a warning about doing too little at the appropriate time, may we now issue another one about being over-ambitious and attempting to do too much when the calendar, but not the weather, beckons. We have seen more than one good boat with a good coat of paint in most places, mercilessly stripped or sanded down by enthusiasm rather than necessity, and then repainted in the worst possible conditions for the job, with rain laden wind whipping the paint off the end of the brush. It cannot be over-emphasized that the usual English early Spring is not a very suitable time to undertake major work in the open, and those owners who have not the benefit of good cover should be wary of the exposure of bare wood and metal for any lengthy period. If you are in the open do not strip it one week and come back to prime it a week or fortnight hence. Only strip as much as you can prime with a protective coat before you leave the job for the next occasion. Remember that a boat mouldering in some wet and windy corner of a yard is being attacked by forces much more insidious and destructive than those it will meet during the sailing season. You may conclude from this that it would be better to carry out the major maintenance work when the boat is laid up in the Autumn. You could be right, but no doubt you will still be standing there in March with the wind bringing tears to your eyes and the paint seeping under your mittens, which is why we have prepared for you a list of things to do before you put your boat back into the water.

Even supposing that you have saved all of your fitting out tasks until the Spring, there are some things which, if you failed to do them in the Autumn, must be tackled first so as to give the longest time between first attention and subsequent treatment. The first of these is scrubbing the weed and chitters off the bottom, and the second, opening up the bilges and all lockers and cupboards so that the damp corners can dry out. You will need to arrange for a through draught by adjustment of the forehatch, cabin vents, etc., but all such vents to the open air must be protected against the direct entry of moisture. If the sun shines take advantage of it and open the boat right up using every port and vent but do not leave it that way overnight even if the boat is covered with a tarpaulin. If there is an electric power point handy it is possible to do a crash job on the lower regions inside the hull with the use of a fan heater—which should be arranged to blow through the hull and not directly onto damp areas, but do not overdo it.

Before letting you get on with the schedule of work there is one more point we would like to make. Schedules and maker's instructions frequently tell you what to do without telling why you are doing it. Sometimes recommendations are conflicting and perhaps because of this one might be tempted to cut a few corners. As an instance, most paints need undercoats, but they are not essential and may not even be recommended for some synthetic coverings. The same goes for the variety of anti-fouling paint now available and it is here we would issue a warning. Always apply an undercoat to a wooden boat before using a high copper content anti-fouling.

The penalty for not doing this will vary, but the worst possible case, to use an example, is probably a wooden hull, copper fastened and with galvanized fittings. A direct application of copper anti-fouling will effectively link the heads of all the fastenings and make one pole of a fairly large battery, the galvanized fittings will provide the other pole and with salt water as an efficient electrolyte it is likely that all the galvanized fittings will need to be replaced in two seasons or less. You may know this, but strangely, there are some boatbuilders who do not, and you are unlikely to find it printed on the tin.

There is one other thing we would like to say about anti-fouling whilst we are on the subject because it is a tedious job to renew it, if it becomes necessary during the season. Many are the varieties and the claims that are made for them, and in our experience one is more likely to get through the season without a fresh application of anti-fouling, if an extra coat is put on beyond the maker's recommendation, and this appears to be more important than the brand which is used.

Work Schedules

WOODEN BOATS

The Outside Hull, Deck and Superstructure

1. Remove the weed and the barnacles from the bottom, and if it is a twin keel boat make sure that all encrustations are removed inside the keels where they join the hull as a nice drag-promoting fillet can form here. Weed can be scrubbed off with a stiff brush, or a piece of wet sacking is very effective and will also remove the looser barnacles, the others you will need to scrape off using, preferably, a wooden scraper.

2. Assuming that you do not intend to do a complete repaint from the bare wood out, go around the topsides and mark any damaged areas of paintwork. Rub these down with dry abrasive paper so as to roughly feather the edges of the damaged area. Paint the affected parts with primer or undercoat according to whether the bare wood has been exposed.

3. By now the bottom may be dry enough to do the same as you did on the topsides, dealing with only the affected areas and using dry sandpaper or a steel scraper as necessary to remove loose paint or isolated 'islands' of paint adhering in

the damaged zones. Then prime or undercoat locally as required.

4. Back to the topsides and put some more undercoat on the places being treated. Find another job to do; the undercoat you put on the bottom is probably not yet dry enough for another application, when it is, put some on.

5. Rub down the undercoat lightly on all the patches being treated, but on the topsides only and leave the bottom for the time being. Most undercoat rubs down very easily and the merest whisk over with a medium to fine grade abrasive paper, used dry, should suffice otherwise you will take off the lot. (You have been using coarse paper for the earlier operations.)

6. Give the topside patches a wipe with a turpentine rag, if turps mixes with your topside paint, otherwise use a dry rag and paint them with the topside enamel. (You will have hoped by this time to have filled the patches to the same level as the surrounding paintwork on both topsides and bottom, but you will need to use your own estimate of how many undercoats to apply and have achieved this before putting enamel on the topside patches.)

7. When the enamel on the patches is hard, you can begin to splash water about, and the whole of the topsides and bottom, including the patched places, can be rubbed down with wet and dry paper to give a key for a new coat of paint all over. On the topsides you will then be applying the topcoat of your choice and on the bottom an all over undercoat. However, if there is a considerable amount of work to be done on the deck and superstructure it is advisable to delay 7 until you have completed the following operations 9 to 11.

8. If the deck is painted proceed as for the topsides as far as attention with primer and undercoat. If the deck fittings have not been removed for a number of years, it would be a good idea to take one off to inspect the wood beneath and be guided by that as to the extent of further investigation. Whenever fitting or replacing deck fittings put a good coat of sealing compound underneath and in the bolt holes before attachment. This inspection applies whether the deck is marine plywood, laid planking or canvas covered and a sealant should be used on all when refixing fittings. On ply decks, check

where possible for delamination at the edges.

9. If your deck is laid and you have not experienced any leaks an inspection of the seams will confirm the soundness or otherwise of the caulking. If you have leaks, you might have quite a task scraping out the seams and refilling with one of the proprietary caulking compounds, since a leak appearing down below can be a long way from its source on deck.

10. Decks which are canvased are fine excepting that when they start to go, it may not be apparent, and water held beneath the canvas can cause a great deal of damage. The first places to look, are in dead areas where the water may collect behind fillets and other woodwork which has been put on top of the canvas, and also areas which the scuppers cannot clear, as in the angles of coamings, etc. There is no treatment for wood which has started to rot and the only thing to do is to cut out the affected parts well back beyond the seat of the rot and scarph in new wood with one of the resin glues which are impervious to water (the same applies of course to any rot found beneath fittings as mentioned in 8). The canvas can have a patch let in where ripe or torn and it may then be put down again on a good layer of wet paint, but unless you are handy with tools it might be better to get professional assistance if you are in trouble as indicated in this paragraph. The final paint job on the deck can, if you wish, be left until the boat is finished completely or even when it is afloat, when all of the feet and bodies helping to raise the mast, etc., have departed.

11. The brightwork on the superstructure is one of the testing places which shows whether or not you are skilled with a brush, but even more important to the job is the degree of care that goes into the preparation of the area to be re-varnished. Trying to rub down broken areas and patches of moisture and frost-withered skin with abrasive paper, wet or dry, can be a frustrating and thoroughly unsatisfactory procedure. If the area is large and the damage dispersed you will do well to strip it completely with a good paint and varnish remover. If the area is limited, scrape it with a piece of glass and use a fresh piece when the edge dulls. With enough broken glass around you can scrape anything including using selected pieces for inside and outside radii. You will

find that you can roughly feather off the edges of a patch also with the glass and then complete the job with dry paper.

Allow the area to dry thoroughly after rubbing down and then apply a mixture of varnish and 25% turps or white spirit to the bare wood. Let this dry and apply a coat of varnish and so on rubbing down lightly between each coat until you have filled the patch and you are able to rub down the whole of the coaming or whatever it is. After rubbing down with a fine grade of wet paper all over, to make a key for the new varnish coat, take a tack rag (a rag dampened with a mixture of varnish and turpentine) and wipe over the area you intend to varnish immediately. Do not try to apply this final coat on a dull, cold day. In fact it can be one of the last things before the vessel goes back to the water because you are going to get a lot of traffic over the boat whilst you are doing all the other jobs.

So choose your day, ideally, bright, warm and windless, put your tin of varnish in the sun, put water down all over the ground around the boat, dust it down, get moving with the tack rag, and with a brush which has never been used for anything else, start the varnishing. Do not attempt to brush over large areas. Go as fast as you can consistent with not raising bubbles and do a patch at a time if the area is large, working the varnish criss-cross to get an even distribution and then finishing with light strokes in the direction of the grain. If later in the work you find you have missed a bit, leave it, do not try to work it over. Rectify when the first coat is dry.

13. Putting on the anti-fouling is another job that can be left until you are ready to launch, in fact, with some types it is essential that they are immersed as soon as possible after application. There is no need to rub down the undercoat you applied earlier, providing you have achieved a reasonably smooth surface, but if it has stood long enough to get weathered or dirty you can wash it over. Make sure it is dry before putting on the anti-fouling and do not paint over the sacrificial anode.

The Inside Hull and Cabin

1. It is likely that by the time the foregoing has been accomplished the inside of the boat will have been well

ventilated and you can begin the rather long job of prodding out dirt and silt from bilges, nooks and crannies, on lands and in limber holes, and taking the opportunity at the same time to scrape off any loose paint you may find. Suck all of this out with a vacuum cleaner if one is available, otherwise brush and blow it all up to one end and shovel it out as best you can. (Whilst you have been doing all this you will at the same time have been making an inspection of the condition of all the wood for cracks, rot and other deterioration. Engine bearers and frames in way of these should get close scrutiny.) With dry paper sand any bare patches and coat with primer and then undercoat. Where only topcoat has been lost do the same with undercoat. When all is dry you can wash the whole of the interior, using as little water as possible and rinsing with clean water and drying with a cloth as you go along. A sponge cloth is useful for this job. There is never any need to splash water all over the place, and if you do, you may well find it lurking in the odd corner when you do the painting.

Having given the inside a chance to dry and air again, you can start the paintwork, working preferably from the bottom to the top so that all the cabin sole can be put back before you try hopping from floor to floor in order to paint the deckhead. If the old paint has been washed fairly thoroughly with a soap powder there will be sufficient 'key' for new paint without trying to sand everything down. This would be a hopeless task to do properly inside the boat.

2. Varnish work inside the cabin can follow the same procedures as the outside work, and if you have a gas or electric heater you can carry on in adverse weather, but don't forget that tack rag which is essential to a speck-free finish. Unless you are using them continuously, varnish brushes are difficult to keep in good condition but for short periods out of use you can put them in turpentine, otherwise wash and dry them out completely, making sure that you have not left any varnish up in the roots of the bristles which may later appear all over the work as dried specks. One certain way of keeping them in prime condition is to put them in a jar in a mixture of turpentine and linseed oil and make a hole in the lid just big enough to let the handles pass through, any gap is sealed by wrapping round with a rag. Brushes kept in

this way are never permitted to dry out at all from one year to the next.

3. Before leaving the subject of wooden hulls there are two more things to observe: A. Never use rubbing down paper with a rotary motion, or a rotary power sander, an orbital power sander will suffice, otherwise rub a patch first in one direction and then if necessary at a good angle across the first direction. Never try to rub down a large area with long strokes, always do a small patch and move on to the next. With varnish work you must always rub down in the direction of the grain. B. Spend your time in preparation of the surfaces to be painted or varnished. Putting on the final coat of anything is probably the easiest task from the point of view of labour.

GRP BOATS

Hull, Deck and Superstructure

As with wooden hulls we are mostly concerned with two things. Making good, minor damage such as scores and blemishes and giving the hull a good overall protective finish. Serious damage such as penetration of the laminates we will deal with at the end of this GRP maintenance schedule.

1. The first job, as with the wooden hull, is to go round and mark any damage which calls for attention. Scratches and deeper scores which have penetrated the gel coat without significant damage to the glass laminate should be treated by first cleaning out the scores with a rag damped with acetone. Besides cleaning this will also soften the surface slightly and give a key, but if you have no acetone you may very carefully clean out the damage with a corner of sandpaper used dry. Next you will need some gel coat (resin pigmented to the hull colour) with which you fill the damaged area using a putty knife. You can contain the gel resin by putting some strips of Sellotape over the patch, and this will also promote hardening of the surface, otherwise the gel coat may remain at a rubbery consistency for a long time and prevent rubbing down. When the patch has hardened, it should be rubbed down using a pad and successively fine grades wet and dry used wet until, apart perhaps from a slight difference in colour, the damaged area is indistinguishable from the rest.

If you cannot obtain gel coat, polyurethane paint may be used but although this will give protection, it has no filling properties and the scar will remain visible to close inspection.

2. Having attended to damaged areas, all over maintenance for the hull and superstructure surfaces takes the form of a thorough cleaning with soap and water followed by a good, hard wax polish. There are waxes especially suitable for glassfibre which are used to finish moulds and perhaps to give a final touch to your boat when it is new, and if you can obtain one of these it will be greatly superior to a car polish in durability.

3. Crazing of the gel coat is very rarely met with these days and it is only likely to be rife on an old moulding. It is almost impossible to apply large areas of new gel coat without factory conditions so the only answer is to rub down and paint the hull with polyurethane. The rubbing down process is much as for a wooden hull and again you should not use a rotary motion. The reason for this is that you are trying to provide a key for your paint and rubbing unidirectionally and then at an angle across it, is the only way you can be sure of 100% treatment of the surface. Although a rotary motion may produce much more dramatic looking scratches, that is not really what you are after.

4. There is one kind of surface blemish on glassfibre which may arouse interest more than concern and that is the star crack which, as its name implies is a series of fine lines radiating from a centre. This effect can have at least two reasons, first, it can be caused by the impact of a sharp object, and second, it may not be a crack at all but an impression from the mould which itself may have some star cracks through minor ill treatment in releasing mouldings. The treatment is as for other GRP skin blemishes if it is a crack or otherwise you may polish out the impression with the finest grade of wet and dry and then polish.

5. Fittings on glassfibre hulls may cause some damage in the ordinary course of their working life, dependent upon how they have been attached. Chainplates for instance which are deck fixing with bolts in tension (an accepted method for a GRP hull) can, unless the pad underneath is sufficiently large, give rise to some flexing about the point of attachment with

small cracks appearing around the perimeter of the holes. The cracks in the gel coat can be filled as described earlier but the proper answer is to reinforce the area also by a larger pad and washers underneath. Do not forget that any bolt extracted must be well covered with sealing compound when it is re-inserted.

6. In cleaning out the inside lower hull of a GRP boat, one can be a bit more generous with water since there will be fewer places where it may remain and it will cause no harm. But if, when you have cleaned out the bilges, you want to freshen up the appearance, a coat of polyurethane paint will adhere or for that matter any topside undercoat and enamel.

7. Repair to the laminations of a GRP hull can only be effected by cutting out the damaged area and doing a new lay up locally to renew the structure although a deep impact crack, as distinct from a puncture, may be cleaned out, sealed with some layers of chopped strand mat and resin applied to the inside surface. Roughen it up well with coarse paper and fill from the outside with a resin putty pigmented to the gel coat colour, and then rub down when hard. The layers of mat inside the hull should be allowed to cure before knifing in the putty.

8. For a puncture, a rectangle should be cut out of the skin so as to allow a good margin around the actual point of damage. This cutout should have radiused corners and the edges should be filed so as to make a chamfer with its largest side inside the hull. Several layers of chopped strand mat (csm) should be cut to duplicate the material which has been removed from the hole, and also some larger rectangles of csm of increasing size for backing up the patch on the inside. A piece of thin board, semi-rigid plastic or metal is then cut to cover the area of the hole and bolted on from the outside so as to follow the hull contour as far as possible. It must be waxed on its inner side so that the resin will not stick to it. A gel coat is applied to the board from the inside of the hull and allowed to cure. Then the laying up can commence, using first a good application of resin and then mat, repeating the process until the hole is flush with the surrounding skin after it has been consolidated with a small roller, which will also remove any entrapped air. When this has cured the board may be re-

moved from the outside and the bolt holes filled with resin putty. The larger pieces of csm which have been cut are then put on the inside so as to cover the filled area, using the smallest piece first and rolling afterwards to remove air from the resin and consolidate. The last task is to rub down the patch on the outside with fine, wet paper and a pad so as to smooth and blend with the outside contour of the hull (Fig. 16.1).

9. Some GRP boats have a considerable amount of wood joinery inside and some outside trim. The maintenance is as for those parts of a wooden boat described earlier, excepting that recently some preference has been noted for deck and cockpit trim to be in teak. This has the virtue of requiring very little attention and if it is treated at all it should be oiled and not varnished.

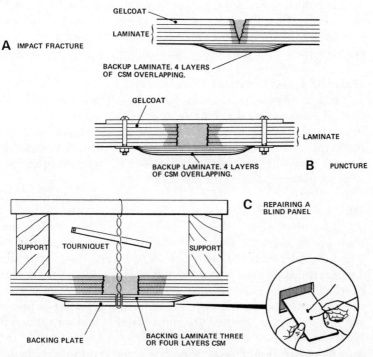

Fig. 16.1   Glassfibre repair A. Impact fracture. B. Puncture. C. Repairing a blind panel.

271

STEEL HULLS

1. Most cleaning off and corrosion removal jobs on a steel hull call for a power tool so that you can use rotary wire brushes and sander heads, otherwise you may be chipping and rubbing for a long time. You can use a rotary sander on a steel hull, and it is advisable to buy the more expensive abrasive discs which will last considerably longer. You will probably need to go down to the metal in many places and these should be primed immediately.

2. If there is any amount of corrosion on the rudder hangings you should give them a fairly vigorous going over with a light hammer, and a small chisel too if you are suspicious. It is possible for a massive lump of corrosion to masquerade as a solid piece of metal. Rectification if necessary is not easy because these fittings will generally be rivetted or welded solidly to the hull. You have the option of getting them off which is quite a task, or having a welding plant brought to the boat so that they can be built up on the spot. This will probably call for some laborious filing afterwards but it is perhaps the easier method.

GENERAL—ALL HULLS

1. If you have a ballast keel draw one of the bolts annually and be guided as to the remainder by what you find.

2. When dealing with the bottom of the boat take the opportunity to closely inspect any instrument heads and skin fittings, also the propeller shaft and any brackets, the propeller and the retaining nut and pin.

DECK FITTINGS

1. The main thing to note about deck fittings apart from their condition is the manner in which they are attached and the metal of which the bolts, screws, washers, etc., are made. In general unless the metal for the fitting and the fixing can correspond, stainless steel is probably the safest universal alternative in order to avoid corrosion through inter-action of the metals. A wire brush is the most suitable tool for removing corrosion residues from fittings made from any metal, and abrasive cloth should only be used if you intend to effect some subsequent protection by painting, re-galvanizing, etc.

2. Wherever possible deck fittings should be bolted down using backing plates or pads and large washers, and no item which is liable to take the weight of a person nor any fitting which could affect the safety of the ship should be otherwise. The only exceptions to this rule might be small cleats for fenders or flag halyards and the like.

3. For cleaning of miscellaneous parts. The slight rust film sometimes found on stainless steel parts and SS lifeline wire, shrouds, etc., can generally be cleaned off with an oily rag, and a surprising amount of dirt will come off too from the wire. Aluminium window frames, if not anodized, can be cleaned with a Brillo pad.

4. Mechanical gear on deck such as the anchor windlass, sheet winches, exposed controls, etc., should be freed off and lubricated as required, but take note of those items which might have plastic bearings, some of which are affected by mineral lubricants.

RIGGING, SPARS AND SAILS

1. Varnished wooden spars are prone to a lot of discolouration and blackening through being flogged by halyards and blocks, but it is only worsening of appearance, not of soundness. Hair cracks or shakes across the grain should be looked into for depth and get a professional opinion if in doubt. Vertical splits, unless gaping and of significant length are not a great threat but they should be filled. The heel of the mast should be examined for rot and also any part of the mast which is encased, such as under wide shroud bands and fittings, again, the professional is needed if you find trouble. If all is well you can proceed to scrape and varnish or if you feel like something calling for less work you can sand it down and paint it. White spars look quite smart and you cannot see the bruised wood as you can with varnish.

If you intend to keep to varnish and the condition is beyond rubbing down and a new coat, you can reduce your labour in scraping by avoiding all fancy scrapers and acquiring a few pieces of broken glass which will remove the old varnish at no cost and twice the speed. Rub down afterwards with a fine grade of dry sandpaper and re-varnish as described for the brightwork on wooden hulls using spar varnish with the first coat diluted by 25% turpentine.

2.   Metal spars of aluminium alloy which are unpainted and not anodized tend to acquire a rough, grey appearance which is the metal's own way of getting some surface protection by oxidation. The way to brighten things up and have a close inspection for cracks around fittings, etc., at the same time is with a cup type wire brush in a power drill. This removes the oxide without removing metal and besides shining things up it also reveals any imperfections. A thin coat of spar varnish applied immediately after brushing will retain the shine and protect the spar for a season, and the next time you clean it you will only be taking off old varnish.

3.   Check electric wiring, light fittings, etc., on the mast whilst it is down.

4.   Rigging screws sometimes have appalling tolerances, some are so tight they cannot be turned and others, often of the same make are so loose that the threaded ends nearly fall out. A rigging screw of the latter kind may have less than half of its quoted tensile strength. If you have any like this and you do not wish to renew, remove them from any strategic positions such as forestay and cap shrouds. Either use them for the lower stays or, better still, for tensioning lifeline wires, for which purpose they are likely to be adequate. If the lead of the shroud from the rigging screw does not allow the screw some free angular movement on the chainplate, you should check that the screw has not been bent by lateral strain, and when refitting put in a toggle or a shackle between the chainplate and the screw. If a rigging screw is bent for any reason check with the maker before trying to straighten it, some are malleable, others are not. Some of the makers of SS rigging screws now have a parts replacement service and you may buy just the piece you need instead of a complete screw. Put some hard grease on the threads before reassembly.

Faults on shackles are fairly obvious. Replace if showing more than superficial wear, and replace with a larger size if the shackle is bent. Never use bronze shackles aloft on anything bigger than a dinghy and never use them for anchors or the mooring chain however big they may be. The soft metal wears very rapidly if there is any movement under load.

Galvanized shackles can do with a bit of grease on the pin, especially the bigger ones. All shackles used aloft should be locked up tight with pliers and moused with a wire. Mousing of rigging screws should include the shackle if one is fitted.

5. Roller reefing gear should be lubricated and if it is of the enclosed gear type with an oil hole on top, put a bit of sticky tape over it, otherwise it is possible for the casing to be filled with rainwater coming down the luff of the sail.

6. All rigging wire, and wire halyards should be checked for broken strands and luff wires in headsails should also be tested by flexing and feeling for stray ends. Very little galvanized wire is used nowadays on yachts but, as with galvanized fittings, it is quite sound and seamanlike stuff. For a sailing boat however we would hesitate to give it the time honoured treatment with linseed, etc., unless you are unconcerned about the colour of your sails. The mainsail in particular will rub the leeward shrouds when off the wind and acquire all the dirt the linseed has collected.

7. Sails and their roping and all soft cordage should be checked down its length, also sail stitching and the security of cringles, particularly clew cringles on headsails. Synthetic ropes such as terylene and nylon do not appear to go ripe suddenly like cotton ropes, and for them to be comfortable to the hand they are normally of larger diameter than is needed for the job, so there is some reserve strength in them, even when they look dirty and tatty. Running rigging can be turned end for end so as to distribute the wear. When renewing, buy pre-stretched terylene for the halyards and sheets.

8. When terylene sails get really dirty they are very difficult to wash with any satisfaction. If you can persuade your family to give up the bath for about three days and you put them in warm water with half a packet of Persil evenly distributed, knead and turn them when you can, and tread them every morning like grapes, and after much rinsing at the end of the prescribed period they are spread flat upon the lawn to dry, you may find, that apart from rust marks and mould spots, you have a more presentable suit of sails. If you do not feel up to all this, it is best to send them to the sailmaker for laundering, but you will have to make up your mind when laying up and not expect them to be dealt with whilst you are fitting out.

NAVIGATION EQUIPMENT

1. There is little you can do yourself about electronic devices except to observe the makers remarks in the manual, if one is provided, and do not go beyond what is recommended. Refer to the maker without hesitation if in any difficulty.

2. Compasses, sextants and charts can be sent away for checking and correction. Send the former when you lay up and the latter whilst you are fitting out.

3. Check wiring and sockets for the navigation lights if electric. Have you got some spare bulbs?

4. Check over loose gear such as towing logs, radar reflector (if folding type), torches, etc.

MOORING GEAR

1. The chain on a permanent mooring wears fairly rapidly due to being dragged around at every tide. But your anchor chain cable, unless you do an awful lot of mooring, does not get a deal of use by comparison and provided it is of ample size for the boat it should last a very long time. Wear, when it occurs will be measurable by the depth of the groove in the end of the links, and whilst we would not like to pontificate on this, we would suggest that if the depth of the groove approaches $\frac{1}{6}$th of the diameter of the gauge of the link, e.g. $\frac{1}{16}$in on a $\frac{3}{8}$in chain, it should be replaced since you are effectively using a cable a size smaller than you require for your boat. A cable which is rusty may not necessarily be dangerously weakened, but it will make a mess on the deck and be a threat to your cordage and sails every time you use it, so if it still has the necessary dimensions get it re-galvanized.

2. When you secure the bitter (inboard) end of the chain cable in the locker it should be lashed not shackled, or better still it can have a lashing far enough up the cable to be on the deck when the cable is all out. The bitter end may then be shackled.

3. Make sure that the shackle holding the anchor to the cable has a thicker section than the chain links. It should be tightened with pliers and moused with a piece of wire but do not be tempted to rivet over the end of the pin to lock it. You can start a crack in the metal and we have seen a vessel

lost from moorings because of it.

4. Your kedge anchor will have a fathom or two of chain and a soft cable. A good knot to join them is the fisherman's bend but it should go on to a shackle somewhat bigger than the chain so that the rope does not get cut. This knot is good because two turns go through the shackle, which spreads the load, and although it is self-jamming it is easily undone. Check your soft cable where the shackle bears on it, cut off and tie again if worn or frayed, and when you have made the knot tie the loose end back onto the standing part with twine.

5. Check all the warps and if you visit quays with sharp concrete edges get some lengths of polythene tube to slip over and take the chafe in the crucial places.

THE DINGHY

1. For hull maintenance see the appropriate earlier items in the schedule.

2. Check buoyancy bags or tanks for airtightness.

3. Replace the painter if it looks stretched or worn. This applies particularly if you are in the habit of towing the tender.

4. Paint or varnish the oars but pay attention to the security of the rowlocks, that the socket chocks are not loose and the lanyards on the rowlocks not rotten.

5. You can check the inflatable for leaks when you wash it. If you use soap and water the bubbles will identify quite small leakages and the final test is to leave it inflated for a few days.

GENERAL GEAR

1. If you use gas for cooking, check for chafe and strain on the pipe through the movement of other gear. Check on all joints and especially at the stove if it is gimballed.

2. Check electric wiring in the hull and particularly any which is fixed low down in the boat as for electric bilge pumps and perhaps some engine wiring. Take one or two of the fittings apart to see the state of things. Salt air and electrical current can gum up the inside.

3. Go over all the seacocks and skin fittings inside the hull checking for tightness of the flange nuts. Grease and repack stopcock valves and glands.

4. Pump some disinfectant through the WC and later strip

it out, clean it, and reassemble with new gaskets and washers as required.

5. Note the maintenance date on fire extinguishers and act if necessary. If they are of the once only, power type, try letting one off; you could be surprised.

6. If flares and other pyrotechnics are more than two years old replace them and use the others on bonfire night at home.

7. Go over lifejackets, harnesses, etc., carefully and give them to your wife to wash in warm (not hot) fresh water. You can do the same with oilskins and sailing jackets and they will not only be cleaner but they will also lose their musty smell. Pass soft furnishings in the same direction for attention.

8. Split pins and other retaining devices should be renewed if they have been disturbed. Those up the mast are the most important and they are cheap enough to replace without question.

ENGINES

Inboard Engines

Apart from routine attention to external equipment such as filters, batteries, etc., it is difficult and perhaps unwise to generalize on what should be the extent of your work on the engine, and this applies to engines of all kinds and not just inboards. We would suggest that you follow the recommendations in the maker's instruction manual closely, and do not exceed these unless you have a particular flair and knowledge as a mechanic.

1. If the battery was not removed on laying up take it out and have it charged and serviced whilst you are fitting out. It depends upon its age, but batteries thrive on use, and if it has been standing all winter it will need a long, slow charge to bring it back into condition. Remember to keep it topped up with distilled water to just above the level of the plates.

2. Check over both high and low tension wiring in the case of petrol engines and renew any HT leads which are oil soaked or cracked.

3. For petrol motors, clean the inside of the distributor head with a petrol damped rag so that it is absolutely clean and clean the outside also. If there is spark erosion on the rotor tip and the contacts scrape clean with a penknife or the end of

a small file and clean out afterwards.

4. Examine the contact breaker points and if they have a level, matt grey appearance do not touch them but adjust the gap to that recommended. If they are pitted or the cam lift pad is badly worn, replace them with new, and remember to put a smear of grease on the cam. If the points appear satisfactory but there is bad arcing across when they open, replace the condenser.

5. Get the plugs sandblasted and reset the gaps and if the earth electrodes have burnt thin or hollow, get new plugs.

6. For petrol or diesel. Drain the oil sump (but warm up the engine first), take off the filter, and with a container under in its place, give the engine a few turns to discharge as much old oil as possible. Replace either the filter or the filter element, according to type and if the latter, clean out the filter casing.

7. On petrol units, replace or clean the air filter according to the manual and also clean out the carburettor bowl and the fuel line filter. If there are signs of excessive dirt and water emulsion, strip out the jets as well and clean these and the jet passages.

8. On diesel engines, if you have had a smoky exhaust or other signs of falling off in performance, remove the injectors and send them for servicing. The same agents will also deal with the fuel pump if it needs attention. Clean fuel filter. Clean air filters as for petrol motors.

9. On all installations drain the fuel tank to remove any water and dirt. Check the fuel lines from the tank and remember, if they are copper, these harden and become brittle with age and vibration. They should have a few turns in them when installed to relieve the stresses but if they have been untouched for a few seasons it would be a good idea to anneal them. The process is very simple and the reverse of that employed for softening ferrous metal. Remove the pipes and drain, heat to cherry red or at least until green flames are given off, and then plunge into cold water. Success will be indicated by the oxide flaking off the pipe to leave a new-looking surface. Do not get the heat near the nipples at the ends of the pipe and if you cannot heat it all at once do the process in stages.

10. If there are any plastic pipes in the system they should be

279

K

kept well away from heat since a melted fuel pipe could be catastrophic. Generally speaking, if flexibility is required it is better to use an armoured flexible pipe.

11. Drain fresh water cooling systems, flush through and refill, and check the circulating pump for output and gland leakage.

12. Examine engine holding down bolts, and couplings for tightness. If you have to do any amount of tightening up on the engine bolts, check freedom of rotation of the propeller shaft afterwards. Examine the stern gland, repack if it seems too hard packed, grease and before replacing fill the greaser cup. Examine the propeller shaft for corrosion and pitting whilst the gland is backed off.

13. Check for play in control linkages, replace any worn pins, and lubricate with grease.

14. On petrol engines with water injected exhausts, check through the system for signs of corrosion and/or leakage.

15. The mileage or hours on your engine will probably be small compared with a road or industrial unit, and therefore the requirement for further attention beyond the items given above must depend upon your knowledge of the unit, but if you think that tappet adjustment or decarbonization is necessary follow the maker's manual closely. Two stroke engines particularly tend to get heavy carbon deposits because of the fuel they burn, and it is fairly certain that if you find excessive carbon in the exhaust manifold there will be a similar deposit in the cylinder ports, and performance will be falling off.

16. Similarly, in the case of gearboxes, clutches and variable pitch systems, unless you have reason to query the function of any part, satisfactory performance should only require the attention recommended in the maker's manual, e.g. a check on the recommended clutch adjustment, oil levels, etc.

Outboard Engines

1. Most of the procedure for checking fuel and ignition systems is as that given for inboard engines and to go much further would involve major dismantlement probably calling for special tools.

2. Corrosion deposits, externally, in the water passages and

on the drive shaft are frequent causes of trouble and the answer to most of it is flushing the unit in fresh water after use, which of course is normally impossible. But it is possible to flush the motor out at the end of the season before putting it away and run a drop of oil into the cylinders (the latter a good practice for all engines on laying up), also you can clean it over with an oily rag.

3. Drive shaft corrosion can cause complete failure if it sets in on the quilldrive between the crankshaft and the drive shaft. The way to check is to take off the lower unit and withdraw the shaft. If it is OK put it back with a liberal coating of underwater grease. Check up on the water pump impellor at the same time for wear, and check that the water orifices in the lower casing and the discharge are not silted up. Recharge the lower unit with the advised lubricant on reassembly.

4. Examine the cylinder head joint for blow by and if there are tell tale signs check the tightness of the cylinder head nuts, but unless you have a torque spanner do not overdo it.

5. Check the propeller and drive pin for signs of damage. Replace the pin and get the screw serviced if there is any significant wear or distortion.

6. Check the fuel line and the steering connections to the engine and examine the attachment of the sheaves to the hull.

7. See that the fuel tanks and the battery, if one is carried, are all secured to prevent movement under way.

Inboard/Outboard Engines

1. These are mostly covered under 'inboard engines' but in addition there is a transom seal to be checked.

2. A general inspection of the outdrive casing for damage, wear in linkages, and tightness of all the attachments and other bolts.

3. Check for action on swivelling and tilting mechanisms and lubricate.

4. Examine the steering connections in the hull as well as on the engine.

chapter 17

Personal Gear

There is a great amount of so-called yachting clothing available nowadays, and most of it is very suitable for the aprés-sail gin and general wear around the club, but its life span is liable to be small if subjected to much bashing around in a boat. We do not feel it wise to discuss any particular fashion in sailing wear but rather to confine ourselves to what is serviceable aboard and reasonably tidy for going ashore. In this respect we are rather like the old member who was asked whether he thought the club ties were better in silk or terylene, and his reply was that silk was OK for holding up your trousers, but terylene was better for starting the outboard.

For those who wish to be warm and dry at sea in indifferent weather the PVC smock and trousers is probably still the best bet for protection, excepting only the overall suit, although the latter can be a hot and inconvenient garment. We are of course, talking of cruising gear and this has nothing to do with our wet-suited dinghy friends. For cockpits which are further from the sea, and with little deck work envisaged, a garment which some call a Cowes coat is, if properly designed, waterproof, warm and generally useful, and if worn with a pair of overtrousers will give reasonable protection. Most of them have a hood built into the collar.

This kind of coat is also tidy enough to wear ashore without people looking for the ring in your ear. But regrettably manufacturers today appear to think the latter use to be of more importance than its proper function and there are many coats offered which fall short of the requirement. Frequently they are made from material which is too soft to withstand snags and tears, and over-sensitive to contact with the various liquids which may be spilt in a boat. Some of them have gratuitous stitching and embellishment, all of which is a potential entry for water. Another feature not to be encouraged is the incorporation of dummy quilting inside which holds, not a loose synthetic down fill, but a sheet of foam plastic bath mat material. The difference is significant for the energetic wearer, for with the foam plastic lining he will sweat like a pig and become rather more wet inside than outside.

Slit pockets, fastened with a Velcro strip are desirable as they are less likely to take in water and the Velcro gives an automatic closure. A thing which even good coats sometimes lack is an inside breast pocket. One of these with a button fastening is really useful when going ashore with passport, travellers' cheques, etc., because frequently the only other garment with pockets which is being worn are one's trousers, the hip pockets of which are not suitable for carrying valuable documents or wallets.

Lightweight, proofed nylon overtrousers are useful for combating spray, they will also keep out the wind and they will pack small enough to go into your pocket, but they are not completely waterproof. If you sit in any water it will come through pretty quickly. PVC trousers are waterproof but not so amenable to being thrust into a pocket.

Footwear is a problem in a small boat which is inclined to be wet. One never knows whether to acknowledge defeat with a pair of deck shoes or try to keep dry with a pair of short sea boots. Short boots are generally handy and much more comfortable than the long ones. Be liberal about size and get a pair of oversocks to go with them. The natural tendency is to tuck one's trouser ends into the boots but if it is really wet and you are wearing overtrousers you will see that it is best that they should cover the boots. It is in any case wise to have more than one change of footwear aboard so that you can be shod according to conditions. The espadrille type of deck shoe is every bit as useful as those with laces and in good weather they are sensible wear in or out of the water or shopping along the quay.

Caps there are aplenty, but if you wear one and wish to

look any further than the traditional pattern, the Chichester baseball variety is very practical aboard, particularly for those who do not wear sunglasses, the long peak being a great help in brilliant weather.

So far we have only discussed the outermost garments. We do not intend to dig too far below, feeling that that is your business, but we suggest that trousers with a good percentage of synthetic yarn are practical, because if they get wet they dry very quickly, and furthermore, for the discerning, they keep their crease. Any sea-going wardrobe must include a number of sweaters both thick and thin, and a couple of them should be of water resistant wool and of considerable weight. There is not much to be said about them except that it would be nice if the sleeves at the wrist clung a bit more closely. After only short wear one frequently has a bell-bottom sleeve up which the wind can whistle unimpeded.

In regard to underclothes, many a staunch cruising man depends upon his longjohns, and string vests are very popular but it really depends upon what you are accustomed to wearing, with the caution that you always need more at sea. A yachting editor (whom we hope we may still call a friend) was presented with a pair of mens stretch tights of winter weight, a dark secret he revealed to us whilst above the North Sea on our way to Sweden. It was November but we will not suggest that he was seeking some moral advantage. Anyway, the stretch tights kept on stretching, which caused a good deal of marionette-like movement and eventually, we presumed, a considerable roll of material under his armpits. In consequence we are not sure whether we should recommend these garments to you.

The thing is, whatever you wear you must take enough to give you a couple of changes otherwise you may be very uncomfortable.

For the night, a sleeping bag is to be preferred above sundry blankets, both the cover and the down filling can be of natural or synthetic material but the latter has the advantage of quicker drying if it gets wet. Loose sheet bag linings can be made up to suit.

The boat you sail in may be very well equipped, but if you are invited to crew in another boat it is advisable to take a few small things, the lack of which at the vital time can be frustrating. A 'housewife' is a useful addition to your bag, also a knife, a shackle key and a bottle opener, some barley sugar, chocolate, and a supply of glucose tablets will take up little room, and are well worth having to fall back upon.

You might wish to have your own binoculars. If you need to buy a pair the desirable specification for sea glasses is 7 × 50 and it is better if they are not centre focussing. Separate eye piece focussing is best because the casing can then be made watertight. Glasses are available now with a built-in compass which may be read whilst focussing on an object so giving an immediate bearing. A good pair of binoculars can be a valuable aid but it is remarkable what poor performance many people accept, one can frequently see better with the naked eye. Unless a really good pair can be afforded it is probably best to acquire reconditioned Service glasses.

In the matter of baggage we find it rather difficult to make a recommendation, except that you should avoid suitcases and any other rigid, hard-cornered receptacles. The situation is eased if the boat has adequate lockers for all crew members. Otherwise it is difficult to find a satisfactory holdall, since after the first rummage therein everything is in one glorious tangle and small items take some finding. A soft Gladstone bag or holdall with lots of pockets inside would be a good idea but so far we have not met one. Similarly, toilet bags with more pockets in them would be an improvement. The traditional kitbag is easy to carry and stow but unless you wish to live rough we would not recommend it as the ideal boat bag.

Personal buoyancy equipment gives a wide choice of lifejackets and buoyancy aids, but it is necessary to make the distinction that whereas buoyancy aids (to SBBNF 1971 standard) are satisfactory for conditions which may result in only a short immersion, the conditions resulting from foundering or being lost overside offshore require a lifejacket to BS 3595. 1969. The further question is: When is it sensible to wear one? A reasonable answer seems to be that children should always wear a lifejacket when leaving the shore, and adults should be prepared to put one on whenever circumstances promote even a remote possibility of use, e.g., if

Fig. 17.1 Howarth waterproof smock and safety harness. Note drain holes in smock pockets and two carbine hooks on harness so that one is always attached whilst the other is being moved to a new position.

leaving the cockpit at sea to work on deck, even in fine weather (a safety harness (Fig. 17.1.) would be an additional requirement in bad conditions). At all times when visibility is poor or there is a rising sea, and, for single handed sailors, always when out of the cabin, plus a harness for deck work.

The required amount of buoyancy can be achieved with either a light vest or waistcoat which is inflatable via a small CO_2 cartridge or by mouth, or both methods (Fig. 17.2.). The buoyancy may be worn separately or built into a garment such as a watch coat or a waterproof jacket. The thing is to choose something in which one feels sufficiently comfortable so as not to want to be rid of it at the first opportunity.

Some buoyancy aids have a permanently buoyant filling and do not necessarily depend upon inflation and some require no inflation at all (Fig. 17.3.). This kind of buoyancy is probably the best equipment for children since it leaves nothing to chance, but it is also important to ensure that the

Fig. 17.2   Beaufort Mk 10 lifevest with CO_2 inflation.

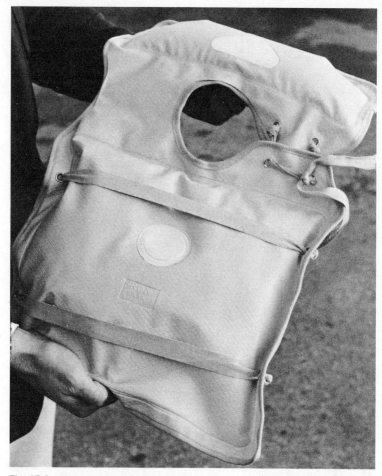

Fig. 17.3   Holtwear Toddler's buoyancy aid.

method of fastening the jacket is strong enough to enable the child to be lifted from the water if necessary by its means.

More freedom aboard can be given to children if they are equipped as suggested, and with a safety harness and a little thought as to its anchorage they can also range on deck without anxiety.

chapter 18

Weather, Wind and Waves

Most articles about weather in boating magazines seem to fall
into two categories, weather lore or discussions of skies and
clouds. Weather lore is normally based on solid fact and
centuries of observation while photography only shows what
we can see with our own eyes. Here we hope to explain
where our weather comes from and what happens in the
atmosphere to cause it to change.

To avoid delving too far into the physics of the matter the
reader will have to accept certain statements without
explanation.

(i) Warm air rises causing surface pressure to fall, the air
pressure falling with increased height, but slowly.

(ii) Cold air descends causing surface pressure to rise, the air
pressure falling with increased height, but more rapidly than
in warm air.

(iii) Air moves from high pressure to low pressure.

(iv) All air contains water vapour.

When talking in terms of air pressure or temperature it is
purely relative. Warm air is warm compared with its cooler
neighbour, similarly, high pressure air is high compared with
air of lower pressure adjacent to it.

On a world wide scale the air over the Equator is subjected
to continual surface heating. The warmed air rises into the
upper atmosphere, creating a low pressure belt around the
Equator, and flows north. Cold air over the pole descends,
creating high pressure, and flows south (we are only considering the northern hemisphere). Under these circumstances we
are left with a continual northerly wind.

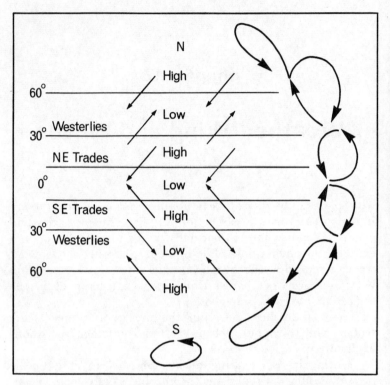

Fig. 18.1 The effect of high and low pressure belts around the earth, which give rise to well defined areas of constant winds like the Trades and the Westerlies.

The rotation of the earth effects the air mass by applying the Geostrophic Force, which deflects all bodies to the right. As the upper warm air from the Equator moves north it is deflected east causing a pile up of air in the region of 30° north, creating a high pressure belt. Air in this high pressure belt moves south-west into the low pressure area around the Equator, where it re-circulates, and north-west where it interacts with the colder polar air. Thus we have permanent areas of pressure giving rise to well defined areas of constant winds, i.e. Trade Winds, Westerlies, etc. The only variation to this wind pattern is seasonal, as the sun moves north and south of the Equator (Fig. 18.1.).

This ideal wind pattern is upset by mountain ranges and

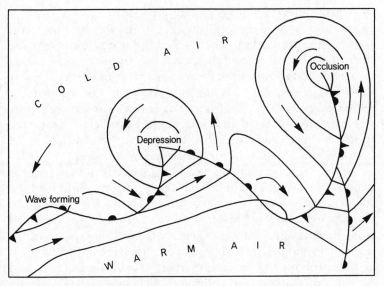

Fig. 18.2 Typical Polar Front with life cycle of warm front depression.

unequal heating over oceans and land masses. An example of this is the intense heating over northern India causing a low pressure area in a high pressure belt, giving rise to the monsoons. In winter rapid cooling of the land mass of Siberia causes a high pressure area in a low pressure belt, the resulting air flow subjecting the British Isles occasionally to bitterly cold easterly winds.

We live in temperate latitudes of low pressure. High pressure over the North Pole sends cold air south, while high pressure over the Tropics sends warm air north. Somewhere over the Atlantic Ocean these two air masses meet to form the polar front. The transition from warm to cold air is usually spread over several miles, but is sufficiently abrupt to be clearly noticeable.

The polar front does not extend vertically upwards from the surface due to the earth's rotation and the fact that the warm air is less dense than the cold air and tends to rise over its neighbour.

The conflicting warm and cold air masses at the front are continually fighting for supremacy, forming waves. Eventually a pronounced wave forms (Fig. 18.2.). As the wave moves eastwards along the front, cold air ahead of the front is constantly being replaced by air from within the front, causing pressure to fall. The further the warm air penetrates the front the greater the fall of pressure, until the penetration is so deep that a depression forms (low). At this point the polar front is renamed. The leading edge becomes the warm front, the trailing edge the cold front. The surface wind travels anti-clockwise around the depression roughly parallel to the isobars (lines of equal pressure). The greater the pressure difference between warm and cold air the stronger the wind.

As the depression moves steadily eastwards the warm air is constantly trying to climb over the cold air, while cold air following the front is trying to undercut the warm air, consequently, the warm air is forced upwards and the cold front catches up with the warm front, forming an occluded front or occlusion. An occlusion is the last stage in the life cycle of a depression. As more and more warm air is lifted and cooled the temperature difference between the two slowly disappears and pressure differences equal out as the depression fills up.

There is a nearly permanent area of high pressure (anti-cyclone) over the Azores which occasionally spreads north, sometimes breaking free from the main area and drifting to form a ridge of high pressure bringing dry, settled weather. As already mentioned high pressure over Siberia can also spread westwards over the British Isles bringing cold, clear weather in winter.

When there is an established high pressure area over the country the depressions, which still form over the Atlantic, are deflected around the British Isles, giving dry weather in one half of the country while it is wet and windy in the other.

High pressure areas are the exception rather than the rule, thus it is not unusual for at least one depression to cross the country each day.

CLOUDS

All air contains a certain amount of water vapour, the maximum amount depending on the air temperature. An amount of water easily absorbed at high temperature may be enough to saturate the same volume of air at a lower temperature. If the air is reduced to this temperature the water vapour will condense out to form water droplets. When air rises it expands and its temperature drops, if it rises until the temperature drops below the saturation point then clouds, which consist of water droplets, will form.

There are three basic cloud formations: Stratiform (Stratus), cloud which forms in flat layers (Fig. 18.3.); Cumiliform (Cumulus), which forms in heaps (Fig. 18.4); Cirriform (Cirrus), layers of ice crystals at high altitude (Fig. 18.5.).

Clouds form in one of five ways: convection, orographic, turbulent, frontal and depression.

Convection clouds are formed by surface heating. The heated air rises in bubbles, is cooled by the surrounding cooler, more dense air and stops rising (Fig. 18.6.). When convection first begins, in the early morning, the bubbles are small, but as heating increases the bubbles rise higher. Eventually they reach a point where the surrounding air is sufficiently cool to cause saturation to occur, resulting in

Fig. 18.3 One of the three basic cloud formations (Stratiform, Cumiliform and Cirriform). This is Stratiform—Stratocumulus with some Stratus visible below.

Fig. 18.4 Cumiliform—Cumulus.

Fig. 18.5 Cirriform—Cirrus.

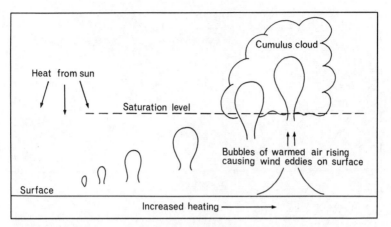

Fig. 18.6 Diagrammatic example of convection cloud formation.

Cumulus clouds. The size of the cloud depends on the temperature of the surrounding air mass. When the clouds are forming and building the edge is clean and sharp, as it starts to decay it takes on a ragged appearance. Cumulus builds to its maximum during the heat of the day, early afternoon. After this peak they start to decay and the dew will start to fall, but not noticeably. A thing to remember when considering painting.

Orographic cloud is formed when air is forced to rise over surface obstructions, i.e., cliffs, hills or mountains. The size of the cloud is dependent upon the height of the obstruction and the wind speed. The most usual type of cloud is Stratiform, covering the hilltop and drifting downwind.

Turbulent cloud is formed by friction between the earth's surface and the atmosphere immediately above (the first 2000ft). The friction causes the air to mix until the distribution of water vapour is almost uniform. If this brings the air to the saturation point then clouds will form. Turbulent cloud normally only forms in a moist airstream, its height and thickness depending on the wind speed and type of surface.

Frontal cloud as its name implies occurs at a warm front. A warm air mass is forced to rise over the cold air mass it is following, the whole mass being lifted as opposed to just the lower levels. At very high altitudes it is always cold with very

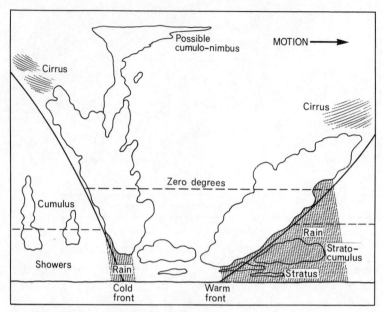

Fig. 18.7   The formation of a frontal depression.

little water vapour, as it is cooled even more thin Cirrus clouds form, always an early warning of the approach of a warm front. As the front approaches, closer cloud at medium and lower levels appears and as the prevailing south-westerly wind is always moist this cloud is thick, wet and layered. At the actual front low Stratus appears, sometimes extending down to the surface (Fig. 18.7.).

On average, a warm front is 200 miles deep travelling at 25 knots, thus the average passage time is in the order of eight hours. This time is prolonged if the front decides to become stationary or is caught up by a succeeding front, as when it meets high pressure from the east. Depending on the weather immediately prior to the front, surface heating can cause convection clouds to form amongst the frontal cloud.

Depression cloud occurs at the centre of an occlusion as the mass of warm air is lifted bodily, cooled below saturation point and condenses out as cloud, usually Stratus and Cumulus (Stratocumulus).

PRECIPITATION

Precipitation is any moisture falling from the atmosphere, the most common being rain.

Rain consists of water droplets which have amalgamated while moving in a column of warm, rising air. Eventually, the droplets become too heavy to be supported by the rising air and fall from the bottom of the cloud as rain.

Drizzle is water vapour or droplets as in a cloud and may be considered as a cloud on the surface.

Snow is formed by water vapour condensing at sub-zero temperatures. The resulting ice crystals coalesce to form snow flakes, which eventually become too heavy to be supported by the rising air and fall to the surface as snow.

Hail only falls from thunder clouds (Cumulonimbus), where intense air currents carry water droplets into sub-zero temperatures until it is disturbed (supercooled) when it immediately freezes to form ice crystals. These crystals then fall into warm air, melt and are lifted again where it freezes and by collision with other drops of super cooled water increases in size. Continual rising and falling causes more and more water to adhere to the stone until it becomes too heavy and falls from the cloud. If a hailstone is cut open it has the appearance of an onion with alternate rings of grey and white ice.

FOG

There are only two types of fog, advection and radiation.

Advection fog is formed in a similar way to turbulent cloud. When warm, moist air is blown over a cool surface the air is gradually cooled to below the saturation level. Turbulence will cause this saturated air to lift and form low Stratus. Continued cooling will cause the base to lower until it reaches the surface. This is the formation of all coastal and sea fog.

Radiation fog forms over land on clear windless nights. The earth radiates its heat into space very quickly. The air near the surface will also cool rapidly eventually reaching saturation point and the water vapour condenses out, initially as dew, but as cooling continues, as fog. In winter, with the air temperature below zero, the dew freezes forming frost.

Radiation fog forms first in low lying areas as the cooling air descends into valleys and hollows. It also forms very rapidly near rivers and marshy ground where evaporation will cause the moisture content to be high.

Both types of fog are normally dispersed by surface heating or wind, although cold and thick fog may persist and require a strong wind to disperse it.

THUNDERSTORMS

Thunderstorms (Cumulonimbus) start as Cumulus cloud, ascend into the atmosphere until reaching an inversion (temperature increase with height instead of decreasing), where it continues to ascend, forming the characteristic anvil top as it is blown downwind. In spring and summer they are not uncommon in this country, but we certainly don't get our share. Every day there are about 45,000 thunderstorms, 1,750 in existence at any one time, mainly in the Tropics. Lightning flashes occur at the rate of one hundred per second although only twenty-five per cent of these reach the surface, the remainder taking place within the cloud.

ICING

Icing only really concerns the intrepid all weather sailor. The air must contain moisture but it need not be freezing. A strong dry wind, several degrees above freezing, blowing on a wet sail will cause the sail to freeze due to the latent heat of evaporation. This reduction in temperature due to wind speed is termed the 'chill factor' and is directly proportional to the wind speed; it is applicable at all temperatures.

Frost will form on rigging, superstructure, etc., as described earlier.

A supercooled water droplet striking something solid will freeze, but only part of the drop freezes initially, the remainder is warmed by the latent heat of crystallization, but as the heat is conducted away by the sub-zero surface the remaining free water freezes immediately after. On a rigging stay ice will build up on the edge into wind and stream backwards forming a shape similar to an aircraft wing section.

The two types of icing which will effect the sailor are rime ice and rain ice.

Rime Ice is formed when small supercooled cloud water droplets (freezing fog), meet a freezing surface. They will adhere to anything solid, but as there is little free water after the initial freezing the ice layer will consist of many small frozen water droplets with much air trapped between them, giving a milky appearance. Larger water droplets, due to the amount of free water filling the air spaces before complete freezing, will form thick, clear ice.

Rain ice is not so common. Rain falling from a non-freezing cloud layer into freezing air below becomes supercooled and freezes on impact. A rain droplet is much larger than the largest cloud water droplet, thus the ice formed is clear with no air spaces. The rate of ice build up can be very great and quite sudden.

If air and sea temperatures are sufficiently low salt spray will also become supercooled and freeze on impact, but will be cloudy in appearance due to the presence of salt.

Any ice forming on a vessel's top hamper can be dangerous since the increased weight above the water line will cause instability as the centre of gravity rises above the normal.

WEATHER PATTERNS

Our weather is governed by one of five air masses when it is not under the influence of depressions. The predominant one is the Tropical Maritime from the south-west. After its long passage over the ocean it is always warm and moist, bringing with it drizzle, low cloud and sea fog on coasts. Generally 'muggy'.

Also from the south-west comes the Returning Polar Maritime giving a very varied weather pattern, low cloud over coasts but clearing inland to give sunny periods and showers and possibly thunderstorms.

From the south-east comes the Tropical Continental, mainly in summer, bringing hot, dry weather with clear skies. After several days thunderstorms are likely to develop during the later afternoon and evening.

The Polar Continental from the north-east gives variable

cloud amounts, sea fog on eastern coasts and snow showers in winter, but rather warm in summer. Should this air stream come from the east it will have travelled less distance over the sea and therefore be somewhat drier, giving dry, sunny, warm and hazy conditions in summer and dry, cold, hazy conditions in winter with moderate to severe frosts at night, occasionally persisting all day.

Air from the north-west, Polar Maritime, is normally unstable leading to showers and thunderstorms during the day and clearing skies at night. The clear skies cause a heavy dew in summer and fog and frost in winter.

INTERPRETATION

The Meteorology Office has access to literally hundreds of 'actual' weather reports. From these reports the Meteorologist compiles his chart and using his professional skill, issues a forecast.

As an isolated observer you cannot hope to match this, but given access to his chart, pictorially on the television or daily press or verbally through the shipping forecasts, you can make your own observations and 'fix' yourself in the weather pattern.

When the wind is from about NNW through E to SSE the expected weather will be as stated earlier for the Tropical Continental, Polar Continental and Polar Maritime. It is only when the prevailing wind from either side of SW starts to blow that a sharp lookout must be kept for the depression.

Consider a depression travelling steadily eastwards across the Atlantic Ocean at 25 knots. Weather reports from aircraft, shipping and satellites indicate the speed and direction are remaining constant. On this basis the forecaster makes his predictions, only to find at the last moment with little or no warning, the front has become stationary, accelerated or changed direction. The basic forecast will be correct, but the timing and placing will be wrong.

Reference to the weather chart will show what is expected to happen in the air mass around us. Thus the observer will be able to make his own short term forecast by studying the sky, wind and barometer.

WIND

Caution should be exercised when assessing the wind direction
on the surface since it can be effected locally by trees, build-
ings, etc., and on a larger scale by hills, mountains, cliffs and
by funnelling in a valley or up a river estuary. Reference to
cloud movement is more accurate but even this can be ten or
twenty degrees in error. Don't confuse the overall air movement with the normal day/night breezes blowing from sea to
land during the day and vice versa at night.

PRESSURE

A barometer is a must for forecasting, but it must be accurately
calibrated and checked periodically. The sailor will normally
be at sea level but if you are cruising inland the barometer
will give artificially high readings as you climb a flight of
locks. One millibar or 00·03in representing thirty feet. The
arbitary change from high to low pressure occurs at 1013·2
millibars; 29·92in of mercury.

Cross references between your barometer and the forecast
chart with its Isobars (lines of equal pressure), will locate you
in the weather pattern and with your assessment of wind speed
and direction as indicated above, your weather position should
be fairly accurate.

Most barometers seem to be calibrated in inches whereas
weather forecast information is mainly in millibars, for this
reason a conversion chart is given below.

mb	0	1	2	3	4	5	6	7	8	9
960	28·35	28·38	28·41	28·44	28·47	28·50	28·53	28·56	28·58	28·61
970	28·64	28·67	28·70	28·73	28·76	28·79	28·82	28·85	28·88	28·91
980	28·94	28·97	29·00	29·03	29·06	29·09	29·12	29·15	29·18	29·20
990	29·23	29·26	29·29	29·32	29·35	29·38	29·41	29·44	29·47	29·50
1000	29·53	29·56	29·59	29·62	29·65	29·68	29·71	29·74	29·77	29·80
1010	29·83	29·86	29·89	29·91	29·94	29·97	30·00	30·03	30·06	30·09
1020	30·12	30·15	30·18	30·21	30·24	30·27	30·30	30·33	30·36	30·39
1030	30·42	30·45	30·47	30·50	30·53	30·56	30·59	30·62	30·65	30·68

SKY

Estimation of the exact time of arrival of a front is very
difficult as variations in land masses and geographical features
control the speed of the front. Observation of the sky however
enables the observer to make his own estimation of the
situation. The classic layer of high thin cloud appearing on

the horizon to be followed by medium level layered cloud announcing the pending arrival of low cloud and rain. The wind falling to calm and the barometer holding steady will indicate that you are very near the centre of the depression. An increase in wind strength, or a definite rapid change in wind direction with an associated rise on the barometer will herald the passing of the front. The sky should become lighter from the West and bring clearer showery weather. At least until the next depression appears on the scene.

Close monitoring of barometer and wind will tell you what should be happening to the weather. The sky will tell you what is actually happening. Similarly the sky and wind will establish the type of air stream affecting you but the barometer will give an early indication when change is on the way.

Part 2

TIDES AND TIDAL CURRENTS

Supposing that you have got your weather sorted out the next major consideration for the small boat man, whose boat speed is reckoned in knots rather than tens of knots, is contemplation of the tidal situations that he will encounter on the voyage.

Very briefly, there are two tide identifications, Springs and Neaps. Spring tides occur when the moon is full and also when it is new, thus they have approximately a two week interval and at midpoint during these periods of waxing and waning the neap tides occur so that they also have a two week interval. Spring tides have the greatest range and they produce the very high High Water and the very low Low Water, whereas with neap tides the maxima are reduced and so we get only modest HW and LW.

The movement from springs to neaps and vice versa is gradual so that from the top of springs the HW will decrease in height with each tide and from neaps it will increase on each tide until it gets up to the highest spring tide for that cycle. There is no consistency in exact measurement between the increments or between the final heights of one cycle and another, and hence it is necessary to consult a tide table such as in Reed's Almanac which predicts the tides over a twelve month period.

Predicted times and heights are popularly given for Dover and London and thereafter for most ports. For those places too small to warrant publication of tidal information except locally, a time difference is given on the nearest major port. These time differences are constant so we may give the difference of the major ports on Dover also.

If the time taken for the tide to ebb and flow is approximately the same for springs and neaps then something must happen to accommodate the much larger volume of water which manifests itself with a spring tide. The variable is the speed at which the body of water moves and so we may expect spring tides to flow more strongly than neaps. Thus if on a tidal atlas the direction of the current is arrowed and marked $1-1\frac{1}{2}$ we can infer that the higher speed of $1\frac{1}{2}$ knots may be expected during spring tides but of course the speed will be a maximum and in fact the actual speed will vary according to the time in relation to HW and LW in that area. As an approximation the tidal stream is generally at its strongest midway between the times of HW and LW, that is, midway between the slack water which occurs on the turns of the tide.

The speed of most tidal streams around the UK are in a range up to about 3 knots, but there are places locally where this is almost doubled and it is clear that if your vessel is good for 6 knots and you meet a 5 knot current and a headwind you will not get very far. Hence it is of the utmost importance that in planning a voyage the tides are 'worked' so that you may add their speed to yours instead of subtracting it. In a sailing vessel particularly, the tidal currents are every bit as important as the wind. For those without an adequate auxiliary engine perhaps even more so, because without the power of your sails the tide may carry you into difficult situations.

If one talks to owners who have attempted the Channel for the first time without spectacular success as to ETA and landfall, it is nearly always the case that they have given insufficient attention to time and tide. No-one may expect the wind to hold good for him in any particular direction but there is a certainty about the tide which calls for complete acknowledgement. So when courses are laid they should be made with reservations and an awareness of what is possible supposing failure of the wind to behave as we would like it, or a sudden seediness in the engine department which causes us to be at point X two hours later than intended.

The alternatives should be known supposing the immediate objective becomes impossible, and by bearing in mind the alternative strategems and safe courses at the planning stage we are less likely to be caught out.

An example which illustrates the point is a small sailing vessel, capable of about 5 knots in still water with its auxiliary, on a crossing from the North Foreland to Calais. On such a course the final approach to this port is preferably made from the west so that, for instance, the first landfall may be a few miles off Cap Blanc Nez which is west of Calais. The tide runs along the coast very strongly here, and in a vessel such as the above it is useless to combat it supposing the wind falls light or is adverse. Hence it is important to be off the coast at the right time for the east-going tide. If you are sufficiently delayed and you find the tidal current has reversed its course you should be aware of the possibilities, which, briefly described, may be: Plod on for several hours on your intended course with very little movement over the ground until the current eases; anchor (consult the chart for prohibited areas); alter course and go with the tide to Boulogne; go home.

Obviously the weather will do much to influence your decision, but if you are alert to the possibilities in advance you will be better armed to cope.

Inshore tidal streams tend to follow shorelines and in consequence they will bend their direction into bays rather than rush straight by, as may be inferred by the small scale tidal atlas. This should be taken into account when cruising close in.

Finally, in regard to chart sounding. These are not wholly reliable in shoal areas and harbour entrances on shallow coasts and the less the depth given the more the likely percentage of error. The reason is that on low shores the sands move about and if you have an extra 2ft of sand or mud on a chart sounding of 1 fathom, then at LW springs you will have only 4ft of water, a discrepancy of 33 per cent. For this reason ports which have tricky entrances at LW should be approached with the aid of the relevant Admiralty Pilot as well as the chart.

WAVES

These are things we could really do without, but since they are a product of the wind, which sailing types require for progress, it is doubtful whether all would approve of their abolition. Waves are raised by the wind and grow in size not only with increasing wind strength but also with the duration of the wind and the distance they have travelled. Around the coast their steepness is also affected by the depth of the water and tidal currents.

Because wave height depends considerably upon fetch (the distance it has travelled), waves of great height are not usual in narrow seas, but with certain slants of the wind very long fetches are possible for some waves which spend themselves on our coasts. The North Sea gives an example of this: East Anglia and the North Kent coast may not experience waves which have travelled further than the width of the North Sea for much of the time, but if the wind direction is such as to bring it straight down the funnel between the Norwegian and the Scottish coasts, the seas can have a fetch all the way from the Arctic, a distance of some thousands rather than hundreds of miles, the effect of which will be to raise the height of the waves significantly without any increase in wind strength. Thus whereas a recorded wave height of 30ft may be the expected maximum in the North Sea in winter, in October 1970 a wave of over 70ft was recorded. No doubt it had travelled a long way to reach such proportions.

The amateur boat owner will not be concerned in the ordinary course of events with weather of that kind, but from time to time he will be impressed by the effects achieved by winds and waves of lesser majesty. As noted earlier, for a given wind strength, the seas encountered in a shoal area or estuary will be shorter and steeper and in any weight of wind that much more vicious.

For a sailing vessel, the question of optimum speed in rough (but not dangerous) conditions barely arises because she will not travel fast enough to strike the seas with great force on any point of sailing (although a heavy sea might strike her occasionally), also the sails will stabilize the vessel. A motor vessel however, may do herself an injury through being driven too hard in conditions which although not exceptional are sufficiently strenuous to require discretion. Some hulls are much more capable than others and it is hardly possible to offer advice in regard to speed and circumstance, but experience tends to show that apart from the overall need for caution with the throttles, there is also room for experiment. The most comfortable speed will proclaim itself to the helmsman, and it will not necessarily be the slowest, since there are so many variables which have an influence, e.g., the heading, the size of the boat, wave length and so on.

Some rough water is man-made through the incidence of piers and other disturbing elements at harbour entrances which can also give rise to sand bars and hence more broken water. The effect due to wind and current can sometimes be much more dramatic than circumstances appear to warrant, and although it is not recommended that any such situation be treated lightly, in any reasonable sailing weather it is mainly a question of knowing what depth of water there is and the strength of the wind, preferably factual rather than estimated.

Onshore and offshore winds and the seas they bring are always misleading in so far as conditions further out are concerned. If there is much weight in the wind you may be sure that you are experiencing the worst of the former whilst surveying the seas from the harbour head, but you will learn very little about the latter from such a position, and the situation calls for caution, forecasts, and perhaps some local advice.

chapter 19

Legal and General

LAW FOR SMALL BOATS

When a motor vehicle is taken on a public road it must conform to 'construction and use' regulations, be licensed and insured, and be driven only by a person who holds a licence to drive. Basically, none of these obligations fall on the 'pleasure yacht' (the phrase used in the Merchant Shipping Act 1894 to cover private vessels which are not used for a commercial purpose).

The present regulations as to minimum safety requirements are set out in the Merchant Shipping (Lifesaving Appliances) Rules 1965 but they apply only to pleasure yachts 45ft long and over. Owners of such vessels should peruse the regulations carefully for they refer to minimum numbers of approved type lifebuoys and liferafts, distress signals, etc.

Registration

There is no national system of compulsory registration for all pleasure yachts, as there is for all motor vehicles, but there are many compulsory local systems applied by conservancy and harbour authorities. For example, the Thames Conservancy has the authority to impose local registration and local enforcement of minimum standards referring, e.g., to sanitary control and fire precautions, will be derived from the Private Acts of Parliament which give the authority its statutory powers.

Registration as a 'British Ship' is no doubt national registration of a sort. If a sea-going vessel (not for example a

307

houseboat) is owned by a British person it is a 'British ship' but whether it must become a Registered British ship depends on its size and use. If it does not exceed 15 net registered tons and is used solely on the coasts and rivers of the UK or Eire it need not be registered. Thus, yachts which make foreign cruises, even if under 15 tons, should in law be registered. Registration of small boats is cumbersome and expensive and very many of them remain unregistered, but registration does provide convenient evidence of title. On the question of title, if the vessel is on charter, the charter agreement should be carried, for this helps to explain, especially abroad, why the Certificate of Registry is in the name of another person. Only a registered yacht can secure an Admiralty Warrant to fly a special ensign. Harbour dues, light dues, etc., are usually charged according to net registered tonnage and this gives a more realistic result than the usual alternative, Thames Measurement tonnage, or an estimate.

There is no penalty in the nature of a fine for failure to register when you ought to. The consequences of failure would be that the owner would be liable for the duties, liabilities, etc., imposed on British ships but would not get the benefits of his British ownership and, apparently, there is power to compel registration by detention of a vessel.

Application for registration can be made to the Registrar at any of the 119 approved registry ports in the British Isles. Details are given in a booklet published by the RYA. If a yacht is issued with signal letters—the 'Ship's Numbers' (being four of the International Code Flags flown in a hoist) these are endorsed on the Certificate of Registry and her radio call signals are identical with her visual signal letters. Notice of change of ownership or of loss must be given to the Registrar as must notice of changes of engine, rig, tonnage, etc.

Insurance
The folly of being uninsured hardly needs stating but insurance is not obligatory for private yachts. The insurance policy for a yacht need not be of any standard form. Many underwriters use their own form of Yacht or Motor Boat or Dinghy policy but, for larger vessels, it is common to use the standard form of Marine Insurance Policy which was adapted to suit

yachts by the incorporation of Institute Yacht Clauses in 1926. There are certain additional Clauses which can be incorporated by negotiation, such as the 'Institute Speed-boat Clauses' (if the vessel's designed speed exceeds 17 knots) and 'Permission to Charter Clauses'. Cruising limits are set out in every policy and these should be borne in mind when planning a voyage. Thus, a dinghy policy is probably restricted to 'inland and coastal waters of the UK' but a large dinghy may cross to France or be trailed abroad.

Dinghy policies usually cover transit risks when a boat is taken by trailer, but loss or damage to the trailer (and risk of theft is appreciable) may need special negotiation. It may be cheaper to arrange this with the car insurance company.

Gear left lying about on hards or in dinghy parks is often stolen, but pilferage of such gear is not usually covered because cover is restricted (as with the Institute Yacht Clauses also) to forceable entry, e.g., into a locked store. A locked cabin may be easily forced but, if you did not have it locked, your subsequent claim under 'forceable entry' may be queried.

If an incident occurs which is liable to cause a claim on your insurance, inform your insurers as soon as possible, and preferably *before* any repairs or replacements are put in hand.

Limitation of Liability

The principle of limiting liability for damage caused by sea collision was designed to save ship owners from the full consequences of the carelessness of their masters or crew. If an owner can prove that an accident was caused 'without his fault or privity', i.e., personal, blameworthy conduct by him, he may limit his liability to pay to maximum figures based on the net registered tonnage of his ship multiplied by a sum internationally agreed in gold francs. This is now about £28 ($68) per ton for property damage and about £86 ($210) per ton in the case of personal injury and death.

Even if the owner be on board as master, and the actual negligence be caused by his crew he could usually hope to prove that this was without his fault or privity.

Maximum liability may therefore be very low. A six ton yacht, for example, may do great damage but the maximum liability for the owner remains at about £28 ($68) × 6.

In recent years the principle of limiting liability was extended to skippers and crews in addition to owners but, until a High Court case in 1967, it was doubtful whether limitation of liability could apply to a negligent owner who was also a skipper, the usual position with small boats. This case decided that he could and today, therefore, the only situation in which an owner who is not also skipper may not limit liability would appear to be where he is personally at fault. For example, if he lent his yacht to a friend and in some way it caused damage through being in an unsuitable condition.

In cases of dispute the right to limit has to be claimed in court and so the expense of obtaining a 'Limiting Decree', together with the presence of 'knock for knock' arrangements among insurers, tends to make for the settlement of small claims in full. The uninsured owner has, however, a remarkable degree of immunity and his uninsured victim may suffer heavily if limitation is claimed against him.

A craft need not be registered as a British Ship to apply for limitation but, if not registered, arrangements would have to be made to get it officially measured.

Fortunately for victims of damage involving injury or death, a 'platform' tonnage of 300 tons is applied to even the smallest vessel so liability in these cases cannot be limited below about £26,000 ($50,000).

Limitation applies to craft even when racing, a fact made clear by the RYA's prescription to rule 72(4) of the IYRU Rules.

Rules of the Road
The 'rules of the road' are the International Regulations for Prevention of Collision at Sea, and they apply on the 'high seas and all waters connected therewith navigable by sea going vessels' unless there are local rules to the contrary. A great number of our rivers have local rules and, in lakes, under the Countryside Act 1967, the local authority may impose special navigation rules. Local enquiries should always be made. It is wrong to assume that the International Regulations give priority to sail in all circumstances. In

narrow channels (and the Courts have defined 'narrow' liberally enough to include areas like the Solent, Southampton Water, river estuaries, and Cherbourg Harbour entrance) this is not so and also, in such waters, powered vessels under 65ft long must now give priority to larger vessels. Even on the high seas 'special circumstances including the limitation of the craft involved may render necessary a departure' from the general rules 'to avoid immediate danger'.

Navigation Rights

The right to navigate and anchor over all tidal water does not include a right to ground or rest on the foreshore. Someone will own the foreshore, probably a local authority on long lease from the Crown, and grounding say, to scrub a yacht, involves technical trespass. This legal position is important when people assert a right to dig in moorings on foreshore, possibly beyond any harbour jurisdiction. There is no legal right to do this without permission.

A local authority, by the Public Health Act 1961, can impose bylaws up to 1000 yards from LWM–OST to control speeds, engines noise, etc., of pleasure boats and the navigation 'without due care' provisions in such bylaws are probably the first extension of 'Road Traffic Law' to the coastal sea.

Navigation rights in inland waters usually derive from statute or long usage. They therefore arise in the same legal way as do rights of passage over land. In fact, many small rivers are private. A navigation right does not give a right to go ashore, moor, or tow along the banks, or fish.

Salvage

Many people are uneasily doubtful about salvage. Salvage is any service which helps to save a vessel or its gear or people on it, when in real danger in tidal water if the service is voluntary and not in performance of an official duty. Thus, lifeboatmen who claim salvage will be doing so as private persons who are, for this purpose, borrowing the lifeboat.

Property salvage may give entitlement to a salvage award but, as the principle is 'no cure, no pay', some property must be saved. If only people are rescued, salvage is not claimable.

Size of awards depends on a consideration of all the facts; value of property, danger, time and skills involved, etc., and

L

awards are usually more modest than generally believed.

If possible, a 'no cure, no pay' salvage agreement should be made when help is needed and this will then fix the sum claimable. One's crew should overhear it, and it should be noted in the log or elsewhere.

REGISTRATION OF YACHTS AS BRITISH SHIPS*
NOTES ON PROCEDURE

*A booklet on registration procedure No. G7/71 is available (free to members) from the RYA).

Registration is primarily a matter for the Registrar of Ships at the port of registry. The Registrar is a Customs and Excise Official and is usually to be found at the port's Custom House.

The first requirement is to decide on a name for the ship and a port of registry. A ship may be registered at any port at which there is a Registrar and not necessarily at the port nearest the owner's residence.

You should then write to the Registrar and ask him for the necessary application forms so that you may (i) apply for approval of the name by the Registrar General at Cardiff and (ii) apply for registration of the ship.

The Registrar will tell you what fees and what documents he will require from you (i.e. If you are not the owner, the owner must give you written authority to apply on his behalf, there must be a Builder's Certificate and/or Bill of Sale, and a Declaration of Ownership).

The Registrar will also require a Certificate of Survey from a BOT Surveyor. The present fee for this is £11 ($27) for a vessel less than 50 tons gross, and it may be paid in with the request for survey, at any convenient Mercantile Marine Office.

After receipt of the fee, the Mercantile Marine Office will forward the application to the appropriate Marine Survey Office. Do not send subsequent correspondence to the Mercantile Marine Office, for apart from receiving the fee it is in no way concerned with the survey and time will be lost in readdressing, etc.

When the Registrar is in all respects satisfied he will issue a Carving Note bearing the Official Number and Register Tonnage which are to be cut in on the main beam. The Carving Note must then be certified by a BOT Surveyor (or sometimes by a Customs Officer specially authorized). Registration will be completed when the Registrar receives the Carving Note.

The vessel must have the name and port of registry marked on the stern, and the marking should be in a permanent form—not paint only, i.e., it should be cut or etched in, or it should be in welded raised lettering. The surveyor is required to certify that this has been done at the time of his survey. Members of certain yacht clubs are permitted to omit this marking, so particulars of yacht club membership should be mentioned on the application for survey.

To summarize the procedure:

(i) Application for registry by owner or authorized agent.

(ii) Approval of name (propose say three names as one may be refused).

(iii) Application for survey.

(iv) Builder's Certificate.

(v) Documents of Sale between intermediate owners if not first owners.

(vi) Declaration of ownership.

(vii) Carving of Official Number and Register Tonnage on the main beam.

(viii) Get Carving Note certified and return to Registrar.

NOTES ON FLAGS

The flags used by British yachts are:

1. The Ensign
2. The Burgee
3. Racing Flag
4. House Flag
5. International Code Flags

British yachts wear the Red Ensign unless otherwise entitled as mentioned in Chapter 1. Yachts of over 15 tons register are required to wear the Ensign at all appropriate times. Yachts under 15 tons, whether registered or not, are, if

313

owned by a British subject, entitled to wear the Ensign and the Red Ensign must, by law, be carried aboard.

The Ensign should be worn when in sight of another vessel and at all times when entering or leaving a foreign port. It must be lowered at sunset, and is hoisted, when in harbour, with other flags, e.g., burgee, house flag, when 'Colours' are made. That is the time of hoisting as indicated by any Royal Navy vessel which may be present or the Yacht Club ashore.

The Ensign is always worn aft, from an ensign staff or, from the after peak of a gaff if carried. Sailing vessels with Bermudan rig may wear it two-thirds up the leach of the mainsail.

Courtesy Ensigns are flown when in the territorial waters of another country. They are flown from a yardarm and unless the flags are identical it is the Maritime and not the National Ensign which should be displayed.

The Burgee distinguishes the vessel as a yacht. It is a triangular flag, most frequently bearing a design particular to a yacht club, which the owner as a member is entitled to fly. Unless racing, when it is replaced by the Racing Flag, the Burgee should be flown during daylight hours, and it should always be flown with the Red Ensign unless the boat is too small to wear an Ensign.

The Burgee is flown at the masthead or at the highest hoist. If an owner belongs to more than one Yachting Body, e.g., his home yacht club and a cruising club, he flies his yacht club Burgee at the masthead and the other from the starboard crosstrees or a shroud at similar height. When visiting another club, the Burgee of that club, may be flown as a courtesy from the yardarm as above.

The Racing Flag is only flown whilst actually taking part in a race and the lowering of that flag signifies retirement. It is flown at the masthead in lieu of the Burgee.

House Flags are personal to the owner of a vessel, they are rectangular and may replace the Racing Flag when racing. Otherwise they may be flown in a power vessel on a lower hoist at any time when the Burgee and the Ensign are worn.

The International Code Flags constitute an alphabet and numbers by which means messages may be sent between vessels at sea and between vessels and shore stations. Besides the facility to spell out messages with flag combinations there are also single flag and two flag signals which have internationally recognized meanings, e.g., the Q flag, which is yellow, indicates that you require quarantine or Customs clearance, the letter G (blue and yellow vertical stripes) means that you want a pilot. The two flags N and C flown together in that order mean: 'I am in distress and require assistance'.

You need not acquire the whole set of code flags for a very small yacht, but it is useful to have a flag manual and sufficient code flags to communicate essential messages, as for example those above. Small boats in any case barely provide a suitable platform from which to send up verbose hoists.

EXTRACTS FROM THE INTERNATIONAL REGULATIONS FOR PREVENTING COLLISIONS AT SEA 1960 (HMSO No. 1525—1965)

Part A.—Preliminary and Definitions

Rule 1

(a) These Rules shall be followed by all vessels and seaplanes upon the high seas and in all waters connected therewith navigable by seagoing vessels, except as provided in Rule 30.
(b) The Rules concerning lights shall be complied with in all weathers from sunset to sunrise, and during such times no other lights shall be exhibited, except such lights as cannot be mistaken for the prescribed lights or do not impair their visibility or distinctive character, or interfere with the keeping of a proper look-out. The lights prescribed by these Rules may also be exhibited from sunrise to sunset in restricted visibility and in all over circumstances when it is deemed necessary.
(c) (i) the word 'vessel' includes every description of water craft, other than a seaplane on the water, used or capable of being used as a means of transportation on water;
   (iv) every power-driven vessel which is under sail and not under power is to be considered a sailing vessel, and every vessel under power, whether under sail or not, is to be considered a power-driven vessel;

  (ix) vessels shall be deemed to be in sight of one another only when one can be observed visually from the other;

  (x) the word 'visible', when applied to lights, means visible on a dark night with a clear atmosphere;

  (xi) the term 'short blast' means a blast of about one second's duration;

  (xii) the term 'prolonged blast' means a blast of from four to six seconds' duration;

  (xiii) the word 'whistle' means any appliance capable of producing the prescribed short and prolonged blasts;

  (xiv) the term 'engaged in fishing' means fishing with nets, lines or trawls but does not include fishing with trolling lines.

Rule 2

(a) A power-driven vessel when under way shall carry:

  (i) On or in front of the foremast, or if a vessel without a foremast then in the forepart of the vessel, a white light so constructed as to show an unbroken light over an arc of the horizon of 225 degrees (20 points of the compass), so fixed as to show the light $112\frac{1}{2}$ degrees (10 points) on each side of the vessel, that is, from right ahead to $22\frac{1}{2}$ degrees (2 points) abaft the beam on either side, and of such a character as to be visible at a distance of at least 5 miles.

  (ii) Either forward of or abaft the white light prescribed in sub-section (i) a second white light similar in construction and character to that light. Vessels of less than 150ft in length shall not be required to carry this second white light but may do so (Fig. 19.1.).

  (iii) These two white lights shall be so placed in a line with and over the keel that one shall be at least 15ft higher than the other and in such a position that the forward light shall always be shown lower than the after one. The horizontal distance between the two white lights shall be at least three times the vertical distance. The lower of these two white lights or, if only one is carried, then that light shall be placed at a height above the hull of not less than 20ft.

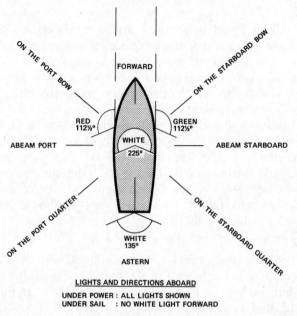

FORWARD

ON THE PORT BOW

ON THE STARBOARD BOW

RED
112½°

GREEN
112½°

ABEAM PORT

ABEAM STARBOARD

WHITE
225°

ON THE PORT QUARTER

ON THE STARBOARD QUARTER

WHITE
135°

ASTERN

LIGHTS AND DIRECTIONS ABOARD
UNDER POWER : ALL LIGHTS SHOWN
UNDER SAIL   : NO WHITE LIGHT FORWARD

Fig. 19.1   Lights and directions aboard.

(iv) On the starboard side a green light so constructed as to show an unbroken light over an arc of the horizon of 112½ degrees (10 points of the compass), so fixed as to show the light from right ahead to 22½ degrees (2 points) abaft the beam on the starboard side, and of such a character as to be visible at a distance of at least 2 miles.

(v) On the port side a red light so constructed as to show an unbroken light over an arc of the horizon of 112½ degrees (10 points of the compass), so fixed as to show the light from right ahead to 22½ degrees (2 points) abaft the beam on the port side, and of such a character as to be visible at a distance of at least 2 miles.

(vi) The said green and red sidelights shall be fitted with inboard screens projecting at least 3ft forward from the light, so as to prevent these lights from being seen across the bows.

317

Rule 5

(a) A sailing vessel under way and any vessel or seaplane being towed shall carry the same lights as are prescribed in Rule 2 for a power-driven vessel or a seaplane under way, respectively, with the exception of the white lights prescribed therein, which they shall never carry. They shall also carry stern lights as prescribed in Rule 10.

(b) In addition to the lights prescribed in section (a), a sailing vessel may carry on the top of the foremast two lights in a vertical line one over the other, sufficiently separated so as to be clearly distinguished. The upper light shall be red and the lower light shall be green. Both lights shall be constructed and fixed as prescribed in Rule 2(a)(i) and shall be visible at a distance of at least 2 miles.

Rule 6

(a) When it is not possible on account of bad weather or other sufficient cause to fix the green and red sidelights, these lights shall be kept at hand lighted and ready for immediate use, and shall, on the approach of or to other vessels, be exhibited on their respective sides in sufficient time to prevent collision, in such manner as to make them most visible, and so that the green light shall not be seen on the port side nor the red light on the starboard side, nor, if practicable, more than $22\frac{1}{2}$ degrees (2 points) abaft the beam on their respective sides.

(b) To make the use of these portable lights more certain and easy, the lanterns containing them shall each be painted outside with the colour of the lights they respectively contain, and shall be provided with proper screens.

Rule 7

Power-driven vessels of less than 65ft in length, vessels under oars or sails of less than 40ft in length, and rowing boats, when under way shall not be required to carry the lights prescribed in Rules 2, 3 and 5, but if they do not carry them they shall be provided with the following lights:

(a) Power-driven vessels of less than 65ft in length, except as provided in sections (b) and (c) shall carry:

> (i) In the forepart of the vessel, where it can best be seen, and at a height above the gunwale of not less

than 9ft, a white light constructed and fixed as prescribed in Rule 2(a)(i) and of such a character as to be visible at a distance of at least 3 miles.

(ii) Green and red sidelights constructed and fixed as prescribed in Rule 2(a)(iv) and (v), and of such a character as to be visible at a distance of at least 1 mile, or a combined lantern showing a green light and a red light from right ahead to $22\frac{1}{2}$ degrees (2 points) abaft the beam on their respective sides. Such lantern shall be carried not less than 3ft below the white light.

(c) Power-driven vessels of less than 40ft in length may carry the white light at a less height than 9ft above the gunwale but it shall be carried not less than 3ft above the sidelights or the combined lantern prescribed in section (a) (ii).

(d) Vessels of less than 40ft in length, under oars or sails, except as provided in section (f), shall, if they do not carry the sidelights, carry, where it can best be seen, a lantern showing a green light on one side and a red light on the other, of such a character as to be visible at a distance of at least 1 mile, and so fixed that the green light shall not be seen on the port side, nor the red light on the starboard side. Where it is not possible to fix this light, it shall be kept ready for immediate use and shall be exhibited in sufficient time to prevent collision and so that the green light shall not be seen on the port side nor the red light on the starboard side.

(f) Small rowing boats, whether under oars or sail, shall only be required to have ready at hand an electric torch or a lighted lantern, showing a white light, which shall be exhibited in sufficient time to prevent collision.

Rule 10

(a) Except where otherwise provided in these Rules, a vessel when under way shall carry at her stern a white light, so constructed that it shall show an unbroken light over an arc of the horizon of 135 degrees (12 points of the compass) so fixed as to show the light $67\frac{1}{2}$ degrees (6 points) from right aft on each side of the vessel, and of such a character as to be visible at a distance of at least 2 miles.

(b) In a small vessel, if it is not possible on account of bad weather or other sufficient cause for this light to be fixed, an electric torch or a lighted lantern showing a white light shall be kept at hand ready for use and shall, on the approach of an overtaking vessel, be shown in sufficient time to prevent collision.

Rule 11

(a) A vessel of less than 150ft in length, when at anchor, shall carry in the forepart of the vessel, where it can best be seen, a white light visible all round the horizon at a distance of at least 2 miles. Such a vessel may also carry a second white light in the position prescribed in section (b) of this Rule but shall not be required to do so. The second white light, if carried, shall be visible at a distance of at least 2 miles and so placed as to be as far as possible visible all round the horizon.

(c) Between sunrise and sunset every vessel when at anchor shall carry in the forepart of the vessel, where it can best be seen, one black ball not less than 2ft in diameter.

(e) A vessel aground shall carry the light or lights prescribed in sections (a) or (b) and the two red lights prescribed in Rule 4(a). By day she shall carry, where they can best be seen, three black balls, each not less than 2ft in diameter, placed in a vertical line one over the other, not less than 6ft apart.

Rule 12

Every vessel or seaplane on the water may, if necessary in order to attract attention, in addition to the lights which she is by these Rules required to carry, show a flare-up light or use a detonating or other efficient sound signal that cannot be mistaken for any signal authorized elsewhere under these Rules.

Rule 14

A vessel proceeding under sail, when also being propelled by machinery, shall carry in the day time forward, where it can best be seen, one black conical shape, point downwards, not less than 2ft in diameter at its base.

Part C.—Sound Signals and Conduct in Restricted Visibility
Preliminary

1. The possession of information obtained from radar does

not relieve any vessel of the obligation of conforming strictly with the Rules and, in particular, the obligations contained in Rules 15 and 16.

Rule 15

(a) A power-driven vessel of 40ft or more in length shall be provided with an efficient whistle, sounded by steam or by some substitute for steam, so placed that the sound may not be intercepted by any obstruction, and with an efficient fog horn to be sounded by mechanical means, and also with an efficient bell. A sailing vessel of 40ft or more in length shall be provided with a similar fog horn and bell.

(b) All signals prescribed in this Rule for vessels under way shall be given:

    (i) by power-driven vessels on the whistle;
    (ii) by sailing vessels on the fog horn;
    (iii) by vessels towed on the whistle or fog horn.

(c) In fog, mist, falling snow, heavy rainstorms, or any other condition similarly restricting visibility, whether by day or night, the signals prescribed in this Rule shall be used as follows:

    (i) A power-driven vessel making way through the water shall sound at intervals of not more than 2 minutes a prolonged blast.

    (ii) A power-driven vessel under way, but stopped and making no way through the water, shall sound at intervals of not more than 2 minutes two prolonged blasts, with an interval of about 1 second between them.

    (iii) A sailing vessel under way shall sound, at intervals of not more than 1 minute, when on the starboard tack one blast, when on the port tack two blasts in succession, and when with the wind abaft the beam three blasts in succession.

    (iv) A vessel when at anchor shall at intervals of not more than 1 minute ring the bell rapidly for about 5 seconds . . . . . Every vessel at anchor may in addition, in accordance with Rule 12, sound three blasts in succession, namely, one short, one prolonged, and one short blast, to give warning of her position and of the

321

possibility of collision to an approaching vessel.

(vii) A vessel aground shall give the bell signal and, if required, the gong signal, prescribed in subsection (iv) and shall, in addition, give 3 separate and distinct strokes on the bell immediately before and after such rapid ringing of the bell.

(ix) A vessel of less than 40ft in length, a rowing boat, or a seaplane on the water, shall not be obliged to give the above-mentioned signals but if she does not, she shall make some other efficient sound signal at intervals of not more than 1 minute.

Part D.—Steering and Sailing Rules

Preliminary

1. In obeying and construing these Rules, any action taken should be positive, in ample time, and with due regard to the observance of good seamanship.

2. Risk of collision can, when circumstances permit, be ascertained by carefully watching the compass bearing of an approaching vessel. If the bearing does not appreciably change, such risk should be deemed to exist (Fig. 19.2.).

3. Mariners should bear in mind that seaplanes in the act of landing or taking off, or operating under adverse weather

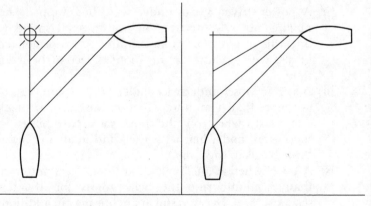

BEARING CONSTANT
ON COLLISION COURSE

BEARING CHANGING
WILL PASS CLEAR

Fig. 19.2   Other vessel's bearing—Collision course. Safe course.

conditions, may be unable to change their intended action at the last moment.

4.   Rules 17 to 24 apply only to vessels in sight of one another.

Rule 17

(a) When two sailing vessels are approaching one another, so as to involve risk of collision, one of them shall keep out of the way of the other as follows:

(i) When each has the wind on a different side, the vessel which has the wind on the port side shall keep out of the way of the other.

(ii) When both have the wind on the same side, the vessel which is to windward shall keep out of the way of the vessel which is to leeward.

(b) For the purposes of this Rule the windward side shall be deemed to be the side opposite to that on which the mainsail is carried or, in the case of a square-rigged vessel, the side opposite to that on which the largest fore-and-aft sail is carried (Fig. 19.3.).

Rule 18

(a) When two power-driven vessels are meeting end on, or nearly end on, so as to involve risk of collision, each shall alter her course to starboard, so that each may pass on the port side of the other. This Rule only applies to cases where vessels are meeting end on, or nearly end on, in such a manner as to involve risk of collision, and does not apply to two vessels which must, if both keep on their respective courses, pass clear of each other (Fig. 19.4a.).

Rule 19

When two power-driven vessels are crossing, so as to involve risk of collision, the vessel which has the other on her own starboard side shall keep out of the way of the other (Fig. 19.4b).

Rule 20

(a) When a power-driven vessel and a sailing vessel are proceeding in such directions as to involve risk of collision, except as provided for in Rules 24 and 26, the power-driven vessel shall keep out of the way of the sailing vessel (Fig. 19.4c.).

(b) This Rule shall not give to a sailing vessel the right to hamper, in a narrow channel, the safe passage of a power-driven vessel which can navigate only inside such channel.

Rule 21

Where by any of these Rules one of two vessels is to keep out of the way, the other shall keep her course and speed. When, from any cause, the latter vessel finds herself so close that

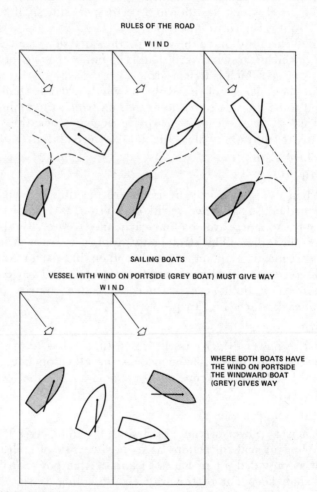

RULES OF THE ROAD

WIND

SAILING BOATS

VESSEL WITH WIND ON PORTSIDE (GREY BOAT) MUST GIVE WAY

WIND

WHERE BOTH BOATS HAVE
THE WIND ON PORTSIDE
THE WINDWARD BOAT
(GREY) GIVES WAY

Fig. 19.3 Sailing Vessels

RULES OF THE ROAD

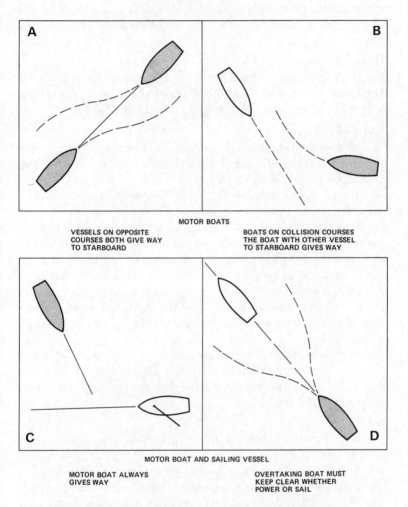

MOTOR BOATS

A	B
VESSELS ON OPPOSITE COURSES BOTH GIVE WAY TO STARBOARD	BOATS ON COLLISION COURSES THE BOAT WITH OTHER VESSEL TO STARBOARD GIVES WAY

MOTOR BOAT AND SAILING VESSEL

C	D
MOTOR BOAT ALWAYS GIVES WAY	OVERTAKING BOAT MUST KEEP CLEAR WHETHER POWER OR SAIL

Fig. 19.4   Rules of the road. Motor vessels. Motor and Sailing Vessels.

collision cannot be avoided by the action of the giving-way vessel alone, she also shall take such action as will best aid to avert collision (see Rules 27 and 29).

Rule 22

Every vessel which is directed by these Rules to keep out of the

325

way of another vessel shall, so far as possible, take positive early action to comply with this obligation, and shall, if the circumstances of the case admit, avoid crossing ahead of the other.

Rule 23

Every power-driven vessel which is directed by these Rules to keep out of the way of another vessel shall, on approaching her, if necessary, slacken her speed or stop or reverse.

Rule 24

(a) Notwithstanding anything contained in these Rules, every vessel overtaking any other shall keep out of the way of the overtaken vessel (Fig. 19.4d.).

(b) Every vessel coming up with another vessel from any direction more than $22\frac{1}{2}$ degrees (2 points) abaft her beam, i.e., in such a position, with reference to the vessel which she is overtaking, that at night she would be unable to see either of that vessel's sidelights, shall be deemed to be an overtaking vessel; and no subsequent alteration of the bearing between the two vessels shall make the overtaking vessel a crossing vessel within the meaning of these Rules, or relieve her of the duty of keeping clear of the overtaken vessel until she is finally past and clear.

(c) If the overtaking vessel cannot determine with certainty whether she is forward of or abaft this direction from the other vessel, she shall assume that she is an overtaking vessel and keep out of the way.

Rule 25

(a) In a narrow channel every power-driven vessel when proceeding along the course of the channel shall, when it is safe and practicable, keep to that side of the fairway or mid-channel which lies on the starboard side of such vessel.

(b) Whenever a power-driven vessel is nearing a bend in a channel where a vessel approaching from the other direction cannot be seen, such power-driven vessel, when she shall have arrived within one-half ($\frac{1}{2}$) mile of the bend, shall give a signal by one prolonged blast on her whistle which signal shall be answered by a similar blast given by an approaching power-driven vessel that may be within hearing around the bend. Regardless of whether an approaching vessel on the farther side of the bend is heard, such bend shall be rounded with alertness and caution.

(c) In a narrow channel a power-driven vessel of less than 65ft in length shall not hamper the safe passage of a vessel which can navigate only inside such channel.

Rule 26

All vessels not engaged in fishing, except vessels to which the provisions of Rule 4 apply, shall, when under way, keep out of the way of vessels engaged in fishing. This Rule shall not give to any vessel engaged in fishing the right of obstructing a fairway used by vessels other than fishing vessels.

Rule 27

In obeying and construing these Rules due regard shall be had to all dangers of navigation and collision, and to any special circumstances, including the limitations of the craft involved, which may render a departure from the above Rules necessary in order to avoid immediate danger.

Part E.—Sound Signals for Vessels in Sight of One Another

Rule 28

(a) When vessels are in sight of one another, a power-driven vessel under way, in taking any course authorized or required by these Rules, shall indicate that course by the following signals on her whistle, namely:

One short blast to mean 'I am altering my course to starboard'.

Two short blasts to mean 'I am altering my course to port'.

Three short blasts to mean 'My engines are going astern'.

(b) Whenever a power-driven vessel which, under these Rules, is to keep her course and speed, is in sight of another vessel and is in doubt whether sufficient action is being taken by the other vessel to avert collision, she may indicate such doubt by giving at least five short and rapid blasts on the whistle. The giving of such a signal shall not relieve a vessel of her obligations under Rules 27 and 29 or any other Rule, or of her duty to indicate any action taken under these Rules by giving the appropriate sound signals laid down in this Rule.

chapter 20

Inland Waterways

It is interesting to ponder that had the internal combustion engine preceded the steam engine, we might by now have abandoned that expensive and troublesome invention known as the automobile, in favour of swift and near-silent journeys behind super steam engines. And one may contemplate our inland waterways system from the same point of view, for it is clear that in view of our present state of disarray in the environmental and economic aspects of road and rail, that if someone were to invent canals tomorrow he would be hailed as a genius.

The fact that an inlands waterway system exists is clearly a disadvantage to its further use for industry, after all, there is little glory in rebuilding a few locks when you can indulge millions on a motorway. However, if the waterways are neglected commercially, there is a growing number of people who are becoming aware of the recreational potential of the waterways, natural and man-made which extend for most of the length and breadth of the country, and offer many of the delights of 'messing about in boats' without most of the hazards which may accompany the pastime on broader waters.

At present, the control of the inland waterways is the subject of much argument, but whether eventually they are the responsibility of one national or several regional bodies it is hardly likely that the momentum behind the movement for wider recreational use will be lost, although the restoration of many sections may be delayed. However, from the more than 2,500 miles of additional navigable waterways recorded in the mid-nineteenth century there is still a large amount left to enjoy, and many of the decayed locks and cuts are being rehabilitated by devoted people with very limited funds but a great deal of enthusiasm and expertise.

Under the jurisdiction of the British Waterways Board, and urged by the interest of the Inland Waterways Association, about 1,500 miles of cruiseways have been designated to date, but this does not prohibit visits to less used corners of the navigations.

The waterways system consists of canals of both broad and narrow gauge which form a network with navigable rivers. The locks on the narrow gauge navigations have a breadth of only 7ft whilst the wider canals will accommodate twice that width or more. The incidence of the narrow canals in the Midlands effectively divides the broad waterways into three approximate divisions within which most of these inland navigations are found, although there may be discontinuity through the dereliction of certain sections: West Country/London/South Midlands, Lancashire/Yorkshire/East Midlands/Lincolnshire, The Fens and East Anglia (these two not connected except by sea).

It is tantalizing to observe that it would require only a length of the Grand Union, together with the Northampton Arm and the Leicester section to be widened in order to link the majority of the broad gauge waterways throughout the country, but one of these includes perhaps the most famous series of locks in the system, the Foxton Flight, the summit of which is 412ft above sea level (Fig. 20.1.).

Apart from the necessary working of the locks, inland waterways offer a kind of boating which is not over-strenuous but quite unique in its appeal. Even to walk along the tow path, whether behind the tall brick walls of a city 'cut', or in a different solitude across quiet fields is to enter another world. It is an accessible new dimension which does not call for much fortitude from the family or the use of many sailing skills. Because of this and a new sense of responsibility for the environment amongst those in high places, it is likely that inland waterway cruising and boat ownership in that sector will develop more rapidly than any other area of pleasure boating.

Fig. 20.1   The Foxton Flight and a steel narrow boat. (Harborough Marine.)

There are an increasing number of marinas and boat stations where craft may either be kept or hired, and for those who have no inclination to command even a narrow boat, there are scheduled voyages by cruise operators whereby you may have the comfort of a hotel with ever changing scenery.

Most of the scenery will be restful, but surprisingly perhaps, it can also sometimes be exciting. Crossing the Chirk aqueduct, with one's boat floating serenely above the valley far below, must cause the blood to circulate a little more rapidly, and the Pontcysyllte aqueduct a little further along the way to Llangollen is even more impressive. As seen from the ground a boat moving slowly across the valley of the Dee at a height of 120ft inspires awe for those who dared to create such an astonishing facility. Both Chirk and Pontcysyllte have stood for about 170 years and there are many other works of like age in the inland waterways system which give similar cause to wonder. The inland navigations have a lot to offer besides peace and unique view of the British countryside.

Many books, factual, historical and evocative are now to be had by those who would like to get the feel of this arm of boating and both the BWB and the IWA have literature available. There are also operator associations who can provide details of marinas and boat stations run by their members.

One of the best inland waterway maps has been produced by the journal *Motor Boat and Yachting*. It is in full colour and covers the whole system in four parts given with issues dating from May 14th, 1971. Back numbers are available.

As regards to what sort of boats are suitable for the inland navigations, the answer could be, almost any boat provided it does not draw much more than 2ft and indeed, the extraordinary variety of craft now to be seen tends to support this view. But it depends where you wish to go. If the answer is 'everywhere' then you will need a narrow boat which, whilst it need not be to the traditional work boat pattern will have a beam of not more than 6ft 10in and a length of under 45ft. Obviously there is plenty of scope inside these dimensions. The height from the waterline to the top of the cabin should preferably not exceed 6ft and if you wish to go through the very lowest bridges and tunnels 5ft 6in is about the limit.

Boats intended for the wider waterways can exceed 14ft and have somewhat more height, but it will hardly ever be necessary to have more than 6ft above the waterline to get the required headroom down below. In fact, as will be plain, with a draft of up to 2ft and a flat bottom you have no need for great height above the water.

Because of their somewhat utilitarian shape, and also because many are the original or the descendants of traditional craft, many boats are built of steel. Flat topsides and flat bottoms are easily constructed from steel plate, which nowadays will be all-welded to give a strong and trouble free hull. Use in fresh water reduces the corrosion problem which may otherwise be encountered. Although some smaller are built, most steel boats will be 30ft or over in length.

The popular material for small and medium size cruisers is GRP, which requires little maintenance, and many of the small cabin cruisers which are offered for inshore and estuary sailing are equally suitable for inland waterways (Fig. 20.2.). There are, however, plenty of boats built especially for the canals which have modern accommodation facilities within a maximum beam of 6ft 10in.

Fig. 20.2 The Elysian 27, a comfortable, modern GRP cruiser.

Engines may have as much variety as the many options which are offered for use in sea-going small craft. The main difference is that speed is not one of the requirements and the engine of your choice, whether petrol or diesel will probably be of low power for the size of the vessel. The reason is that you will rarely wish (or be permitted) to push the boat at more than its optimum speed/length figure. This briefly, is the square root of the waterline length multiplied by an arguable figure according to the shape of your boat which we will say is 1.3 (see design chapter). Hence, if your boat is 25ft on the waterline the square root is 5 which multiplied by 1.3 gives $6\frac{1}{2}$ knots. Up to that speed you may propel your boat with only modest horsepower, but when you try to exceed it you will need vastly more.

Thus it is perfectly feasible, and on the grounds of first cost and installation charges, highly attractive to consider the use of a low power outboard engine if your excursions are to be limited, but if you wish to go on long voyages the fuel cost may be reckoned with.

For the long distance man who will use his boat regularly, a small diesel engine is probably the best choice in any boat of 25ft or more in length, on the grounds of long life and fuel economy. But up to that size of vessel all of the options remain open; inboard, outboard, two stroke, four stroke, petrol, petrol/paraffin or diesel. On the question of cooling for inboard engines, these may be either air or water cooled but having regard to the type of service and their environment, water cooling would seem to be more attractive, especially since fresh water will not give rise to corrosion in the system to the same extent as would be experienced at sea. An efficient, accessible and easily cleared inlet filter is obviously a prime requirement.

1 EMERGENCY SIGNALS

These emergency signals are either used together or separately by vessels in case of emergency to summon assistance from other vessels or from land:

It is forbidden to use these signals except to indicate that the vessel is in need of assistance. It is also forbidden to use any signal which may be confused with these signals.

1. Maroons exploded at intervals of about one minute.

2. Continuous use of foghorn.

3. Rockets with red stars, fired one at a time at short intervals.

4. Signals sent by radio-telegraphy or by other methods of any type with the Morse signal:
   ...———...

5. Signals sent by radio-telephone by using the word "May-day" (a corruption of the French "M'aidez!")

6. Emergency signal NC in accordance with the international signal book.

7. A signal consisting of a square flag with a ball or similar object above or below it.

8. Flame signals on vessel (seldom applicable on leisure craft).

9. Rocket with parachute flare or hand flare with red flame.

10. Smoke signal (orange smoke).

11. Repeated raising and lowering of arms extended sideways.

2 FLAG SIGNALS

One-letter signals

A   I have divers down. Keep well clear and reduce speed.

B   I am loading/discharging/carrying dangerous material.

C   Yes (positive).

D   Keep your distance, I can only manoeuvre with difficulty.

E   I am altering course to starboard.

F   I am disabled.

G   I need a pilot.

H   I have a pilot on board.

I   I am altering course to port.

J   I have a fire on board.

K   I wish to contact you.

L   Stop making headway immediately.

M   My vessel has stopped and is not making headway.

Two-letter signals
(*type example*)

N   No (negative).

O   Man overboard.

P   In port: All men aboard, I am preparing to leave port.

P   At sea (to be used by fishing vessels): My gear has jammed.

Q   My ship is free from infection.

R   "Received" (reception signal).

S   My engines are running astern.

T   Keep clear of me, I am engaged in tandem trawling.

U   You are heading for danger.

V   I require assistance.

W   I require medical assitance.

X   Cease what you are doing and pay attention to my signals.

Y   My anchor is dragging.

Z   I need a tug (Fishing vessels: I am laying out fishing gear).

NC   I am in distress and require assistance.

3 INTERNATIONAL MORSE CODE

The following table shows the
international Morse code signals
which are used for optical and
acoustic signalling.

Morse Code

Signal		Signal		Signal	
A	·—	I	··	*R	·—·
B	—···	J	·———	S	···
C	—·—·	*K	—·—	T	—
CH	————	*L	·—··	*U	··—
D	—··	M	——	*V	···—
E	·	N	—·	W	·——
*F	··—·	*O	———	X	—··—
G	——·	*P	·——·	Y	—·——
H	····	Q	——·—	Z	——··

Figures

1	·————
2	··———
3	···——
4	····—
5	·····
6	—····
7	——···
8	———··
9	————·
0	—————

Other signs

Full stop (period)	·—·—·—
Comma	——··——
Colon	———···
Question mark	··——··
Brackets (parenthesis) ..	—·——·—
Hyphen or dash........	—····—
Double dash (=)........	—···—
Underline sign	··——·—
Apostrophe	·————·
Spacer between whole figures and fractions	·—··—·
Start transmitting (Over!)	—·—
Starting sign............	—·—·—
Concluding sign for a telegram	·—·—·
Wait!	·—···
Understood!	···—·
Error erasing sign	········
Signing off	···—·—

*These single letters may be flashed in emergency; their meaning being as in
single letter flag signals.

4 SOUND SIGNALS

Sound signal		Vessel
With whistle		
▬	F	Motorships in motion.
▬ ▬	F	Motorships with main engines stopped and stationary.
▬ ··	F	Tugs, cable vessels, unmanoeuvrable vessels, vessels engaged in fishing, etc.
▬ ···	F	Vessels under tow.
R · ▬ ·	A	Vessels lying at anchor.
G ▬ ▬ ·	P	I require pilot.
·	M	I am altering course to starboard.
··	M	I am altering course to port.
···	M	I am running astern.
····	D	Distinctive signal for motor-driven pilot-boat.
·····	A	Appeal to meeting vessel to act.
With foghorn		
▬	F	Sailing vessels on starboard tack.
▬ ▬	F	Sailing vessels on port tack.
▬ ▬ ▬	F	Sailing vessels with the wind abaft the beam.
▬ ···	F	Vessels under tow.
Ship's bell and gong		
Bell-ringing	F	Vessels lying at anchor.
Bell-ringing + gong	F	Vessels lying at anchor.
···Bell-ringing ···	F	Vessels aground.
···Bell-ringing ···+gong	F	Vessels aground.
At least six single strikes after regular fog signal	F	Dredger. Passage marked with funnel-shaped beacon.
At least six single strikes after regular fog signal	F	Dredger. Passage marked with cone-shaped beacon.
Double strike on the ship's bell	F	Lightship marking wreck. Passage north or east of the lightship.
Single strike on the ship's bell	F	Lightship marking wreck. Passage south or west of the lightship.

F = Fog signal
M = Manoeuvring signal
D = Distinguishing signal
P = Pilot signal
A = Attention signal

5 UNIFORM LATERAL SYSTEM (G.B.)

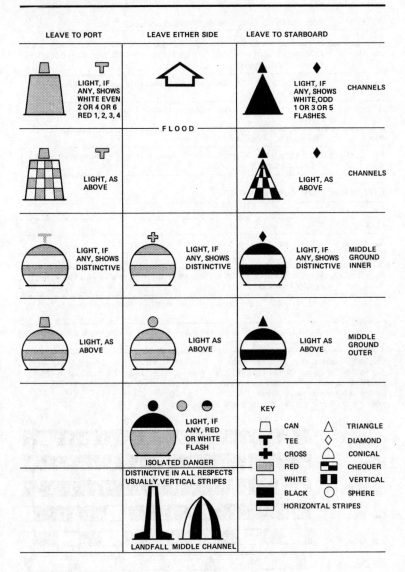

LEAVE TO PORT	LEAVE EITHER SIDE	LEAVE TO STARBOARD	
LIGHT, IF ANY, SHOWS WHITE EVEN 2 OR 4 OR 6 RED 1, 2, 3, 4	FLOOD	LIGHT, IF ANY, SHOWS WHITE, ODD 1 OR 3 OR 5 FLASHES.	CHANNELS
LIGHT, AS ABOVE		LIGHT, AS ABOVE	CHANNELS
LIGHT, IF ANY, SHOWS DISTINCTIVE	LIGHT, IF ANY, SHOWS DISTINCTIVE	LIGHT, IF ANY, SHOWS DISTINCTIVE	MIDDLE GROUND INNER
LIGHT, AS ABOVE	LIGHT AS ABOVE	LIGHT AS ABOVE	MIDDLE GROUND OUTER

LIGHT, IF ANY, RED OR WHITE FLASH

ISOLATED DANGER

DISTINCTIVE IN ALL RESPECTS USUALLY VERTICAL STRIPES

LANDFALL MIDDLE CHANNEL

KEY

	CAN		TRIANGLE
	TEE		DIAMOND
	CROSS		CONICAL
	RED		CHEQUER
	WHITE		VERTICAL
	BLACK		SPHERE
	HORIZONTAL STRIPES		

Appendix 6

6 LIGHT CHARACTERISTICS.

Qk. Fl.	Quick flashing, each flash being not more than 0.7 sec.
Fl.	Flashing.
Dk. Occ.	Dark occulting, the duration of light being 2 seconds or more but shorter, however, than the duration of darkness.
Eq. Occ.	Equally occulting, the duration of light always equal to the duration of darkness.
Li. Occ.	Light occulting, the duration of light always greater than the duration of darkness.
Mo.	Morse light, indicating a Morse sign.
Alt. F. (Co.)	Alternating fixed, (Colour), a fixed light showing alternating colours in the same sector.

Example of light characteristics

Qk. Fl. 60/m	60 quick flashes per minute.
Fl. 3 s	One flash every third second.
Gp. Fl. (2) 6 s	A group consisting of two flashes every sixth second.
Dk. Occ. 10 s	Dark occulting showing light every tenth second.
Eq. Occ. 5 s	Equally occulting with half the time (2.5 seconds) dark and half light at regular intervals.
Li. Occ. 5 s	Occulting light totally eclipsed every fifth second by a short period of darkness.
Li. Occ. (2) 10 s	Occulting light totally eclipsed every tenth second by a group of two short periods of darkness.

The light characteristics include numbers of seconds (does not apply to **quick flashing**) which indicate the time taken for the entire variation sequence. For example **Li. Occ.** (2) 10 s means that it takes 10 seconds between the first (or second) eclipse in a group and the first (or second) eclipse in the following group.

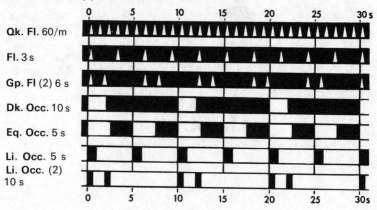

7 WIND STRENGTH

Beaufort Scale

Beaufort Scale	Wind velocity			Definition
	Metres/sec.	km./h	knots	
0	0–0.2	less than 1	less than 1	Calm
1	0.3–1.5	1–5	1–3	Light air
2	1.6–3.3	6–11	4–6	Light breeze
3	3.4–5.4	12–19	7–10	Gentle breeze
4	5.5–7.9	20–28	11–16	Moderate breeze
5	8.0–10.7	29–38	17–21	Fresh breeze
6	10.8–13.8	39–49	22–27	Strong breeze
7	13.8–17.1	50–61	28–33	Moderate gale
8	17.2–20.7	62–74	34–40	Fresh gale
9	20.8–24.2	75–88	41–47	Strong gale
10	24.5–28.4	89–102	48–55	Whole gale
11	28.4–32.6	103–117	56–63	Storm
12	32.7–36.9	118–133	64–71	Hurricane

8 SPEED TABLE

Time Factor

Time taken to travel 1 nautical mile

Min.	1	2	3	4	5	6	7	8	9
Sec.					Speed of boat in knots				
0	60.00	30.00	20.00	15.00	12.00	10.00	8.57	7.50	6.67
2	58.06	29.51	19.78	14.88	11.92	9.95	8.53	7.47	6.64
4	56.25	29.03	19.56	14.75	11.84	9.89	8.49	7.44	6.62
6	54.55	28.57	19.36	14.63	11.76	9.84	8.45	7.41	6.59
8	52.94	28.13	19.15	14.52	11.69	9.78	8.41	7.38	6.56
10	51.43	27.69	18.95	14.40	11.61	9.73	8.37	7.35	6.54
12	50.00	27.27	18.75	14.29	11.54	9.68	8.33	7.32	6.52
14	48.65	26.87	18.56	14.17	11.47	9.63	8.29	7.29	6.50
16	46.37	26.47	18.37	14.06	11.39	9.57	8.26	7.26	6.48
18	46.15	26.09	18.18	13.95	11.32	9.52	8.22	7.23	6.45
20	45.00	25.71	18.00	13.85	11.25	9.47	8.18	7.20	6.43
22	43.90	25.35	17.82	13.74	11.18	9.42	8.15	7.17	6.41
24	42.86	25.00	17.65	13.64	11.11	9.38	8.11	7.14	6.38
26	41.86	24.66	17.48	13.53	11.04	9.33	8.07	7.12	6.36
28	40.90	24.32	17.31	13.43	10.98	9.28	8.04	7.09	6.34
30	40.00	24.00	17.14	13.33	10.91	9.23	8.00	7.06	6.32
32	39.13	23.68	16.98	13.24	10.84	9.18	7.97	7.03	6.29
34	38.30	23.38	16.82	13.14	10.78	9.14	7.93	7.00	6.27
36	37.50	23.08	16.67	13.04	10.71	9.09	7.90	6.98	6.25
38	36.74	22.79	16.51	12.95	10.65	9.05	7.86	6.95	6.23
40	36.00	22.50	16.36	12.85	10.59	9.00	7.83	6.92	6.21
42	35.29	22.22	16.22	12.77	10.53	8.96	7.79	6.90	6.19
44	34.62	21.95	16.07	12.68	10.47	8.91	7.76	6.87	6.16
46	33.96	21.69	15.93	12.59	10.40	8.87	7.73	6.84	6.14
48	33.33	21.43	15.79	12.50	10.35	8.82	7.69	6.82	6.12
50	32.73	21.18	15.65	12.41	10.29	8.78	7.66	6.79	6.10
52	32.14	20.93	15.52	12.33	10.23	8.74	7.63	6.77	6.08
54	31.58	20.69	15.38	12.25	10.17	8.70	7.60	6.74	6.06
56	31.03	20.45	15.25	12.16	10.11	8.65	7.56	6.72	6.04
58	30.51	20.23	15.13	12.08	10.06	8.61	7.53	6.69	6.02
60	30.00	20.00	15.00	12.00	10.00	8.57	7.50	6.67	6.00

8 SPEED TABLE

Formula for calculating speed, time and distance

$$S = \frac{D \times 3600}{T} \qquad T = \frac{D \times 3600}{S} \qquad D = \frac{S \times T}{3600}$$

S = Speed in knots   D = Distance in nautical miles (minutes of latitude)
T = Time in seconds. Example: If the distance is 1.5 nautical miles and the time is 7 min. 30 sec. (450 seconds), then the speed is as follows:

$$S = \frac{1.5 \times 3600}{450} = 12 \text{ knots}$$

Distance Factor

If a boat travels 1 nautical mile in:

60 m.	then the speed is	1 Knot	3 m. 45 s. then the speed is 16 Knots
30 „	„ „ „ „ 2 „		3 „ 32 „ „ „ „ „ 17 „
20 „	„ „ „ „ 3 „		3 „ 20 „ „ „ „ „ 18 „
15 „	„ „ „ „ 4 „		3 „ 9.5 „ „ „ „ „ 19 „
12 „	„ „ „ „ 5 „		3 „ 0 „ „ „ „ „ 20 „
10 „	„ „ „ „ 6 „		2 „ 51.4 „ „ „ „ „ 21 „
8 „ 34 s.	„ „ „ „ 7 „		2 „ 43.6 „ „ „ „ „ 22 „
7 „ 30 „	„ „ „ „ 8 „		2 „ 36.5 „ „ „ „ „ 23 „
6 „ 40 „	„ „ „ „ 9 „		2 „ 30 „ „ „ „ „ 24 „
6 „ 0 „	„ „ „ „ 10 „		2 „ 24 „ „ „ „ „ 25 „
5 „ 27 „	„ „ „ „ 11 „		2 „ 18.5 „ „ „ „ „ 26 „
5 „ 0 „	„ „ „ „ 12 „		2 „ 13.3 „ „ „ „ „ 27 „
4 „ 37 „	„ „ „ „ 13 „		2 „ 8.6 „ „ „ „ „ 28 „
4 „ 17 „	„ „ „ „ 14 „		2 „ 4.1 „ „ „ „ „ 29 „
4 „ 0 „	„ „ „ „ 15 „		2 „ 0 „ „ „ „ „ 30 „

341

9 SPEEDS

Comparison Table

km./h.	m.p.h.	metres/sec.	knots
10	6.22	2.78	5.40
20	12.4	5.56	10.8
30	18.7	8.34	16.2
40	24.9	11.1	21.6
50	31.1	13.9	27.0
60	37.4	16.7	32.4
70	43.6	19.4	37.8
80	49.8	22.2	43.2
90	56.0	25.0	48.6
100	62.2	27.8	54.0
120	74.7	33.3	64.8
140	87.1	38.9	75.6
160	99.5	44.5	86.4
180	112	50.0	97.2
200	124	55.6	108
220	137	61.2	119
240	149	66.7	130
260	162	72.3	140
280	174	77.8	151
300	187	83.4	162

1 statute mile = 1 609 m.
1 nautical mile = 1 852 m.
1 knot = 1 nautical mile per hour.

10 KNOTS AND SPLICES

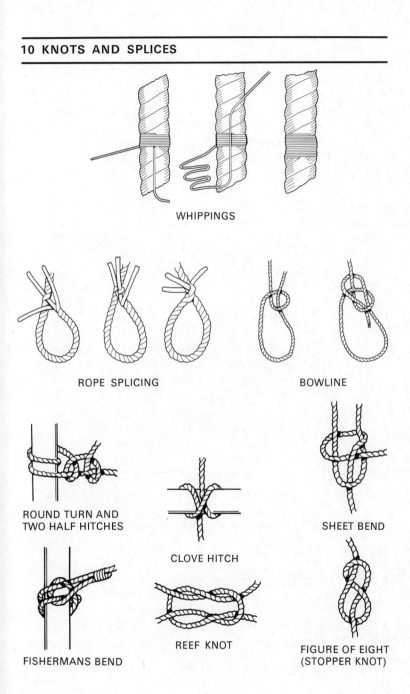

WHIPPINGS

ROPE SPLICING

BOWLINE

ROUND TURN AND
TWO HALF HITCHES

CLOVE HITCH

SHEET BEND

FISHERMANS BEND

REEF KNOT

FIGURE OF EIGHT
(STOPPER KNOT)

343

M

11 ROPE

Tensile strength and weight for various types of rope

Dimensions

Circumference in mm	Diam. mm	Tensile strength kg	Weight per 100 m	Tensile strength kg	Weight per 100 m
		Manilla		**Hemp**	
19.	6	320	3	350	3
25.4	8	600	5.5	550	5.5
31.7	10	800	8	850	8
38.1	12	1,200	12	1,200	12
44.4	14	1,600	16	1,600	16
50.8	16	2,300	20	2,100	20
63.5	20	3,500	30	3,200	30
76.2	24	5,000	42	4,400	42
101.6	32	8,600	73	7,400	73
		Drawn nylon		**Nylon wool**	
19.	6	550	2.3	250	1.7
25.4	8	950	4.0	400	3.0
31.7	10	1,400	6.2	600	4.6
38.1	12	2,000	9.0	800	7.0
44.4	14	2,600	12	1,100	9.5
50.8	16	3,500	16	1,400	12
63.5	20	5,400	25	2,000	18
76.2	24	8,000	36	2,700	26
101.6	32	14,000	66	4,500	46

(25.4 mm = 1 inch   0.45 kg = 1 lb)

Braided

Size of circumference in mm	Breaking strain in kg	Breaking strain in kg
	Nylon	**Terylene**
19.	952.3	657.5
25.4	1451.2	1179.1
38.1	3401.2	2584.9
50.8	5442.	4535.

11 ROPE

3 Strand

Size of circumference in mm	Breaking strain in kg	Breaking strain in kg
	Nylon	**Terylene**
19.	748.2	566.8
25.4	1351.4	1015.8
38.1	2997.6	2267.5
50.8	5282.3	4063.3
	Polypropylene Multifilament	
19.	548.7	
25.4	961.4	
38.1	2031.6	
50.8	3453.8	

12 CABLES (STAINLESS STEEL WIRE)

Cross-section areas, tensile strength and weights concerning lines in standing rigging.

The 19-strand line (1 × 19) has the least stretch and is therefore used on modern boats with top rigging. In its heavy gauge dimensions it is difficult to splice and the eyes must be pressed, soldered or screwed.

The 49-strand line (7 × 7) is more flexible and easier to splice but has, on the average, a tensile strength which is about 25% lower for the same diameter.

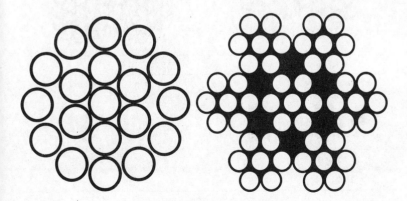

12 CABLES

Diam. mm	1 x 19 non-flexible		7 x 7 flexible	
	Approximate weight, kg	Calc. tensile strength, kg	Approximate weight, kg	Calc. tensile strength, kg
2	0.02	380	0.015	250
3	0.04	800	0.033	630
4	0.087	1,500	0.061	1,130
5	0.14	2,350	0.095	1,790
6	0.20	3,400	0.14	2,600
7	0.26	4,600	0.185	3,460
8	0.34	6,100	0.24	4,445
10	0.54	9,500	0.36	6,810

Cross-section areas, tensile strength and weights for lines in running rigging.

As far as the halyards are concerned, the 133-strand line (7 × 19) is considered to be superior to other types with respect to strength and resitance to deformation.

The best alternative if the sheaves have a small diameter, is to use the very flexible 114-strand line with a fibre core (6 × 19 + 1). Both these types are easy to splice.

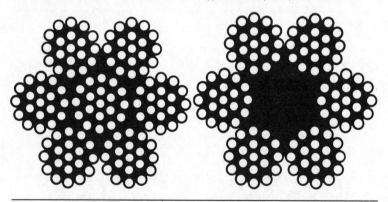

Diam. mm	7 x 19 very flexible		6 x 19 flexible	
	Approximate weight, kg	Calc. tensile strength, kg	Approximate weight, kg	Calc. tensile strength kg
2	0.025	280	0.01	240
3	0.03	550	0.03	570
4	0.06	1,130	0.06	965
5	0.09	1,715	0.09	1,465
6	0.13	2,540	0.13	2,175
7	0.18	3,390	0.17	2,895
8	0.22	4,175	0.22	3,710
10	0.35	6,635	0.34	5,870

13 RIGGING SCREWS

Rigging screws dimensions, 19-strand line

Line diameter, mm.	4	5	6	7	8	9	10
Rigging screw, thread diameter	$\frac{5}{16}$	$\frac{3}{8}$	$\frac{7}{16}$	$\frac{1}{2}$	$\frac{5}{8}$	$\frac{5}{8}$	$\frac{3}{4}$

14 ELECTRICAL CABLES

Current ratings for single and twin
core cables, rubber and plastic insulated.

Cable	Current rating	Cable	Current rating
1/.044	5 amperes	7/.052	37 amperes
3/.029	5 „	7/.064	46 „
3/.036	10 „	19/.044	53 „
1/.064	10 „	19/.052	64 „
7/.029	15 „	19/.064	83 „
7/.036	24 „	19/.083	118 „
7/.044	31 „		

Appendix 15

15 ELECTROLYTIC CORROSION

The list is arranged in the reversed
order of resistance to electrolytic
action, i.e. magnesium is the least and
18/10 stainless steel the most
durable.

Metal or alloy	Potential (volts negative to AG/AG.Cl. $\frac{1}{2}$ cell)	
Magnesium	1.65	
Zinc	1.10	
Galvanised steel	1.10	
Cadmium plating		
Alclad 3 S	0.94	
Aluminium	0.82	
Aluminium alloys	0.73–0.75	
Mild steel	0.60	
Cast iron		
Stainless steel 18/8	0.53	active, passive 0.084
Lead		
Muntz metal	0.40	
Manganese bronze, Naval brass,		
Nickel, Nickel-Chromium alloy		Ni.-Chr. active, passive 0.17
Copper	0.36	
Red brass	0.33	
Aluminium brass	0.32	
Admiralty brass	0.29	
Phos. bronze, Sil. bronze,		
Gunmetal		
Cupro-Nickel alloy	0.25–0.28	
Silver solder		
Nickel	0.20	Metals whose potentials are
Stainless steel 18/14	0.18	widely separated should not be used together in sea water
Monel	0.075	
Stainless 18/10	0.050	

(List courtesy of M. G. Duff & Partners)

(Where no figure is given the potential will be approximate as indicated by position in the scale)

16 TONNAGE

Definitions of tonnage and displacement

Ships

Deadweight tons = Cargo capacity = Max. weight of cargo on board stated in long tons (1 long ton = 1.016 metric tons).

Registered tons = (1 ton = 100 cubic feet = 2.83 cubic metres) stated in the form of both gross registered tons and net registered tons.

Gross registered tonnage = The combined volume of all space on board the ship.

Net registered tonnage = The actual cargo space available.

Displacement = The total weight of the vessel—normally used only in connection with warships.

Pleasure craft

Displacement = The total weight of the boat calculated at the waterline and stated in kg, pounds (USA) and long tons (Great Britain).

T.M. = Thames Measurement is stated in tons but is not a figure of displacement. It is merely a comparison factor between the sizes of various sailing boat types and is based on overall length and beam measurements.

$$\text{T.M.} = \frac{(L-B) \times B \times \frac{1}{2}B}{94}$$

Where L = length and B = Beam, both in feet.

17 WEIGHTS AND MEASURES

Conversion tables
For conversion of British weights and measures to metric units
Multiply by the factors below

Length

Millimetres to inches	0.03937	Inches to millimetres	25.4
Centimetres to inches	0.3937	Inches to centimetres	2.54
Metres to feet	3.281	Feet to metres	0.3048
Kilometres to miles	0.6214	Miles to kilometres	1.609

Area

Square metres to square feet	10.76	Square feet to square metres	0.0929
Square kilometres to square miles	0.3861	Square miles to square kilometres	2.59

x = relationship between the circumference of a circle and its diameter = 3.1416.

Vx = relationship between the diameter of a circle and its circumference = 0.31831.

Volume

Litres to pints (Imp)	1.76	Pints (Imp) to litres	0.568
Litres to gallons (Imp)	0.220	Gallons (Imp) to litres	4.546
Cubic metres to cubic feet	35.31	Cubic feet to cubic metres	0.02832

Weights

Grams to ounces	0.03527	Ounces to grams	28.35
Kilograms to pounds	2.205	Pounds to kilograms	0.4536
Kilograms to long tons	0.000984	Long tons to kilograms	1016

Output: 1 h.p. = 1.0139 metric horsepower (cheval vapeur = cv).
Horsepower standards: SAE = maximum output on the shaft when the engine is only fitted with the components essential for its function = gross output.
DIN = maximum output on the shaft with all standard ancillaries connected to engines as when it is installed = net output = braked output (bhp.) = shaft output (shp.).

Fuel consumption: 1 lb./h.p. hr. = 447.4 grams/h.p. hr.

18 BRITISH-METRIC CONVERSION

Corresponding Metric Units

1 mile	1.609 km
1 nautical mile	1.852 km
1 cable length	0.185 km
1 fathom	1.829 m
1 yard (yd)	0.914 m
1 foot (ft.)	0.305 m
1 inch (in.)	25.4 mm
1 square inch (sq. in.)	6.452 cm^2
1 square foot (sq. ft.)	0.093 m^2
1 square yard (sq. yd.)	0.836 m^2
1 cubic inch (cu. in.)	16.39 cm^3
1 cubic foot (cu. ft.)	0.02832 m^3
1 cubic yard (cu. yd.)	0.765 m^3
1 Imp. gallon	4.546 litres
1 Imp. pint	0.568 litres
1 US gallon	3.785 litres
1 US pint	0.472 litres
1 ounce (oz.)	28.35 grams
1 pound (lb.)	0.454 kg
1 pound-foot (lb. ft.)	0.138 kgm
1 mile per hour (m.p.h.)	1.609 km/hour
1 Imp. gallon/mile	282.5 litres/100 km
1 US gallon/mile	235.2 litres/100 km

Fuel consumption in litres/100 km from miles/gallon is obtained from the following formula:

$$\text{litres/100 km} = \frac{282.5 \text{ (Imp. gall.) or } 235.2 \text{ (US gall.)}}{\text{number of miles per gallon}}$$

In connection with sail-making, when converting from gram weights of canvas to British or American ounce (oz.) weights, divide the weight in grams by 34 for British canvas and by 42 for American canvas.
Example: The gram weight is 300. British oz. weight is then 300:34 = approx. 8.8 oz.
American oz. weight is then 300:42 = approx. 7.1 oz.

METRIC—BRITISH

1 km	0.621 miles
1 nautical mile	6,076 feet
1 cable length	608 feet
1 fathom	6 feet
1 m	1,094 yards
1 m	3,281 feet
1 cm	0.394 inches
1 cm^2	0.155 sq. in.
1 m^2	10.76 sq. ft.
1 m^2	1,196 sq. yd.
1 cm^3	0.061 cu. in.
1 m^3	35.315 cu. ft.
1 m^3	1,307 cu. yd.
1 litre	0.219 Imp. gallon
1 litre	1.761 Imp. pints
1 litre	0.264 US gallon
1 litre	2.119 US pints
1 kg	35.27 ounces
1 kg	2.205 pounds
1 kgm	7.233 lb. ft.
1 km/hour	0.621 m.p.h.
10 litres/100 km	0.035 Imp. gallons/mile
10 litres/100 km	0.042 US gallons/mile

Fuel consumption in miles per gallon from litres/100 km is obtained from the following formula:

$$\text{miles/gallon} = \frac{282.5 \text{ (Imp. gall.) or } 235.2 \text{ (US gall.)}}{\text{number of litres per 100 km}}$$

In connection with sail-making when converting ounce (oz.) weights of canvas to gram weights, multiply by 34 in the case of British canvas, multiply by 42 in the case of American canvas. Example:
British 8 oz. canvas corresponds to $8 \times 34 = 272$ g/m^2.
American 8 oz. canvas corresponds to $8 \times 42 = 336$ g/m^2.

Index